INTERNET AND E-COMMERCE AGREEMENTS

Drafting and Negotiating Tips

Lisa K. Abe

Butterworths

Toronto and Vancouver

Internet and E-Commerce Agreements: Drafting and Negotiating Tips

June 2001

The Butterworth Group of Companies

Canada:
75 Clegg Road, Markham, Ontario L6G 1A1
and
1721-808 Nelson St., Box 12148, Vancouver, B.C. V6Z 2H2
Australia:
Butterworths Pty Ltd., Sydney, Adelaide, Brisbane, Canberra, Melbourne and Perth
Ireland:
Butterworth (Ireland) Ltd., Dublin
Malaysia:
Malayan Law Journal Sdn Bhd, Kuala Lumpur
New Zealand:
Butterworths of New Zealand Ltd., Wellington and Auckland
Singapore:
Butterworths Asia, Singapore
South Africa:
Butterworth Publishers (Pty.) Ltd., Durban
United Kingdom:
Butterworth & Co. (Publishers) Ltd., London and Edinburgh
United States:
LEXIS Publishing, Charlottesville, Virginia

National Library of Canada Cataloguing in Publication Data

Abe, Lisa K., 1967-
Internet and e-commerce agreements : drafting and negotiating tips

Also published in loose–leaf format as part of Canadian forms & precedents. Includes index.
ISBN 0-433-41585-1

1. Internet (Computer network)–Law and legislation–Canada. 2. Electronic commerce–Law and legislation-Canada. 3. Contracts–Canada. 4. Computer contracts–Canada. 5. Contracts–Canada–Forms. I. Title. II. Title: Canadian forms & precedents.

KE936.C36A23 2001 346.7102 C2001-900997-6

Printed and Bound in Canada.

ACKNOWLEDGMENTS

I would like to thank my partners Chris Hale and Brian Gray and my colleagues Greg Segal, Parna Sabet and Szab Gall, for their assistance in reviewing the manuscript and helpful comments. I would also like to acknowledge the contributions by Blake, Cassels & Graydon LLP's e-commerce and privacy committees, including my partners Sheldon Burshtein, Martin Fingerhut, Mark Selick, Beth Gearing, Alan Aucoin and Elizabeth McNaughton. In addition, I would like to thank my assistant Rosemary McLaughlin for her dedication to completing the administrative tasks associated with finalizing the manuscript. Furthermore, it deserves mentioning that this book would not have been possible without the support of everyone at Blake, Cassels & Graydon LLP, in particular my partners, associates, students and staff in our Intellectual Property and Technology Group.

I wish to dedicate this book to my husband and best friend Gabriel Larouche, my mother Tiiu, my brother Andres and my grandmother Selma, all of whom have helped me achieve my dreams through their love, support and encouragement.

Lisa K. Abe
Toronto
June, 2001

DISCLAIMER

While every effort has been made to ensure the completeness and utility of the material contained in this book, there is no warranty, express or implied, that the user will achieve the desired end. The publisher and author disclaim any liability for loss, whether direct or consequential, flowing from the use of the precedents and other materials contained in the work.

BUTTERWORTHS SPEEDFORMS DISK INFORMATION

INTRODUCTION

The enclosed Butterworths SpeedForms disk contains forms and precedents and is designed to be used in conjunction with *Internet and E-Commerce Agreements: Drafting and Negotiating Tips.*

SpeedForms will facilitate the completion of forms and the preparation of precedents. Once the selection of the appropriate form or precedent is made, a lawyer need only provide the information to be inserted and an assistant can then easily locate and complete the form on a computer.

Please note that although most of the forms and precedents included in *Internet and E-Commerce Agreements: Drafting and Negotiating Tips* have been successfully used, there is no warranty, express or implied, that these documents are appropriate for the reader. Liability for the use, or misuse, of any documents is hereby waived.

SYSTEM REQUIREMENTS

The files on the enclosed disk have been designed for use on a personal computer with the following capabilities and configuration:

IBM or IBM-compatible with a hard drive and 3 ½ inch floppy disk drive
Windows 3.1 or higher operating system
Microsoft Word for Windows 97 or higher software
At least 4.5 MB of hard disk space

INSTALLING BUTTERWORTHS SPEEDFORMS ON YOUR HARD DISK DRIVE

Note: The *Internet and E-Commerce Agreements* files are compressed and will be inflated (unzipped) during the installation procedure described below. After installing the files, we recommend that you maintain them on your hard drive under the same file names as the originals. In this way you will ensure that your file names correspond with *Internet and E-Commerce Agreements*. Once you have completed a file, rename the amended file as appropriate for a specific client matter.

Installation Procedure

1. Place the diskette into the floppy disk drive of your computer.
2. Click on Start, then Run on the Taskbar. (In Windows 3.1, open the Program Manager and select Run from the File menu.)
3. In the Open command line of the Run dialog box, type
   a:\ecom.exe
   (where A is the letter of your floppy disk drive) and click the OK button.
4. The WinZip Self-Extractor [ecom.exe] dialog box will open. The default drive and folder to which the files will be installed is **c:\ecom**. You may change the defaults by typing another drive and folder name in the "Unzip To Folder" command line. You must have read/write access privileges to any network drive chosen.
5. Click the Unzip button in the dialog box. The files will then be inflated and installed into the drive and folder you have specified.
6. When the installation is complete, close the dialog box by clicking the Close button.

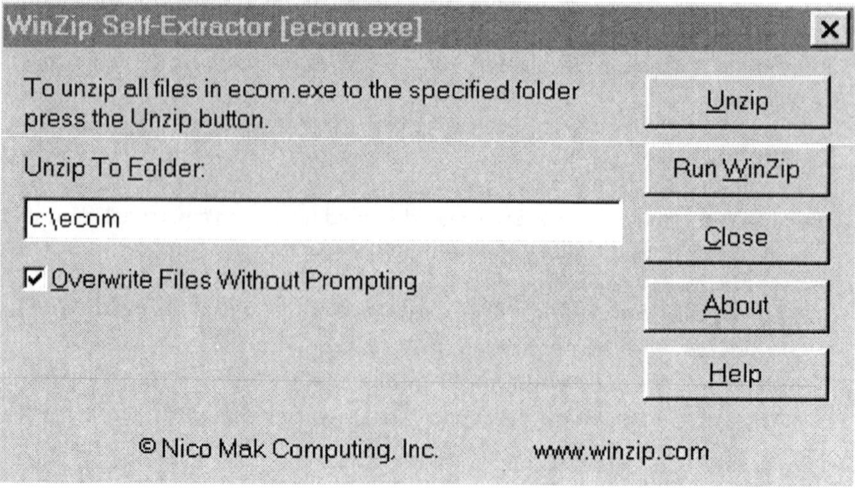

USING BUTTERWORTHS SPEEDFORMS

WHAT'S ON THE DISK?

File names on the diskette correspond to the form names in the book. The Table of Contents lists all forms by form number and form name.

The forms and precedents are set out in a way that makes them easy to use and, wherever possible, a standard and consistent style has been adopted.

NUMBERING

Recitals are not numbered
Sections are numbered 1, 2, 3, etc.
Subsections are numbered 1(a), 1(b), 1(c), etc.
Paragraphs in subsections are numbered 1(1)(a), 1(1)(b), 1(1)(c), etc. 1(a)(i), (ii), (iii), etc.

ROUND BRACKETS

Round brackets are used in the following instances:

(a) to indicate pieces of information known only to the end user of the form, such as names, addresses, dates, descriptions of fixtures, etc.
For example, Whereas (*principal*) has entered into a contract with you dated (*date*) for the supply of (*specify goods or as the case may be*);

(b) to give the user specific instructions.
For example, (*State clearly the name of the franchise or area franchise in the form in which the offer will be made to the public*);

(c) to enclose explanatory notes/text provided by the contributor and which directly relate to a specific form or precedent. These notes appear in roman type within round brackets directly underneath the title of the form and preceding the form itself.

SQUARE BRACKETS

Some precedents contain alternative or optional wordings. If the alternative or optional word or phrase is singular, it will appear in italics within square brackets directly following the existing word or phrase as follows:

head office [*principal place of business*]

If an entire optional clause or paragraph is presented, it will appear in italics within square brackets, following the existing clause or paragraph, with the word "OR" in between as follows:

> The Licensor shall install the Computer program on the Designated Hardware at the Designated Location.
>
> OR
>
> [*The Licensee shall be responsible for the installation of the Computer Program and the Licensor shall perform the installation services specified in the service specification.*]

If several optional words or phrases are offered, they all appear in italics within square brackets with the word "or" in between each option as follows:

> We the undersigned authorize and request you to open an account or accounts in our joint names as [*either or anyone* or *both or all*] of us shall direct.

COMPLETING THE FORMS

Retrieving a Form

Butterworths SpeedForms files are accessed in the same way as any other Word file. Within Microsoft Word, select Open from the File menu, choose the drive and folder into which the files were installed, and then select the file you wish to complete.

Using a Form

We have created the files using certain defaults, such as line margins, tabs, spacing, and justification, but you are free to change the page layout, edit the forms, add or delete information, or make other client-specific modifications, just as you would with documents you create from scratch.

Saving a Form

Once the form has been completed for a specific client matter, it is ready to save or print. Save the form under a new file name to preserve the text of the original file.

Printing a Form

Depending on the application you are using, you may have different print options available to you. The type of printer you use will also have an effect on the final appearance of the form. Any style changes you elect to use may require adjustment or realignment to achieve desired page lengths or page layout.

INTERNET AND E-COMMERCE AGREEMENTS: DRAFTING AND NEGOTIATING TIPS

TABLE OF CONTENTS

PAGE NO.

TABLE OF CASES

INTERNET AND E-COMMERCE AGREEMENTS: DRAFTING AND NEGOTIATING TIPS*

CHAPTER 1

AN INTRODUCTION TO THE INTERNET AND E-COMMERCE

1.1 INTRODUCTION

In order to be able to draft and negotiate effective Internet and e-commerce agreements, one must have an understanding of the Internet and how it works. This chapter will describe the basics of information technology and the common terminology that is essential for contract drafting. In order to draft contracts effectively, one should not be afraid to ask the client to clarify any unfamiliar terminology. For reference, a Glossary is included at the end of this book, which provides definitions of all of the italicized terms.

1.1.1 What is the Internet?

The Internet is a world-wide *network* of computers that communicate with one another. Communication is accomplished by the exchange, transfer or access to information, data, files or programs. One can visualize the Internet's structure as a giant spider web of computers, joined together by various telecommunications connectors or links, such as phone lines, satellites, cables and other devices. Hence the reason why the *Internet* is also sometimes referred to as the *World Wide Web*.

A few computers connected together over a close distance are often referred to as a *local area network* (*LAN*). A LAN is often comprised of a central *server* (a main hardware component) to which individual computers, or *clients*, are linked.

---

* Note that the content of this book reflects the views of the individual author, is intended to be used for discussion and educational purposes only and does not constitute legal advice. Also, since the Internet, e-commerce and its underlying technology are constantly evolving, the terms and concepts referred to in this book are also evolving and at the time of writing this book, are being developed and explored by the courts.

Computers and servers connected together over a larger distance create a *wide area network* (*WAN*) or a *regional network*. Networks may also be connected to one another in various ways. On the Internet, larger networks are connected via high-speed backbones, long distance, high-capacity telecommunications conduits, that can transport large amounts of electronic data at extremely high-speeds.

Various private companies and government agencies have built high-speed backbones, which they lease to Internet access providers, such as ISPs. A high-speed backbone can transfer as much as 155 mega (millions of) bits per second (Mbps).[1]

Networks may be private or public. The Internet is a public network, whereby local computers (such as PCs), known as *clients* and more powerful computers on which information resides, known as *servers*, allow themselves to communicate on an *open system* with other computers and *servers* in the public domain. Private networks, also known as *Intranets*, are networked computers and servers in a *closed system*. An *Intranet* is formed by connecting or allowing access to only specified computers, *servers* or users. For example, in a company, computers can be linked together to form an *Intranet* whereby they share information with one another. *Intranets* generally limit communication with external computers or networks. Networks external to an *Intranet* are referred to as an *Extranet*. The *Internet* is also sometimes referred to as an *Extranet*, when contrasted with an *Intranet*.

1.1.2 Electronic Communications

In order to communicate over a network, computers must speak the same language, known as a telecommunications *protocol*. The most common telecommunications protocol is known as the *Transmission Control Protocol/Internet Protocol* (*TCP/IP*). *TCP/IP* has become a standard as a result of the support of a variety of Internet groups and organizations[2] who have been studying and developing network technology.

---

1 For example, the very high-speed Backbone Network Services (vBNS) which links the research and education community.

2 The Internet Society, the Internet Activities Board, the Massachusetts Institute of Technology Laboratory for Computer Science and the World Wide Web Consortium (W3 Consortium) have all assisted with the direction and growth of new technological developments and standards for the Internet.

Using certain software[3] that understands and interprets *TCP/IP*, the information to be transferred from one computer to another is broken into *packets* by the *Transmission Control Protocol*. Each *packet* is given a *header* that contains a variety of information, such as the address of the recipient computer and the order of reassembling the packets. The *packets* are then sent out onto the *Internet*. The *packets* can take any route available and as they come into contact with various pieces of hardware, they are processed and routed to their proper destination. The *Internet Protocol* handles the routing of the *packets*. At the recipient end, the information is reassembled into its original form using the *Transmission Control Protocol*.

The most important hardware components on the *Internet* are *routers, hubs, gateways, bridges* and *repeaters*. *Routers* act as switches, reading the address in a *packet* and sending it to another *router* using the most efficient path leading towards the *packet's* ultimate destination. *Hubs* and *bridges* link groups of computers or networks with one another, as do *gateways*, which also function to translate data between different types of networks. If the destination of a packet were outside a geographic area, such as a *regional network* or *wide area network* (*WAN*), the *router* would send the packet across a *high-speed backbone*.

One of the benefits of the *Internet*, and the reason why it was initially created by the US military as a communication system, is that if one or more of the computers in a network fails, the other computers can still communicate with one another over a different path.

Another benefit of the *Internet* is that it reduces the cost of world wide communication. Typically, the owner of each computer on the Internet pays for its own connection to a local network that connects to other networks and computers on the Internet, thereby spreading the cost of communications among all Internet participants.

1.1.3 Connecting to the Internet

Internet Service Providers (*ISPs*) and *On-line Service Providers* (*OSPs*) sell connections to various telecommunications systems and high-speed backbones that link the world wide network of computers. The terms *ISP* and *OSP* are often used interchangeably, however, there is a technical difference between them. An *OSP* only offers the service of an *Internet* connection, while an *ISP* offers a variety of additional services and content to its customers, such as news groups, e-mail, web site hosting, bulletin boards, chat lines and help desks.

---

3 This software is referred to as a *TCP/IP* stack or *socket*. Many different sockets are available for PCs, such as *Winsock* or *MacTCP*.

Internet connections occur over various forms of telecommunications systems, for example telephone lines, coaxial cables, fiber optics, microwave links and satellite transmissions. Dedicated telephone lines (which transfer data at up to 56 kilobits per second (Kbps)), T1 lines (which transfer data at 1.544 Mbps) and T3 lines (which transfer data at 44.746 Mbps) can be leased to connect to the *Internet*. Cable, Integrated Services Digital Network (ISDN) telephone lines or high-speed Digital Subscriber Lines (DSL) are also available connections.

In order to ensure that the ISP's or OSP's customer has quick *Internet* access, the ISP or OSP usually leases space on various established lines or backbones, the cost of which is passed on to the customer. In the case of a large customer, an ISP or OSP may allocate a dedicated high-speed line to such customer.

Content Providers provide content to either *Internet* users directly (who are surfing the web and enter a content provider's web site) or to ISPs who add the content to the ISP's other services. For a further discussion on Content Providers, see paragraph 1.5.3, below.

1.2 WHAT ARE DOMAIN NAMES, WEB SITES, WEB PAGES AND WEB BROWSERS?

1.2.1 Domain Names

As discussed above, packets of data communicated over the *Internet* contain an address of the recipient computer that is requesting the data. Each *Web Site* on the *Internet* has a numerical address (known as the *IP address*) in the form of a series of numbers separated by periods (dots). Since numeric addresses are difficult to remember and since web site hosts are often changed while the owners of the sites remain the same, the *Domain Name System* (*DNS*) was developed to keep track of numeric web site addresses.

The *DNS* gives computers and web sites on the *Internet* alphanumeric addresses, much like postal addresses, known as *Domain Names* or *Uniform Resource Locators (URLs). Domain Names* are organized in an hierarchy of levels. The top level specifies the type of entity, or country of registration, e.g., .gov, .com, .ca. In Canada, the .ca domain name system is operated by a not-for-profit corporation known as the *Canadian Internet Registration Authority* or *CIRA*.[4] *CIRA*

---

[4] For more information on Canada's Internet domain name registration system, refer to Blake, Cassels & Graydon LLP, Special Edition of the *Blakes Report* on *Domain Names*, September 2000, a copy of which can be found at www.blakes.ca (referred to herein as the "*Blakes Report*").

has central servers that contain the master database of all registered .ca domain names and their corresponding IP addresses. To register or effect any transaction involving a domain name, one must deal with a *CIRA*-certified registrar. Registrars have entered into registrar agreements with CIRA to provide the services of domain name information, registration, transfer, renewal and modification to Internet users.[5] Persons who have registered domain names are known as registrants. Registrants must enter into agreements with CIRA for the service of a domain name.[6] The domain name registration agreement is, in effect, a service agreement for a limited time period of one to ten years. It does not convey, and expressly excludes, any ownership rights in the domain name to the registrant. However, domain names may acquire trade-mark rights if they meet the common law or statutory requirement for trade-marks.

1.2.2 Web Sites, Web Pages, Content, Hyper-Links and Web Browsers

A *Web Site* is a simple computer program (software) written in a language such as *Hypertext Markup Language (HTML).* The *HTML* tells a *Web Browser* how (with the use of *HTML Tags*) to display data and files and how to run embedded software (such as *Java Applets, ActiveX* or *JavaScript*). *Web Browsers,* such as Netscape Communicator or Microsoft's Internet Explorer, are software that usually reside on a local computer or "*Client*". A *Web Site,* on the other hand, is run on a host computer or "*Server*" that processes requests from *Web Browsers* to send Web Site *Content* to local computers or *Clients*. Sometimes, *Web Browsers* cannot run or display certain *Content,* for which other software (e.g., "plug-ins") or files (e.g., "metafiles") are required. The data, files and embedded software on a *Web Site* are commonly referred to as *Content* and will result in the display and hearing by the *Client* computer of text, video, pictures, sound or other multimedia. The *Content* may be embedded directly into the *Web Site,* or it may be retrieved indirectly via a *hyper-link* from another *Web Site, Web Page,* database or file source.

---

5. Registrars must meet the following conditions to be certified by CIRA: (1) qualify under CIRA's Canadian Presence Requirements for Registrars, set out on CIRA's web site at www.cira.ca and summarized in the *Blakes Report,* referred to in footnote 4 above; (2) enter a Registrar Agreement; (3) have the requisite technical capacity; and (4) pay certification fees.
6. Registrants must satisfy the Canadian Presence Requirements for Registrants, set out on CIRA's web site at www.cira.ca and summarized in the *Blakes Report,* referred to in footnote 4 above.

A *Hyper-Link* is an HTML code embedded into a *Web Site* that directs the *Web Browser* to retrieve information from another location either on the same *Web Server* (known as a *"relative link"*) or on an external *Web Server* (known as an *"absolute link"*). *Hyper-Links* must generally be activated by the *Internet* user by clicking on an icon, highlighted or underlined text that is displayed on the *Client*'s screen by the *Web Browser*. However, sometimes, hyper-linking occurs seamlessly with the *Web Browser*, such as in the case of advertisements or *Content* displayed on a *Web Site*.

A *Web Site* is usually organized into multiple *Web Pages* or sections, which are linked together in layers to permit users to efficiently find what they are looking for on the *Web Site*, using their *Web Browser*. *Homepage* is the term used for the first page of a *Web Site*, which page usually acts as the introduction to the *Web Site* and should contain the legal terms and disclaimers.

1.3 WHAT ARE COOKIES, SHOPPING CARTS, PASSPORTS AND SNIFFERS?

Cookies are data files that are put into an Internet user's computer when the Internet user visits a web site. Each time the Internet user visits a web site, the Internet browser examines the URL of the site being visited and searches for a *Cookie* file in the local hard drive. Information that is stored in the *Cookie* file is sent to the web site's server to be used for a variety of purposes. The types of information that are stored in *Cookie* files includes user names, passwords or any other information that the Internet user has entered or information about the activity that occurred while the user was visiting the web site that created the *Cookie*. The purposes for which the information may be used include enabling users to log on to the site without having to re-register or enter passwords each time; keeping track of purchases selected or completed on the web site, also known as an electronic *shopping cart*; and storing the name of the web site. Internet users can control the placement of *Cookies* on their computers by configuring their Internet browser to not accept *Cookies*, to pop-up a message each time a *Cookie* is being placed on the hard drive or to delete *Cookies* after a certain period of time.

Internet *Passports* are like *Cookies* in that they are both files used for gathering and sharing information about Internet users. However, the main difference is that a *Cookie* is created by the web site's server, while the *Passport* is created by the Internet user him- or herself. The user completes a personal profile (the *passport*) within the user's web browser, which specifies the type of information that can be shared among web sites. When the Internet user visits web sites, those sites will add information to, and read the information from, the *passport* about the user and the user's Internet activities, based on the type of information that the user has permitted to be shared.

Sniffers are computers that sit on the Internet between Internet users and web sites. Through the use of certain software, *Sniffers* can analyze Internet traffic (i.e., TCP/IP packets) to and from web sites. They collect information from *Cookies, Passports* or IP addresses about Internet users, such as their identities, when and what actions are taken, where requests for web pages are coming from and where pages are sent. The information is then stored in a database and used for reporting many kinds of statistical data, such as number of visits to a site or web page and how much time spent there.

1.4 WHAT IS E-COMMERCE?

E-commerce is commercial activity, such as the delivery of information, products, services, or payments, using computer systems, information technology and communications. More narrowly, e-commerce is business to consumer (B2C) and business to business (B2B) transactions conducted over computer networks, whether public (such as the Internet) or private networks.[7]

Examples of e-commerce include:

- the purchase of products and services on the Internet;
- the exchange of financial assets between financial institutions;
- electronic data interchange between manufacturers, wholesalers and retailers;
- on-line auctions; and
- telephone banking.

1.5 WHO ARE THE COMMON INTERNET AND E-COMMERCE PLAYERS AND WHAT SERVICES DO THEY PROVIDE?

It has been suggested that the advent of the Internet and e-commerce will simplify business transactions and eliminate "the middle man". It may appear to the user that products and services are purchased "directly" from suppliers without having to deal with any intermediate parties and giving rise to a misconception that e-commerce will result in the elimination of jobs and economic shrinkage.

---

7 Ministry of Revenue Advisory Committee, *Report of the Committee on Electronic Commerce*, (Ottawa: Industry Canada, April 30, 1998).

However, the Internet and e-commerce has in fact created entirely new businesses and considerably more intermediate players than one would ever have imagined. As an example, when one purchases a product on-line, it may appear that the transaction is occurring directly with the supplier and that there are no others involved. However, one's web browser is responsible for making this appear seamless. Behind the scenes are a plethora of third parties that make the transaction happen. The supplier would likely have contracts with many network and technology infrastructure providers (such as ASPs and web site hosts, discussed below), context and marketplace providers (such as portals, discussed below), content providers and enablers (such as transport companies, distributors, banks and credit card providers).

1.5.1 Network and Technology Infrastructure Providers

In the on-line world, the Internet and e-commerce would not be possible without the network and technology infrastructure providers. These parties include hardware and equipment manufacturers, internet service providers (as discussed above) that provide Internet connectivity, Application Service Providers (ASPs) who are also commonly called hosts or outsourcers, web site hosts, customer relations Management providers (CRMs), telecommunications providers and, of course, software and web site developers.

ASPs host software on their servers and, for a fee, provide a service to others who do not have the software. ASPs may run software on their own systems and allow others to access their systems to process data, alternatively the ASPs will simply receive data from others, process the data, and return output. Web site hosts are also ASPs, which operate web sites (which are software) on their servers that are connected to the Internet, for the benefit of other parties. CRMs play an important role in e-commerce. In many ways, they too act as hosts in running software on their servers to process customer data for businesses. They may also provide additional customer relations services for businesses, such as help desks for customer questions or service.

1.5.2 Context and Marketplace Providers

Context and Marketplace Providers provide web sites where businesses and consumers can meet to enter into transactions among themselves. These providers include web site owners, e-malls, on-line exchanges and auctions. Their web sites are often referred to as *Portals* and the providers typically act much like ASPs, in that they provide a service to buyers and sellers. The service is largely one of access to a web site with the ability given to buyers and sellers to add content, submit and process data, offer and accept contracts for the purchase and sale of products and services on their own terms. Usually, the context and marketplace providers are not party to the transactions and do not act as agents for the buyers and sellers, in order to minimize their exposure to liability related to the transactions, products or services.

1.5.3 Content Providers

Content providers are generally parties who supply data, files and/or embedded software to their customers who have web sites. Content may consist of text, video, pictures (e.g., gif files), sound or other multimedia. The *Content* may be embedded directly into the customer's *Web Site*, or it may be retrieved indirectly via a *hyper-link* to the content provider's *Web Site*, or other data or file source. The content providers may:

(i) either act as service providers providing access to their content to customers who have subscribed to the content provider's service;

(ii) license their content to their customers for use on customers' web sites; or

(iii) may develop content specifically for a particular customer and transfer ownership of all intellectual property rights in the content to such customer.

1.5.4 Enablers

Enablers provide an important service in e-commerce, in that they assist with the processing of e-commerce transactions and help to minimize the risks of e-contracting.[8] They include payment service providers, electronic clearing and settlement networks established by credit card issuers world wide, logistics solutions providers and *Certification Authorities.*

Certification Authorities or *Trusted Third Parties* (*TTPs*) maintain records of private and public *"keys"*, or *algorithms*, for identifying, encrypting, decoding and authenticating electronic documents and their authors. A *Public Key Infrastructure* (*PKI*) acts as a central repository for administering certificates and keys.

[8] For a discussion of the risks of e-contracting, please see Chapter 2.

CHAPTER 2

INTERNET AND E-COMMERCE LEGAL ISSUES

2.1 INTRODUCTION

Over the past few years, there has been exponential growth of electronic commerce and business on the Internet. Businesses whose sales outlets have traditionally been based in bricks and mortar, are opening up new virtual offices on-line where they are selling a wide range of goods and services, including books, toys, groceries, music, clothing, computers, software, investments and shares, just to name a few. Forecasts indicate Internet revenue in Canada is growing each year by billions of dollars. The Internet is becoming the new global marketplace.

However, the Internet and e-commerce raise complex legal issues. In order to effectively draft Internet and e-commerce agreements, one needs to understand these legal issues. This chapter will address the issues that commonly arise when conducting business electronically. However, one should appreciate that electronic transactions, like any other commercial dealings, raise many other legal issues, outside the scope of this book, which also need to be considered, such as those governed by advertising, competition, consumer protection, defamation, securities regulation, taxation and export control laws.

2.2 INTERNET AND E-COMMERCE LEGAL ISSUES

The following are key legal issues arising from the Internet and e-commerce:

2.2.1 Intellectual Property Issues

As discussed in Chapter 1, web sites and e-commerce activities involve the use of many forms of technology and content, such as software, hyper-links and multimedia, which may contain multiple intellectual property rights. In Canada, copyrights and patent rights can exist in the software, processes and content that are used or displayed in web sites and e-commerce. As well, trade-mark rights can exist in domain names, logos, word designs or other devices (e.g., sounds) used in web sites to distinguish goods or services.

The Internet and associated technology have made the storage, reproduction, modification, use and wide-spread distribution of copyright works, patentable subject matter, trade-marks, trade secrets or other intellectual property extremely easy, inexpensive and fast. As a result, authors, inventors and other intellectual property rights owners became and remain highly concerned about the unauthorized use of their works and infringement of their intellectual property rights.

Infringement is also a concern for Internet and e-commerce participants, such as network and technology infrastructure providers, context and marketplace providers, content providers, enablers[1] and their customers and Internet users. If any of these parties engage in the unauthorized use of any software, content, trade-marks, processes or other subject matter which, under local or international intellectual property laws, contains rights exclusive to third parties, these users could be liable for infringement or other violations.[2] The specific risks faced by parties involved in Internet and e-commerce activities, are discussed in the chapters that follow.

2.2.2 Recommendations on What needs to be Done to Minimize the Infringement Risks and to Protect Intellectual Property

To minimize the risks of unauthorized use and infringement of intellectual property rights, one needs to ensure that the owners of such rights (which could be the original developers, their employers, assignees or successors) have either transferred or licensed their rights to the user.

A transfer of intellectual property rights generally requires an assignment in writing, signed by the owner. As well, under the *Copyright Act*, authors of copyright works also have moral rights that can only be waived (not assigned) in writing.[3]

If a license is granted, the scope of the license should be carefully drafted to be consistent with the rights of the intellectual property owner as specified under the applicable intellectual property legislation. Some of the rights that are capable of being licensed include the right to copy, perform, publish, translate, convert, present, communicate, rent, make, construct, use, sell, advertise, distribute and/or display. Consideration should also be given to limitations on the licensee's rights, such as territory, quantity, term and other restrictions.

---

1 See Chapter 1, Section 1.5 for an explanation of Internet and e-commerce participants.

2 In addition to intellectual property infringement, liability may arise for breach of duties of confidentiality, trespass, violation of privacy ad possible criminal theft.

3 Moral rights are described in s. 14.1(1), R.S.C. 1985, c. C-42, as am., as the right to the integrity of the work, to be associated with the work as its author by name or under a pseudonym, and the right to remain anonymous.

In order to effectively draft intellectual property assignments and licenses, one should have a thorough understanding of the applicable intellectual property laws, such as the Canadian *Copyright Act*,[4] the *Trade-marks Act*[5] and the *Patent Act*,[6] and their respective regulations and rules, the analysis of which is outside the scope of this book.[7]

Proper drafting of an assignment or license also requires knowledge of the owners, which may require intellectual property searches in numerous jurisdictions.[8]

To minimize the risks of unauthorized use and infringement of one's own intellectual property rights, one should also do the following:

- register one's interests with the appropriate registrar, such as copyright, patent, trade-mark registrations, with the applicable federal authority in Canada and domain names with domain name registrars;
- post intellectual property notices on web sites (See Chapter 9);
- obtain representations and warranties from contracting parties as to their right to assign or license (as applicable) and that the subject matter does not infringe upon third-party intellectual property rights (specific representations and warranties that should be obtained in various contexts are explored in subsequent chapters);
- obtain indemnities from contracting parties as to any infringement claims brought by third parties in respect of the subject matter (specific indemnities that should be obtained in various contexts are explored in subsequent chapters).

2.2.3 Privacy Issues

Internet and e-commerce activities often involve the exchange of personal information or data. Such information or data is often collected through direct submissions by Internet users when completing registration forms or *Passports*,

---

4 R.S.C. 1985, c. C-42, as am.

5 R.S.C. 1985, c. T-13, as am.

6 R.S.C. 1985, c. P-4, as am.

7 Please refer to *Canadian Copyright Issues on the Internet: What Every Corporate Counsel Must Know*, by Sheldon Burshtein, Canadian Corporate Counsel Association, 1998, Annual Meeting, August 24-25, 1998. See also S. Burshtein, *The Corporate Counsel Guide to Intellectual Property Law*, with E. McNaughton, *Advertising and Deceptive Trade Practices* (Toronto: Canada Law Book, 2000).

8 Searches have many limitations: they are not always accurate and do not always show pending applications (e.g., US patents).

or less obviously through Internet use tracking methods, such as *Cookies*, *Sniffers* or Internet logs.[9]

Personal data about users may be subject to the federal *Personal Information Protection and Electronic Documents Act, Part I*[10] (the "*Privacy Act*") and applicable provincial privacy legislation (See Chapter 4). Under the *Privacy Act*, anyone who collects, stores, uses or discloses personal information about others, needs to satisfy numerous conditions. One of these conditions is obtaining the consent of the individual user for using his or her personal information for the specific purposes that have been disclosed to the user. The implications of privacy legislation must be considered when advising or drafting agreements for Internet and e-commerce players who collect information about individuals, whether openly, through the use of on-line registration forms or *Passports*, or more covertly, such as with *Cookies* or *Sniffers*.

If an Internet user submits information to a web site and the web site owner wants to be able to use or circulate such information in the future, the web site owner will need:

(i) the express consent from the user, for which the owner may also need to incorporate an assignment, license and/or waiver if the submission has intellectual property rights;

(ii) an acknowledgment that such information will not be kept confidential; and

(iii) an indemnity from the user for any claims the web site owner may suffer as a result of using such material.

Privacy rights and obligations may also exist under contract (e.g., non-disclosure agreements),[11] in common law where there is an expectation of privacy,[12] criminal[13] or other legislation[14] and regulations.

---

9 For an explanation of how *Cookies* and *Sniffers* work, see Chapter 1.

10 S.C. 2000, c. 5.

11 See S.C.C. decision in *Cadbury Schweppes Inc. v. FBI Foods Ltd.* (CLAMATO formula) at [1999] 1 S.C.R. 142, 59 B.C.L.R. (3d) 1, 167 D.L.R. (4th) 577, 235 N.R. 30, [1999] 5 W.W.R. 751, 42 B.L.R. (2d) 159, 83 C.P.R. (3d) 289.

12 See *Saccone v. Orr* (1981), 34 O.R. (2d) 317, 19 C.C.L.T. 37 (Co. Ct.) and *Palad v. Pantaleon* (June 14, 1989), York 266930/86 [unreported] where both cases awarded damages for invasion of privacy.

13 See, for example, s. 184(1) of the *Criminal Code*, R.S.C. 1985, c. C-46, as am., dealing with interception of private communications. In the U.S., the *Children's Online Privacy Protection Act*, 15 U.S.C. s. 6501 *et seq* and related Rules 16 C.F.R. Part 312, govern the collection and use of personal information requested from and provided by children under the age of 13.

14 For example, the federal *Personal Information Protection and Electronic Documents Act*, S.C. 2000, c. 5.

2.2.4 Criminal Law Issues

Criminal liability could arise from Internet and e-commerce activities in many ways. As noted above, in Canada, the interception, use or disclosure of private communications could be a criminal offence.

Possession, distribution or creation of content containing illegal materials, such as child pornography, hate literature or obscenities, may also result in criminal liability.[15] Fraud is also becoming increasingly prevalent on the Internet.

2.2.5 e-Contracting Legal Issues

a. Enforceability of e-Contracts

With e-contracts, the legal requirements for creating enforceable agreements are the same as with traditional contracts. However, given that the on-line world is "paperless", it is more difficult to determine whether the traditional contract law requirements have been met to create an enforceable e-contract. A binding contract can be formed in several ways, such as by oral agreement, in writing or implicitly, as a result of the conduct of the parties. Generally, Canadian contract law provides that a valid and enforceable contract will be made if one party makes a proper offer to another party who then unconditionally accepts that offer. In e-commerce, offers and acceptances are communicated electronically and e-contracts may be formed on the Internet or by other on-line means. As a result of these new technologies, there may be uncertainties as to when an offer has been made and when it has been accepted.

There must also be an intention between the parties to create legally binding obligations. If the parties do not intend to be legally bound, no enforceable contract will result. The relationship between and the conduct of the parties has to be examined to determine if the intention was to create an enforceable contract.

b. When and How is an Offer to Form an e-Contract Made?

With e-commerce and on-line communications, questions arise as to whether such communications constitute "offers" and whether Internet users can be construed as "offerees". Terms on a web site may or may not constitute valid offers, depending upon whether they meet the legal requirements of a valid offer or not. To make a valid offer, it must contain all of the material terms of a contract with reasonable specificity, or alternatively, the terms of a contract must

---

15 See *Criminal Code*, R.S.C. 1985 c. C-46, as am., ss. 184 and 193.

reasonably be ascertainable by an agreed upon formula, method or principle of determination.

An important distinction exists between an offer and an "invitation to treat". An "invitation to treat" is merely a solicitation for offers rather than an offer, which is capable of being accepted to form a legally binding contract. For example, advertising products on a web page with a price quotation may merely be an "invitation to treat", i.e., to solicit offers to buy at the indicated price. However, a price quotation may be construed as an offer if it contains sufficient contractual terms (such as delivery, quantity or other payment terms) to indicate an intention to form a legally binding agreement.

c. How are Offers to Form e-Contracts Accepted?

Generally, an offer is accepted if the acceptance is unconditional, relates to the terms of the offer and is communicated to the offeror. Canadian courts have recognized acceptance by various methods, such as orally, by conduct or other methods as may be prescribed in the applicable offer. An offer cannot be accepted if it is no longer outstanding, i.e., if it has been revoked or rejected. An offer can only be accepted by the persons to whom the offeror intended to make the offer. If an acceptance contains additional or different terms or conditions (such as an agreement to purchase an offered item but at a different price) then that communication will constitute a counter-offer rather than acceptance. It will then be up to the original offeror to decide whether to accept the counter-offer or provide another counter-offer.

The making of an offer by electronic means may be viewed as an implied authorization to communicate the acceptance by similar means. Likewise, placing an icon on a web page containing an offer with instructions that Internet users can click on the icon to indicate their acceptance of the offer will likely be viewed by the courts as an authorization to communicate the acceptance by "click".

d. When and Where is an e-Contract Formed?

The requirement that acceptance be communicated raises the issues of when and where an e-contract is formed. In the off-line world, there are two legal principles for determining contract formation. Under the "instantaneous communication rule", contracts formed by means of instantaneous communication are considered formed when and where the offeror receives notice of the acceptance. Canadian courts have applied this rule to facsimile transmissions.[16]

Under the "mailbox rule", contracts formed by correspondence are made when and where the acceptance is sent.[17] This rule applies to both acceptances mailed or given to a courier. Note, however, that under Quebec's civil law system, there is no "mailbox rule", and contracts are formed under the general principle of when and where acceptance is received by the offeror.

In Canada, it is not clear whether the "instantaneous communication rule" or the "mailbox rule" will apply to electronic communications and e-contracts, since it is not always clear whether the form of electronic communication is instantaneous. For example, e-mail is not as instantaneous as communications by phone, since there is no direct continuous line of communication between sender and receiver. When sent over the Internet, e-mail messages are broken down into digitized packets, sent over different routes and servers, and reassembled before reaching the intended recipient. E-mail messages may also be encrypted and may result in unreliable or "garbled" messages being received by the recipient. On the other hand, communications on a web site are more interactive and instantaneous, particularly when immediate feedback is provided and the interaction occurs in real time.

Although the new Canadian e-commerce legislation (see Checklist 2A) does not fully solve the issue of when and where e-contracts are concluded, it does provide some guidance. For example, generally under the provincial e-commerce legislation, if a person has designated or uses an information system for the purpose of receiving particular documents, then such documents are presumed to be received when they enter that system and become capable of retrieval, whether they are actually viewed or not. If there has been no such designation, then such documents are deemed to be received only when the addressee actually becomes aware of the documents and is able to retrieve them. This second test is a rebuttable presumption under the Ontario legislation, so that a recipient has some room to claim that it did not actually receive the documents. The Ontario provincial e-commerce legislation also clarifies that the mere posting of information on a web site may not be sufficient to confirm delivery of that information to another person.

---

16 *Eastern Power Ltd. v. Azienda Communale Energia & Ambiente* (1999), 187 D.L.R. (4th) 409, 125 O.A.C. 54, 50 B.L.R. (2d) 33, 39 C.P.C. (4th) 160, [1990] O.J. No. 3275; *Brinkibon Ltd. v. Stahaag Stahl G.m.b.H.*, [1983] 2 A.C. 34 (H.L.); *Re Viscount Supply Co.*, [1963] O.R. 640 (S.C.).

17 *Imperial Life Ansurance Co. of Canada v. Colmenares*, [1967] S.C.R. 443 at 447.

The rules of offer and acceptance will depend upon the law applicable to the parties. There have been international attempts to harmonize the different rules of contract formation. For example, the *United Nations Convention on Contracts for the International Sale of Goods* provides that acceptance of an offer occurs when and where the acceptance reaches the offeror, so long as acceptance reaches the offeror within a reasonable time or the time specified by the offeror.

In order to avoid any possible confusion, on-line offers should specify the methods of acceptance, and when and where e-contracts will be formed. Offerors may choose to expressly exclude the application of the convention.

e. Do e-Contracts Have to be in Writing?

As discussed above, contracts may be formed orally, in writing, by conduct or other methods specified in the offer. However, several Canadian federal and provincial statutes and regulations impose writing and signature requirements for certain types of contracts to be valid, such as contracts for the sale of land, guarantees and certain "consumer" contracts. These requirements have posed barriers to electronic commerce.

"Writing" and "written" have been defined by legislation to mean words that have been printed, typewritten, painted, engraved, lithographed, photographed, or otherwise represented or reproduced. The Canadian federal and provincial e-commerce legislation, by giving legal recognition to e-contracts and electronic signatures, attempts to clarify that information in machine-readable form will constitute a "writing". Under the provincial e-commerce statutes, electronic contracts and signatures shall not be denied legal effect or enforceability solely on the grounds that they are in electronic form, save for specific exceptions. Under most of the provincial e-commerce statutes, the writing requirement is satisfied if the e-contract is accessible to another person so as to be usable for subsequent reference.

Where prior law requires that a document must be provided to someone in writing, the provincial e-commerce statutes provide that:

(i) the document must be capable of being retained for subsequent reference in the format in which it was created or provided; and

(ii) the information, if any, concerning the document's origin, destination, time and date of sending can also be retained.

The Ontario *Electronic Commerce Act, 2000*, also states that an electronic document is not "provided" to any person if "it is merely made available for access by the person, for example on a web site"[18]. Therefore, merely providing a link to a web site containing an e-contract might not satisfy a legal requirement to provide a person with a copy of the contract. Furthermore, in order to ensure retention of an e-contract in its original form, it is necessary to implement methods to retain the integrity of the e-contract.

The federal *Personal Information Protection and Electronic Documents Act*[19] (the "*Privacy Act*") also permits e-contracts to satisfy writing requirements if both parties to the e-contract have agreed that it be in electronic form and if the e-contract is under the control of the person to whom it is provided and is readable or perceivable so as to be used for subsequent reference. The *Privacy Act* only applies to writing requirements under the federal laws listed in Schedules 2 or 3 of the *Privacy Act*.

f. How Do You Sign an e-Contract?

In general, contracts do not have to be signed in order to be enforceable. However, there are some situations where the law requires signatures.

Statutes which contain legal signature requirements might well be interpreted as not permitting "electronic" signatures. The provincial e-commerce statutes have attempted to deal with this by:

(i) defining an "electronic signature" as electronic information that a person has created or adopted in order to sign a document and which is attached to or associated with the relevant document; and

(ii) providing that statutory signature requirements are satisfied by reliable electronic signatures.

Similarly, the *Privacy Act* defines "electronic signature" as "a signature that consists of one or more letters, characters, numbers or other symbols in digital form incorporated in, attached to or associated with an electronic document." The *Privacy Act* also provides that any signature requirements under federal laws listed in Schedules 2 or 3 are satisfied if the regulations have been complied with. Although no regulations have been passed yet and no courts have interpreted these provisions, it is likely that the electronic signature requirements will be satisfied by simply typing one's name at the end of an e-contract and indicating that it constitutes an electronic signature. Similarly, including one's name at the end of an e-mail may constitute a signature if it is

---

18 S.O. 2000, c. 17, s. 10(1).

19 S.C. 2000, c. 5.

apparent that it is so intended. Also, clicking on an "I Agree" icon will likely satisfy a legal requirement for a signature.[20]

g. Are e-Contracts "Original" Contracts?

Many Canadian statutes require documents to be "original", such as trade documents and certificates, insurance certificates, documents of title and negotiable instruments. Generally, under the provincial e-commerce statutes, e-contracts will be equivalent to original contracts if:

(i) reliable assurances exist as to the integrity of the information contained in the e-contract from the time it was first created in its final form; and

(ii) the e-contract is accessible by the person so as to be usable for subsequent reference and capable of being retained by the person.

In Quebec, the originality test varies depending on whether the need to establish originality is to assure that the document:

(i) is the first form from which copies are made;

(ii) is unique; or

(iii) is the first form of a document associated with a person.

In each case, the integrity of the document must be assured. In the first case, the components of the source technological document must be identified upon reproduction and must remain intact. In the second case, the components of the document or its medium must be structured using a process that makes it possible to assure that the document is unique. In the third case, the components of the document or its medium must be structured using a process that makes it possible to assure that the document is unique, to identify the person with which the document is associated and to maintain the association during the entire life-cycle of the document.

Under the *Privacy Act*, an originality requirement under a federal law listed in Schedule 2 or 3 is satisfied by an e-contract if:

(i) the e-contract contains a secure electronic signature that was added when the e-contract was first generated in its final form and that can be used to verify that the e-contract has not been changed since that time; and

(ii) relevant regulations have been complied with.

---

[20] See footnote 18.

h. How Does One Identify the Other Party to an e-Contract?

E-contracting over an open network such as the Internet raises the issue of uncertainty as to the other party with whom one is communicating and contracting. An Internet user may be able to disguise his or her identity, age, geographic location, or may operate under an alias.

At present, there is no national or international standard for electronically identifying oneself or for signing e-contracts. However, various methods of digital certification and authentication are available that allow parties to enter into e-contracts and exchange documents with a high degree of comfort and security. The following are some examples:

E-Mail	Many e-mail programs use encryption technology to securely transmit e-mail across public networks. The e-mail address may suitably identify the e-mailing party.
Digital Signatures	A digital signature is a cryptographic transformation of data which, when associated with an electronic file or other data unit, can confirm both the origin and the integrity of the data.
Trusted Third-Party Certification	Trusted third parties or certification authorities maintain records of private and public algorithms ("keys") for identifying, encrypting, decoding and authenticating electronic documents and their authors. A Public Key Infrastructure (or "PKI") acts as a central repository for administering certificates and keys.

i. Are Errors in e-Contracts, or e-Contracts Made with Electronic Agents, Enforceable?

Contracts formed by mistake are in many situations not enforceable because the requisite intention to form a binding legal agreement is lacking. In e-contracting, particularly where electronic agents automatically enter into contracts or accept offers on behalf of businesses without further interaction, it may not be possible to correct errors. For this reason, the provincial e-commerce statutes provide that contracts will be void in cases where an individual makes a material error while contracting with an electronic agent of the other party if, after becoming aware of the error, the individual promptly informs the other party. While this provision was intended to promote consumer confidence and encourage e-commerce, it may also increase the frequency of customer repudiation. In most provincial e-commerce statutes, this option to repudiate in the case of error will not be available if the customer has been given "an opportunity to prevent or correct the error" at the time the contract is entered into with the electronic agent. Even in jurisdictions where no such safeguard is stipulated, it is good business practice to ensure that a web site that concludes contracts automatically (such as through electronic agents) is designed to allow parties to review and reconfirm contract terms and to correct errors at the time the contract is formed.

j. How Does the Canadian e-Commerce Legislation Change On-Line Contracting?

The e-commerce legislation in Canada (See Checklist 2A) may in fact have marginal impact on the conduct of e-commerce, since it does not purport to change the general law of contracts. In fact, courts already recognize that if two parties clearly express or imply an intention to enter into a contract through electronic communication, such as e-mail or web-based submissions, then their communication will produce an enforceable agreement. In Ontario, the recent case of *Rudder v. Microsoft* held that contracts made on the Internet (also known as "click-wrap" agreements) are enforceable.[21]

The primary purpose of the Canadian e-commerce legislation is to formally recognize that the legal effect or enforceability of a contract will not be denied solely because the communications resulting in the contract are electronic. Although there may be many reasons to challenge the validity of an e-contract, the electronic form alone will not affect the e-contract's legality or enforceability. The e-commerce legislation recognizes electronic communications, documents and signatures as functionally equivalent to their paper counterparts. This is particularly important where certain statutes, such as

---

21 The *Rudder v. Microsoft* (1999), 47 C.C.L.T. (2d) 168, 2 C.P.R. (4th) 474, 40 C.P.C. (4th) 394 (Ont. S.C.J.), case involved an application by Microsoft for a permanent stay against an Ontario class action arising from a dispute involving the Microsoft Network (MSN). The plaintiffs, who brought the action on behalf of all resident Canadians who subscribed to MSN since 1995, claimed $75 million in damages. Microsoft applied for a permanent stay based on the governing law clause in the click-wrap agreement. The clause provided that the MSN service agreement was governed by the laws of Washington state and that all disputes arising out of the agreement would occur in that state's courts. The court granted the application on the basis of this clause, noting that new members of MSN were required to click the "I Agree" button presented on the computer screen at the same time as the contract terms. It added that to rule against the enforceability of the clause "would lead to chaos in the marketplace, render ineffectual electronic commerce and undermine the integrity of any agreement entered into through this medium". For further information on the enforceability of on-line contracts, please see the February/March 2000 edition of the *Blakes Report on Intellectual Property – Focus on "E-Commerce"* entitled *"That's a Click-Wrap"* by Lisa Abe.

consumer protection legislation and statutes of frauds, require the existence of a "written" agreement or "signature". Nevertheless, electronic contracts will remain subject to basic contract law principles.

The new e-commerce legislation attempts to codify the legal recognition of information and documents communicated electronically. The provincial legislation and bills (collectively the "provincial e-commerce statutes") are fairly similar given that they are all based on the proposed *Uniform Electronic Commerce Act* which was published by the Uniform Law Conference of Canada following consultations with all of the provinces.

The proposed *Uniform Electronic Commerce Act* was itself modeled on the *United Nations Model Law on Electronic Commerce,* which Model Law has served as the basis for drafting e-commerce laws in other countries. Therefore, many foreign e-commerce statutes, such as in the United States and Europe, whether in force or pending, resemble the provincial e-commerce statutes.

The following concepts are addressed in most of the provincial e-commerce statutes (See Checklist 2A):

Functional Equivalency	Electronic communications and documents are recognized as legal, functional equivalents of traditional paper documents in most cases.
Electronic Contracting	Parties can agree to communicate contract terms by exchanging electronic documents and can create binding agreements by simply clicking on an on-screen icon.
Electronic Agent	An electronic agent can contractually bind its principal and other people who are interacting with the agent will likewise be bound.
Official Filings	Governments are committed to providing and accepting most official documents electronically (subject to format requirements).
Paper Form Requirements	Laws requiring paper documents (e.g., for bills of lading or sale, affidavits and trial evidence) will recognize the validity of electronic files.
Electronic Signatures	If a commercial party or governmental agency requires a signature, a properly formatted and authenticated e-signature should suffice.

In addition to these concepts, the Quebec bill deals with identification, authentication of documents and domestic and international legal harmonization.

The federal *Personal Information Protection and Electronic Documents Act* (the "*Privacy Act*")[22] also sets out a legislative scheme by which requirements in federal statutes and regulations that contemplate the use of paper or do not expressly permit the use of electronic technology, may be administered or satisfied in the electronic environment. The *Privacy Act* authorizes regulations to be made as to how those requirements may be satisfied using electronic means. It also addresses, among other matters, the following issues:

Secure E-Signatures	Part 2 describes the characteristics of secure e-signatures and grants authority to make regulations prescribing technologies or processes for the purpose of the definition "secure electronic signature".
Automating Bureaucracy	Federal departments and agencies are authorized to use electronic means to manage information, to receive certain filings and to publish certain official documents.
Personal Privacy	Controls have been placed on private sector collection, use, storage and disclosure of personal information. Retention and exchange of certain personal data without consent can be illegal.

For constitutional reasons, the *Privacy Act* does not directly address general contract law matters, such as when an electronic contract is binding.

For an extensive discussion of the new federal privacy provisions and those sections of the *Privacy Act* concerning the retention and exchange of personal information, please see the April/May 2000 edition of the *Blakes Report on Intellectual Property* entitled "Focus on Privacy". See also Chapter 4 on Privacy Policies.

k. To What Electronic Contracts and Documents Does the Canadian e-Commerce Legislation Apply?

The provincial e-commerce statutes apply generally to all types of contracts and documents. Exceptions include:

---

22 S.C. 2000, c. 5.

(i) wills and codicils;

(ii) living wills and powers of attorney concerning personal health or financial matters;

(iii) documents transferring land; and

(iv) negotiable instruments.

These excepted documents must be in traditional written form to be effective. The provincial e-commerce statutes generally recognize all other electronic documents to be "a writing". The *Privacy Act* applies more restrictively to situations in which federal laws contemplate the use of paper to record or communicate information or transactions.

l. Will e-Contracts Meet Document Retention Requirements?

The provincial e-commerce statutes provide that provincial statutory requirements to retain a paper document will be satisfied by the retention of an electronic document that provides reasonable assurance of its integrity. The standard for reviewing whether there is a reasonable assurance of the integrity of the documents will be assessed in light of the purpose for which the document was created. The provincial e-commerce statutes also provide that documents that were originally generated in electronic form will be deemed retained if they are accessible for future reference and the dates and times at which they were originally sent or received are recorded.

The *Privacy Act* provides that, where a federal law requires someone to retain a document for a specified period, an electronic document will satisfy the requirement if:

(i) the electronic document is retained for the specified period in the format in which it was made, sent or received, or in a format that does not change the information contained in the electronic document that was originally made, sent or received;

(ii) the information in the electronic document will be readable or perceivable by any person who is entitled to have access to the electronic document or who is authorized to require the production of the electronic document; and

(iii) any information that identifies the origin and destination of the electronic document and the date and time when it was sent or received is also retained.

2.2.6 Jurisdictional Issues

One of the primary issues arising from Internet and e-commerce activities pertains to jurisdiction. Given the global reach of the Internet, it is not always clear which laws of which jurisdictions or countries will apply. Determining the jurisdiction may be different for each of the issues that are involved. For example, the laws of one jurisdiction may apply to civil matters, such as contract or tort issues, but the laws of a different jurisdiction may apply to criminal law matters. There are many cases in Canada and abroad that deal with jurisdictional issues involving Internet and e-commerce activities, the detailed discussion of which is beyond the scope of this book.[23]

2.2.7 Tort Liability

Internet and e-commerce activities could also result in tort liability where there is a breach by one party of a duty owed to the other, which gives rise to injury.

A tort may occur when content on a web site is misrepresented and relied upon by another party to their detriment. Other torts that tend to be relevant to Internet and e-commerce inculde libel and slander, invasion of privacy, appropriation of personality, breach of confidence, passing off, defamation, negligence and trespass.

2.3 How Can the Risks be Reduced?

Many of the foregoing risks can be reduced through careful planning of the structure and content of web sites and the drafting of appropriate Internet and e-commerce contracts. A discussion on the specifics of such contracts follows in the subsequent chapters.

---

[23] Generally speaking, the courts have asserted jurisdiction where there is a real and substantial connection with the state and where there is commerical activity. See *Braintech v. Kostiuk* (1998) BCJ No. 622; *Proc-C Ltd. v. Computer City Inc.*, June 30, 2000 (Ont. S.C.J.), Court File No. 929/98, both of which applied *Zippo Manufacturing Co. v. Zippo Dot Com Inc.*, 952 F.Supp. 1119 (W.D. Pa.1997). For a discussion on jurisdiction and other Internet legal issues, please see *Internet Law, A Practical Guide for Legal and Business Professionals* by Alan M. Gahtan, Martin P.J. Kratz and J. Fraser Mann (Toronto: Carswell, 1998); and *Sookman: Computer, Internet and Electronic Commerce Law*, by Barry B. Sookman (Toronto: Carswell, 1991).

CHECKLIST 2A – NEW CANADIAN E-COMMERCE LEGISLATION

FEDERAL AND PROVINCIAL LEGISLATION IN FORCE IN CANADA	
Federal – The Personal Information Protection and Electronic Documents Act, S.C. 2000, c. 5 (Bill C-6):	Parts II and III (electronic documents and evidence) and IV came into force May 1, 2000. Part I came into force January 1, 2001.
British Columbia – Electronic Transactions Act, S.B.C. 2001, c. 10 (Bill 13):	Came into force April 19, 2001.
Manitoba – The Electronic Commerce and Information Act, S.M. 2000, c. 32 – Cap. E55 (Bill 31):	Parts 1, 3 (Electronic contracts and communications) 4, 5 and 7 came into force October 23, 2000. Part 2 (using electronic means) expected to come into force Spring, 2001. Part 6 to come into force March 19, 2001.
Nova Scotia – Electronic Commerce Act S.N.S. 2000, c. 26 (Bill 61):	Came into force November 30, 2000.
Ontario – Electronic Commerce Act, 2000, S.O. 2000, c. 17 (Bill 88):	Came into force October 16, 2000.
Prince Edward Island – Electronic Commerce Act, 2001 (Bill 25):	Came into force May 15, 2001.
Saskatchewan – The Electronic Information and Documents Act, 2000, S.S. 2000, c. E-7.22 (Bill 38):	Ss. 2-24 came into force November 1, 2000. S.1, Part 3 and s. 31 came into force June 21, 2000. C. E-7.22, Reg. 1 – The Electronic Information and Documents Regulations effective November 23, 2000.
Yukon – Electronic Commerce Act, S.Y. 2001, c. 10 (Bill 29):	Came into force March 27, 2001.
PROVINCIAL LEGISLATION PENDING	
Ontario – Private Member's Public Bill 70 (2000):	*An Act with respect to Electronic Information, Documents and Payments, 2000 – Referred to Committee.*
Alberta – Bill 21:	*Electronic Transactions Act, 2001* – First reading May 28, 2001.
New Brunswick – Bill 70:	*Electronic Transactions Act, 2001* – First reading May 23, 2001.

Quebec – Bills 122 and 161:	Bill 122, *An Act to amend the Act respecting Access to documents held by public bodies and the Protection of personal information, the Act respecting the protection of personal information in the private sector, the Professional Code and other legislative provisions*, and Bill 161, *An Act to Establish a Legal Framework for Information Technology*, were re-introduced in the 2nd Session, 36th Parliament, April 5, 2001. Bill 161 was debated in the Assembly on May 22, 2001.

Note: As of May 28, 2001, Newfoundland, Northwest Territories and Nunavut have not proposed any legislative or regulatory initiatives that might affect the use of electronic signatures, records and contracts.

CHECKLIST 2B – WEB SITE LIABILITY ISSUES

The following is a checklist of the common risks and liabilities that businesses with web sites face.

- The content on the web site might not be the most current, could contain errors and might not be complete (e.g. only a summary), and if users rely on the content, the web site owner could be negligent or in breach of implied warranties.
- If the web site contains the principal terms of a contract, such as a description of a product or service, delivery terms and a price, there is a risk that the Internet user might treat this information as an offer as opposed to mere advertising. Once the user accepts this offer, the web site owner will be bound to deliver on the terms of the offer, unless it has specified that the information on the web site is not to be construed as an offer.
- The web site might contain an unknown virus.
- There could be transmission problems, server outages or downtimes.
- The content and hyper-links on the site could contain inaccuracies or problems such as material, which infringes someone else's copyright, or trade-mark rights, or is defamatory or illegal.
- Many web sites permit users to communicate with the web site operator or other users or collect information about users with *Cookies, Passports, Sniffers* or logs and could be subject to consumer protection and privacy issues (See paragraph 2.2.3 and Chapter 4 for a discussion on privacy legislation).
- Jurisdictional issues such as where will a transaction be taxed? Is the web site, its content, the activity conducted on or through the web site, its legal terms or any other related agreements enforceable or illegal in particular countries? Can local laws impose terms into a contract, which one has not expressly agreed to?
- Criminal liability.
- The content on the web site of a public company could contain inaccurate or overly optimistic "investor relations" information that can mislead investors and draw the attention of security regulators. Furthermore, during public offerings, web site content may become subject to security laws and regulations.

CHECKLIST 2C – HOW TO MINIMIZE THE RISKS OF WEB SITE LIABILITY AND RISKS ASSOCIATED WITH E-CONTRACTS

- consider physical location of server and web site;
- specify in the e-contract: the physical location of the server and which governing laws and forum apply; the acceptance methods, what constitutes a "signature" and that an electronic document is equivalent to paper;
- establish security procedures to verify the identity and authority of contracting parties, e.g., using passwords, cryptography or keys;
- set out who the web site is intended to be read by, e.g., age of majority only;
- establish controls on who has access to the web site to buy the products – implement technical controls for unfavourable jurisdictions;
- provide for mechanisms to allow customers to retain copies of e-contracts, to exit the web site and to make corrections;
- specify what rights and licenses the user is granted in accessing the web site and what restrictions are imposed on their use;
- disclaim liability for content and hyper-links;
- disclaim implied representations, warranties (and conditions in Canada), such as merchantability and fitness for a particular purpose (and quality in Canada); and disclaim liability for indirect damages or loss of profits, inaccuracy, incompleteness or timeliness of the web site, viruses or data corruption and damages arising as a result of the transmission, use or inability to use the web site;
- ensure readers scroll through terms and highlight/accept onerous terms of e-contracts;
- have customers type "I accept" rather than merely clicking on a button

CHAPTER 3

INTERNET ACCESS SERVICE AGREEMENTS

3.1 INTRODUCTION TO THE DIFFERENT FORMS OF INTERNET ACCESS SERVICES

As discussed in Chapter 1 (see paragraph 1.1.3) *Internet* connections occur over various forms of telecommunications systems, for example telephone lines, cable, fiber optics, microwave links and satellite transmissions. *ISPs* and *OSPs* lease space on such lines or backbones and sell, to businesses and consumers, connections or access to the Internet.

3.2 WHAT RISKS DOES A CUSTOMER FACE IN OBTAINING INTERNET ACCESS SERVICES AND HOW TO AVOID THEM?

As discussed in Chapter 2, the Internet is an open system where confidentiality and privacy issues are one of the biggest concerns for a customer using the Internet. In addition, a customer obtaining Internet access services from an ISP or OSP may want to obtain certain assurances as to service levels, addressing issues such as continuity of access and minimization of system down-time. A customer also faces the risk that his or her use of Internet access is not secure and that someone could misuse his or her password or other identification. Furthermore, there is the risk that the web sites visited by the customer are inaccurate, incomplete or have other problems.

To allocate some of these risks to other persons, customers would seek covenants, representations, warranties and indemnities from their ISP, OSP (see paragraphs 3.4.9 and 3.4.10 below) as well as any web site or content provider (see Chapter 5) with whom they have direct contractual relationships, that the customers' use of the Internet services are secure, confidential and meet certain service levels or other customer requirements. Correspondingly, this would require the service providers to establish security and content control mechanisms to ensure compliance with their contractual obligations to the customers.

3.3 WHAT RISKS DOES AN ISP FACE IN PROVIDING INTERNET ACCESS SERVICES AND HOW TO AVOID THEM?

As discussed in Chapter 2, an ISP might be found liable for its customers' activities, particularly if the Internet access services include services such as e-mail or interactive web pages (such as chat rooms or bulletin boards) where Internet users can upload their own content. The risks of potential liability increase with the amount of control or knowledge[1] that an ISP has of its customers' activities, and include liability for defamation, intellectual property infringement (such as copyright and trade-mark infringement), violation of privacy and *Criminal Code* offences such as obscenity, child pornography and hate propaganda.

Although an ISP cannot contract out of statutory liability to third parties or criminal liability, the risks faced by the ISP can be reduced with an Internet Access Services Agreement (See Forms 3A and 3B) and Internet Policies (See Chapter 4). The Internet Access Services Agreement and Internet Policies increase customer awareness of potential liabilities. If the customer is in the best position to deal with the risks, there is a good argument that the agreement and policies should be drafted to shift the risks onto the customer and should contain indemnities from the customer for damages that the ISP may suffer.

Another common risk faced by the ISP is the failure of third party software, hardware, telecommunications backbones or other products or services that were not developed or supplied by the ISP and over which the ISP has little or no control. ISPs can manage this risk by ensuring any limitations on the liability of and disclaimers by their suppliers are reflected in the ISPs' contracts with its customers. In addition, when acting for an ISP, one should negotiate limitations on the ISP's liability for events outside the control of the ISP, such as disclaimers of any liability for damages or losses resulting from any third party, including, without limitation, telecommunications service providers, the ISP's contractors and the Internet backbone.

3.4 Principal Terms of Internet Access Service Agreements

In drafting the Internet Access Service Agreement, or any other Internet and e-commerce agreements, it is helpful to have representatives from different areas of the business, such as marketing and technical personnel, provide input as to the business issues and risks that will shape the terms of the agreements. Technology, such as encryption techniques and passwords, may also be implemented to reduce the risk of breach of obligations under the agreement. In any event, the Internet Access Services Agreement between the ISP and the customer should contain the following principle terms:

---

1 Note that certain offences, such as strict liability offences, do not require any knowledge by the offender to be found liable.

3.4.1 Internet Access Services

The Internet Access Services Agreement must clearly describe the type of Internet access services being provided. If the services to be provided include more than mere Internet access (e.g., additional services such as the use of browser software, the hosting of the customer's web site, or the maintenance of a telephone support help desk) the terms of the Access Services Agreement should also include the terms of other agreements (such as software license terms (see C. Ian Kyer and Mark J. Fecenko, *Kyer and Fecenko on Computer-Related Agreements: A Practical Guide* 2nd ed. (Toronto: Butterworths, 1997), Chapter 5), web site hosting terms or support terms) (see Chapter 7 and Form 7A). The agreement should describe: how the services are being provided (e.g., by customer dial-up connection or dedicated high-speed line connected from customer to the ISP and from the ISP's server to an Internet backbone); how many users have access; when the services are available (e.g., 24 hours a day, seven (7) days a week, except during scheduled maintenance periods, or by a certain number of users or from a particular location); and what additional obligations each party has (e.g. to provide certain hardware, software or security technology). (See Form 3B Section 2)

The customer may want to obtain performance guarantees from the ISP. Such guarantees could be similar to the obligations and representations found in web site hosting or software hosting agreements (See Chapters 7 and 8).

If applicable, the terms regarding other obligations, rights and restrictions of the parties, such as: sending and purging of e-mail; privacy (e.g. how data can be collected and stored and whether Internet use will be monitored), (See paragraph 3.4.6, below, and Chapter 4); access to data or web pages; and use of bulletin boards, chat rooms or other Internet services, should also be specified in the Internet Access Services Agreement.

3.4.2 Restrictions

The purpose of setting out restrictions in the Internet Access Services Agreement is to draw to the attention of the customer, prohibited and potentially illegal activities. Although an ISP cannot contract out of statutory liability to third parties or criminal liability, the risks faced by the ISP will likely be reduced if the customer is made aware of potential liabilities, and if the customer covenants not to engage in activities that could create liability for the ISP and if the ISP has contractual remedies against the customer for breach of the customer's covenants.

Common restrictions on a customer using Internet access services are set out in Checklist 3, below, and Form 3A, Section 3.

From the ISP's perspective, it is important that the customer be responsible for any activity that occurs through the customer's account. (See Form 3A, Section 4) This is of particular concern where customers may allow third parties to use their passwords to access the ISP's Internet services. Where security controls, such as encryption technology, are used, customers are in a better position to manage the risks of someone else using their Internet connection.

As well, an ISP may want to include restrictions on customers subleasing or reselling the Internet access services or allowing simultaneous access by more users than are specified in the agreement.

However, from the customer's perspective, particularly where the Internet access services being provided by the ISP are via a dedicated connection, it is important that the ISP be obligated to prevent unauthorized access to the dedicated line by other customers and implement appropriate security controls. (See Form 3B, Section 2.3)

3.4.3 Customer Obligations

The agreement should specify the customer's responsibilities for telecommunications access, software (such as web browsers and connectivity software), computer hardware (such as routers, workstations and servers), and peripherals (such as modems and other communications equipment), which are needed to be able to obtain Internet access services.

To the extent that the customer is in a better position than the ISP to maintain control over its access passwords, it is arguable that the customer should be responsible for maintaining the confidentiality of its passwords and should be responsible for all activities and charges resulting from the use of the customer's account or passwords, including unauthorized use. However, if the ISP's obligations include the requirement to maintain adequate security measures to prevent unauthorized access to the services, the customer may not want to agree to such obligation. The customer should also be obligated to use the Internet access services for lawful purposes. Restrictions on customer's use are discussed in paragraph 3.4.2, above.

3.4.4 Ownership and Licensing

With respect to any equipment, hardware, software, data or other materials used in the provision of the Internet access services, ownership of such materials and, if applicable, terms commonly found in hardware leasing and software licensing agreements (See C. Ian Kyer and Mark J. Fecenko, *Kyer and Fecenko on Computer-Related Agreements: A Practical Guide*, 2nd ed. (Toronto: Butterworths, 1997), Chapters 4 and 5), should be included in the agreement. The scope of any license granted should be carefully drafted. Consideration should be given as to what specific rights are required to be licensed (e.g., the right to run, copy, modify, sublicense, distribute, etc.), whether the license is exclusive, sole or non-exclusive[2] and whether there are any territorial, usage or other restrictions or limitations.

Assignment of any intellectual property rights and waivers of moral rights that a customer may acquire by virtue of their use of the systems, might also be required (e.g., if the customer is given the right to make modifications to software and the ISP desires to own all modifications).

3.4.5 Fees and Reporting

There are many different ways to structure fees in Internet access service agreements. Some of the possibilities upon which fees can be based include each of the following or a combination of the following:

(i) one-time charges, e.g., for implementing access;

(ii) fixed rates, e.g., $x per month or $x per size of access line; or

(iii) variable rates based on:

  (a) total on-line access time in a given time period;

  (b) ISP's variable fee schedules as provided to its customers from time to time; or

  (c) number of users receiving access services.

The agreement should also specify whether the fees are inclusive or exclusive of applicable taxes and duties.

It may also be reasonable to impose an obligation on a party to provide regular reports as to the criteria upon which the fees are based and to allow audits of a party's records to verify fees.

---

2 An "exclusive" license means only the licensee can exercise the rights granted, even to the exclusion of the licensor. Exclusivity can be limited in scope. A "sole" license means no one other than the licensee and licensor can exercise the rights granted.

3.4.6 Confidentiality and Privacy

In order to comply with any applicable legislation or regulations, to facilitate co-operation with law enforcement agencies and to ensure that customers are complying with the Internet Access Services Agreement, it is important that the agreement permit (but not obligate) the ISP to monitor, intercept and disclose the customer's use of the Internet access services.

In the situation where the parties to the Internet Access Services Agreement are exchanging personal or confidential information, such as users' names and addresses, or if the ISP may be monitoring the customer's activities, it is recommended that the agreement contain confidentiality and privacy provisions (See Chapter 4).

3.4.7 Remedies

The Access Services Agreement should also set out the remedies that each party has if the other party is in breach of the agreement. Such remedies may include the right for the non-breaching party to terminate the agreement, to receive liquidated damages and to be indemnified for any third party claims or damages. (See paragraph 3.4.10, below, and Form 3A, Sections 4 and 12)

3.4.8 Term

If applicable, a distinction should be made between the date the agreement becomes effective and the date the Internet access services commence (e.g., when the ISP receives the first payment). As well, it is important to distinguish suspension of services from termination of the entire agreement. For example, if the ISP needs to conduct maintenance work on its servers, it would need the right to suspend services as opposed to terminate them.

From the customer's point of view, it is important that the term of the agreement is not too long, especially as technology is becoming less expensive and ISPs are offering better Internet access rates. Therefore, one should consider whether an option for early termination should be provided in the agreement.

On the other hand, the ISP may have incurred significant costs in setting up the access services and connectivity, particularly for a dedicated line that is being leased on a long-term basis from a third party. Therefore, an ISP would likely want to negotiate a longer agreement term. In order to free-up access lines, an ISP may also want to have the ability to terminate the agreement early if a customer is in breach of this agreement, fails to pay or becomes bankrupt or insolvent.

Careful consideration should also be given to the survival of terms in the Internet Access Services Agreement, such as obligations of confidentiality, privacy, and representations, warranties and indemnities relating to title or non-infringement.

Consideration should also be given to the effects of termination, e.g., whether any software or hardware has to be returned and whether any transitional services need to be provided.

3.4.9 Representations and Warranties

In addition to the usual representations and warranties given by parties to a contract, such as that each party has the right to enter into the agreement and that the agreement does not and will not conflict with any other agreement or obligation that a party may have, Internet Access Services Agreements require some additional representations and warranties to minimize the risk of unique liabilities that arise in Internet access, as discussed in paragraphs 3.2 and 3.3 above.

When acting for the ISP, it is recommended that the following warranties be obtained from the customer:

- if applicable, that the customer has the right to license or provide access to (as the case may be) any software, hardware, data, web site, content or other materials provided to or accessible by the ISP;
- that such materials provided to or accessible by the ISP do not and will not infringe on any copyright or any trade-mark, patent, trade secret or other intellectual property right of any third party, in countries where the ISP will be using or accessing the materials or where the ISP is at risk of being sued for infringement. However, customers will be relatively reluctant to give representations or warranties for any third-party items which were not created by the customer (such as third-party hardware, software or content); which the customer does not own; or over which the customer has no control or has not received similar representations or warranties from the customer's developers, suppliers or licensors;
- if the customer is an individual, that he or she is the end user of the Internet access account and has reached the age of majority.

When acting for the customer, it is recommended that the following warranties be obtained from the ISP:

- in the case of a dedicated, high-speed access line, that the line is of a certain speed and is not shared with other customers;

- that the security or firewall technology is of a certain standard;
- where software is also being licensed as part of the access services, software warranties as to title, right to license, non-infringement, performance and no disabling mechanisms;
- where other services such as web site hosting are being provided by the ISP, warranties pertaining to such services (see Chapter 7);
- that performance of the services under the agreement will be done in a competent manner by qualified personnel; and
- that the ISP has the right to license or provide access to (as the case may be) any software, hardware, or other materials provided to or accessible by the customer in obtaining the Internet access services.

3.4.10 Indemnities

In drafting any indemnity, it is important to consider whether the indemnity should apply only to the contracting parties, or whether it should extend to the relevant party's directors, officers, agents, subcontractors and affiliates as well. If the financial ability or viability of a contracting party is of concern, it may be worthwhile to seek a guarantee from a parent or related company.

If either party is supplying or allowing access by the other party to assets, such as software, hardware, servers, telecommunications systems or other materials (for the purposes of this paragraph 3.4.10, the "supplying party"), then the agreement should provide for an indemnity by the supplying party to protect the other party (for the purposes of this paragraph 3.4.10, the "receiving party") from any liability arising out of the receiving party's use of such assets. The indemnities generally given are indemnities for losses resulting from intellectual property infringement or trade secret misappropriation claims. However, a supplying party will be relatively reluctant to indemnify the receiving party for any items which were not created by the supplying party (e.g., which were supplied to the supplying party by third parties or by the receiving party), which the supplying party does not own; or over which the supplying party has no control or corresponding indemnities from the supplying party's developers, suppliers or licensors.

The receiving party will generally seek an indemnity from the supplying party that the materials received or accessed do not infringe any intellectual property right of any third party, in jurisdictions where the receiving party will use or access such materials, or where the receiving party may otherwise be subject to a claim or judgment. However, it is reasonable for the parties to agree upon limitations upon the scope of the indemnity for example, by having it apply only in territories where the supplying party has conducted intellectual property ownership searches and registrations, or where it would be reasonable to expect the supplying party to do so. Furthermore, since patent and trade-mark applications are generally not publicly available until the patent or trade-mark has been issued, indemnities for patent or trade-mark infringement should be limited only to valid patents or trade-marks that have been issued as of the effective date of the agreement. (See additional discussion in Limitations on Liability and Disclaimers, below)

An indemnity for a claim of infringement of a third party's rights could also include the ability on the supplying party to, at its option:

(i) modify the infringing material so that it becomes non-infringing;

(ii) replace the infringing material (with consideration given to the criteria for such replacement);

(iii) obtain from the third party claiming infringement the right to use the infringing material (provided that such rights can be obtained on terms satisfactory to the indemnifying party); or

(iv) request that the receiving party cease using, remove, return or destroy the infringing material and terminate this agreement.

When acting for the receiving party, however, one should carefully review the agreement to ensure that the supplying party's options, referred to above, do not limit any other remedies that the receiving party may have against the supplying party for breach of a non-infringement warranty. The parties should also consider whether the agreement should provide for a refund of amounts paid under the agreement (especially if amounts were paid for unaccrued services), in the event of early termination as a result of an infringement claim.

To the extent that the customer is in a better position than the ISP to maintain control over its access passwords, the ISP may want to seek an indemnity from the customer for any damages or claims arising from statements or other content transmitted, posted, received or created through the customer's Internet access account, even if transmitted, posted, received or created by someone else (especially intellectual property infringement claims). However, if the ISP's obligations include the requirement to maintain adequate security measures to prevent unauthorized access to the services, the customer may not want to agree to such indemnity.

3.4.11 Limitations on Liability and Disclaimers

When negotiating Internet Access Agreements, consideration should be given as to any limitations on either party's liability for breach of any obligations, representations or warranties in the agreement; for any tortious acts or omissions; or for any other damages that the other party may suffer.

As with most commercial agreements, it is common to cap the liability of both parties for breach of the agreement or negligence to a specified amount, e.g., the amount paid or payable under the agreement over a specified time period. However, with respect to intellectual property infringement claims or breach of confidence, the liabilities a party may suffer could significantly exceed such pre-determined amounts and therefore one may reasonably argue that any liability for breach of an intellectual property warranty (such as a warranty as to title, right to license or non-infringement); intellectual property infringement indemnities (see discussion in paragraph 3.4.10 above); and liability for a breach of confidence should not be limited to direct, quantifiable damages.

Exclusions are, however, often drafted for intellectual property infringement indemnities if:

- the infringement occurs as a result of unauthorized use or modification of the material that is determined to be infringing;
- the indemnified party continues to use the infringing material after such party has been notified of the infringement or such party has been provided with modifications that would have avoided the infringement;
- the indemnified party fails to notify the indemnifying party of any infringement claim that comes to the indemnified party's attention;
- the indemnified party fails to co-operate with the indemnifying party in the investigation and defence of any infringement claim; or
- the indemnifying party does not have sole control over the defence and settlement of any infringement claim.

Subject to any performance warranties, an ISP providing Internet access services will generally disclaim any requirements to provide uninterrupted, confidential, private, secure, dedicated or error-free access services.

As in other commercial agreements, all other representations, warranties and conditions not expressly included in this agreement, whether statutory or otherwise, will often ordinarily be disclaimed, including, without limitation, warranties of merchantability, quality, fitness for a particular purpose, and those arising out of a course of dealing or usage of trade.

Unforeseen circumstances or events beyond a party's control are also commonly included in an excusable delays clause (also known as Force Majeure). As with many types of Internet contracts, ISPs often rely on third parties, such as telecommunications providers, in providing Internet access services. It is up to the contracting parties to negotiate between them who is in the best position to bear the risks of failures or delays by such third parties.

In drafting the Internet Access Services Agreement, one should consider including a provision that exculpates the ISP from responsibility for any problem with the customer's equipment, software, peripherals, telecommunications lines or other materials, that was not caused by any of the services performed by the ISP under the agreement. Furthermore, the ISP may want to attribute responsibility to the customer, in the form of payment to the ISP at the ISP's then standard service rates, for all costs incurred in the evaluation, correction or performance of services relating to problems with the customer's equipment, software, peripherals, telecommunications lines or other materials.

As in other commercial agreements, it is common for the parties to disclaim indirect, consequential, special and punitive damages unless such damages are likely consequences that a party may suffer and would be concerned about, such as in the case of a breach of intellectual property warranties, indemnities or breach of confidentiality. It is important to clearly set out the types of indirect damages that are intended to be excluded, such as loss of profits, savings or data.

3.4.12 General Clauses

As with other commercial agreements, in Internet and e-commerce agreements, one should consider including notice clauses, non-waiver, currency, severability, assignability, entire agreement, further assurances, force majeure, time of the essence, interpretation, independent contractors, binding on successors, survival, governing law and choice of language clauses.

CHECKLIST 3 – FOR DRAFTING INTERNET ACCESS SERVICE AGREEMENTS

- Ensure parties are clearly identified by their full legal names and for on-line agreements, see also checklist in Chapter 9;
- describe the Internet access services, e.g. speed, number of users, connection point, e-mail services, news services, file transfer, remote login, firewall and back-up services;
- specify how and when the services are available or any exceptions to availability, e.g., suspension of services;
- include ISP performance obligations, e.g., that the ISP prevent unauthorized access to the dedicated line by other customers and implement appropriate security controls;
- include any additional obligations that ISP, may have, such as to provide ancillary services (e.g., web site hosting), software, hardware, tools or other materials required for Internet access;
- if applicable, include web site hosting, ownership, software licensing or hardware leasing terms;
- include any additional obligations that customers may have, such as:
  - compliance with ISP's policies,
  - use of the Internet access services for lawful purposes,
  - adherence to the laws of a particular jurisdiction,
  - compliance with court ordered publication bans,
  - responsibility for telecommunications access, software (such as web browsers and connectivity software), computer hardware (such as routers, workstations and servers), and peripherals (such as modems and other communications equipment);
- set out restricted customer activities such as:
  - publishing, printing, distributing, possessing, selling, advocating, promoting, or exposing, obscene material, child pornography, or hate propaganda,
  - the use of trade-marks or trade names,
  - the use of copyright works,
  - defamation, libel, harm to reputation, invasion of privacy, misuse or failure to protect personal information, violation of secrecy, unfair competition and other situations that could generate civil liability,

- export and import restrictions,
- subleasing or reselling the Internet access services or allowing simultaneous access by more users than are specified in the agreement;

- allocate responsibility for activities through customer's accounts or using customer's passwords;
- draft fee and payment terms and specify currency and whether taxes are extra;
- include confidentiality and privacy provisions and consent by customers to ISP's monitoring and disclosure of customer's activities;
- set out the remedies that each party has if the other party is in breach of the agreement, e.g., to receive liquidated damages and to be indemnified for any third-party claims or damages;
- representations, warranties and indemnities given by a customer:
  - that it has the right to enter into the agreement,
  - that the agreement does not and will not conflict with any other agreement or obligation,
  - that it has the right to license or provide access to (as the case may be) any software, hardware, data, web site, content or other materials provided to or accessible by the ISP,
  - that such materials provided to or accessible by the ISP do not or will not infringe on any copyright or any trade-mark, patent, trade secret or other intellectual property right of any third-party, in countries where the ISP will be using or accessing the materials or where the ISP is at risk of being sued for infringement (and consider exceptions for any third-party items which were not created by the customer; which the customer does not own; or over which the customer has no control or has not received similar representations or warranties from the customer's developers, suppliers or licensors),
  - indemnities for losses resulting from intellectual property infringement or trade secret misappropriation claims (and consider exceptions and limitations on indemnities),
  - if the customer is an individual, that he or she is the end user of the Internet access account and has reached the age of majority;
- representations, warranties and indemnities given by an ISP:
  - that it has the right to enter into the agreement,

- that the agreement does not and will not conflict with any other agreement or obligation,
- in the case of a dedicated, high-speed access line, that the line is of a certain speed and is not shared with other customers,
- that the security or firewall technology is of a certain standard,
- where software is also being licensed as part of the access services, software warranties as to title or right to license, non-infringement, performance and no disabling mechanisms (and consider exceptions for any third-party items which were not created by the ISP; which the ISP does not own; or over which the ISP has no control or has not received similar representations or warranties from the ISP's developers, suppliers or licensors),
- where other services such as web site hosting are being provided by the ISP, warranties pertaining to such services (see Chapter 7),
- that performance of the services under the agreement will be done in a competent manner by qualified personnel,
- that the ISP has the right to license or provide access to (as the case may be) any software, hardware, or other materials provided to or accessible by the customer in obtaining the Internet access services,
- indemnities for losses resulting from intellectual property infringement or trade secret misappropriation claims (and consider exceptions and limitations on indemnities);

• disclaimers and limitations on liability to be considered:

- as applicable to indemnities,
- for performance, uninterrupted, confidential, private, secure, dedicated or error-free access services,
- disclaimer of implied warranties,
- force majeure events,
- third-party products, acts or omissions,
- liability by ISP for problems with customer's products,
- indirect damages (should be described),
- draft the term, termination and suspension provisions and consider which terms of the agreement survive termination or expiry,
- consider post-termination or expiry provisions, e.g., return of software or materials and transitional services;

- boilerplate provisions, e.g., notice clauses, non-waiver, currency, severability, assignability, entire agreement, further assurances, force majeure, time of the essence, interpretation, independent contractors, binding on successors, survival, governing law and choice of language clauses.

FORM 3A – DIAL-UP ACCESS AGREEMENT

[NAME OF ISP] INTERNET ACCESS AGREEMENT

This Internet Access Agreement is between you the customer ["You"] and [insert ISP's full legal name] [the "*[NAME OF ISP]*"]. "We" and "Us" means both You and *[NAME OF ISP]*. The effective date of this Agreement is when You accept this Agreement in accordance with the procedure set out [below].

IMPORTANT! CAREFULLY READ THIS AGREEMENT. [BY CLICKING ON THE "I ACCEPT" ICON] [BY USING *[NAME OF ISP'S SERVICES]*] [BY SIGNING BELOW] [BY TYPING "I ACCEPT" IN THE BOX BELOW], THAT ACTION IS THE EQUIVALENT OF YOUR SIGNATURE AND INDICATES THAT YOU HAVE READ THIS AGREEMENT, UNDERSTAND AND ACCEPT ALL THE TERMS AND CONDITIONS AND THAT YOU INTEND TO BE LEGALLY BOUND BY THEM. IF YOU DO NOT AGREE WITH THE TERMS OF THIS AGREEMENT, [CLICK ON THE "EXIT" ICON].

In consideration for You being granted access to the Internet, We understand and agree to the following:

1. You will comply with all *(NAME OF ISP)*'s Use Policies, attached as Schedule A, which Policies may be amended by *(NAME OF ISP)* ("*(NAME OF ISP)*") from time to time.

2. You represent and warrant that You are the end user of this account and have reached the age of majority.

3. You shall adhere to the laws of *[insert province]* and Canada in using *[NAME OF ISP]*, including but not limited to those laws regarding:

(a) court ordered publication bans;

(b) restrictions on publishing, printing, distributing, possessing, selling, advocating, promoting, or exposing, obscene material, child pornography, or hate propaganda and You understand that these situations could generate criminal liability;

(c) restrictions on the use of trade-marks or trade names;

(d) restrictions on the use of copyright work, including without limitation, software;

(e) restrictions on defamation, libel, harm to reputation, invasion of privacy, misuse or failure to protect personal information, violation of secrecy, unfair competition and other situations which could generate civil liability; and

(f) export and import restrictions.

4. You shall be solely responsible for any and all items or statements transmitted, posted, received or created through Your account, on *[NAME OF ISP]*'s system or any other system, and their content, even if transmitted, posted, received or created by someone else, and You agree to indemnify and hold *[NAME OF ISP]*, its directors, officers, employees, agents, contractors and affiliates, harmless from any loss, damage or liability which may result therefrom.

5. You agree and acknowledge that:

(a) payment in advance is required for service, unless otherwise agreed to in writing;

(b) unused connection time cannot be transferred; and

(c) prepaid fees are non-refundable.

6. You acknowledge that invoices are due and payable immediately upon receipt. Interest will be charged on outstanding balances at [*RATE, PERCENTAGE*] per year.

7. *[NAME OF ISP]'s*, it's directors, officers, employees, agents, contractors and affiliates will not be liable for any loss or damage that may result from the use or inability to use *[NAME OF ISP]*'s system or any other system through which services may be provided.

8. *[NAME OF ISP]s* services are not guaranteed and there are no representations or warranties of any kind, including without limitation, uninterrupted or error free service, accessibility, privacy of files or e-mail.

9. Any software which You receive from *[NAME OF ISP]* shall not be used and shall be returned to *[NAME OF ISP]* unless You agree to accept and be bound by the applicable software license agreement.

10. *[NAME OF ISP]* may modify the terms of this agreement and/or rates charged at any time, upon e-mail notice being sent to Your account. Rate changes will take effect on the renewal of this agreement.

11. The term of this agreement shall be for the same term as the payment plan which You applied for and it will automatically renew at the end of the term on the then current terms except that *[NAME OF ISP]*'s then current rates shall apply. If You do not want this agreement to renew, You must advise *[NAME OF ISP]* in writing *[METHOD OF NOTIFICATION, E.G., BY E-MAIL, POST, FAX OR COURIER]* prior to the end of the then current term.

12. *[NAME OF ISP]* may terminate Your access to the Internet and this agreement at any time and without warning, if in *[NAME OF ISP]*'s sole discretion You are in breach of any term of this agreement.

13. If paying by credit card, You agree to provide a copy of Your signature for *[NAME OF ISP]* to maintain on file for billing the credit card. Should You wish to stop payment by credit card, You must advise *[NAME OF ISP]* in writing *[METHOD OF NOTIFICATION, E.G., BY E-MAIL, POST, FAX OR COURIER]*, *[NUMBER]* days in advance.

14. You hereby consent to the exchange of information and documents between Us electronically over the Internet or by e-mail, if to You to [insert address of Internet user] or if to Company [insert address of Company] and that this electronic Agreement shall be the equivalent of a written paper Agreement between Us.

15. If any part of this agreement is held to be unenforceable or invalid, it will be severed from the rest of this agreement which shall continue in full force and effect.

16. *[NAME OF ISP]* and its server is physically located within the Province of [*insert province*], Canada. This agreement will be governed by the laws of the Province of [*insert province*] and the federal laws of Canada and shall be treated in all respects as a [*insert province*] contract, without reference to the principles of conflicts of law. In the event of a dispute, We agree to submit to the non-exclusive jurisdiction of the [*insert province*] courts. We expressly exclude the *UN Convention on Contracts for the International Sale of Goods,* and the *[insert name of provincial International Sale of Goods Act]* as amended, replaced or re-enacted from time to time. We have required that this Agreement and all documents relating thereto be drawn-up in English. Nous avons demandé que cette convention ainsi que tous les documents qui s'y rattachent soient rédigés en anglais.

[I ACCEPT BUTTON] [I DECLINE BUTTON]

FORM 3B – HIGH-SPEED, DEDICATED LINE INTERNET ACCESS AGREEMENT

THIS AGREEMENT is made effective as of the *[DATE]* day of *[MONTH, YEAR]*

BETWEEN:

[*CUSTOMER'S FULL LEGAL NAME*]
"Customer"

-and-

[*ISP'S FULL LEGAL NAME*]

"Supplier"

For good and valuable consideration, the receipt and adequacy of which are hereby acknowledged, the Customer and Supplier agree as follows:

1. INTERPRETATION

1.1 Definitions. — In this Agreement, the following expressions will have the meanings set out below unless the context requires otherwise:

"Business Day" means any day except Saturday, Sunday, or any day on which banks are generally not open for business in the city of *[insert city]*;

"Internet" means the world-wide network of computers commonly understood as the Internet;

"Party" means either Customer or Supplier as the context requires; and "Parties" means both Customer and Supplier;

"Person" is to be broadly interpreted and includes an individual, a corporation, a partnership, a trust, an unincorporated organization, the government of a country of any political subdivision thereof, or any agency or department of any such government, and the executors, administrators or other legal representatives of an individual in such capacity; and

"Web Server" means the computer or computers that the Supplier uses to make web sites accessible to Internet users.

1.2 Headings and Table of Contents. — The division of this Agreement into Articles and Sections, the insertion of headings, and the provision of any table of contents are for convenience of reference only and will not affect the construction or interpretation of this Agreement.

1.3 Number and Gender. — Unless the context requires otherwise, words importing the singular include the plural and vice versa and words importing gender include all genders.

1.4 Business Days. — If any payment is required to be made [or other action is required to be taken] pursuant to this Agreement on a day which is not a Business Day, then such payment [or action] will be made [or taken] on the next Business Day.

1.5 Currency and Payment Obligations. — Except as otherwise expressly provided in this Agreement, all dollar amounts referred to in this Agreement are stated in *[INSERT CURRENCY]* and any payment contemplated by this Agreement will be made by *[INSERT METHOD OF PAYMENT, E.G., CASH, CERTIFIED CHEQUE, DIRECT DEBIT, ETC.]* [or any other method that provides immediately available funds]. All payments due on a particular day must be received and available not later than *[INSERT TIME]* on the due date and any payment made after that time will be deemed to have been made and received on the next Business Day.

1.6 Calculation of Interest. — In calculating interest payable under this Agreement for any period of time, the first day of such period will be included and the last day of such period will be excluded.

1.7 Statute References. — Any reference in this Agreement to any statute or any section thereof will, unless otherwise expressly stated, be deemed to be a reference to such statute or section as amended, restated or re-enacted from time to time.

1.8 Section of Schedule References. — Unless the context requires otherwise, references in this Agreement to Sections or Schedules are to Sections or Schedules of this Agreement.

2. INTERNET ACCESS SERVICES

2.1 Access and Services Provided by Supplier. — The Supplier shall provide the Customer with Internet access services consisting of the following:

(a) a dedicated [*SPEED OF LINE, E.G. T1*] speed [or better] connection from [*POINT OF CONNECTION CLOSEST TO THE CUSTOMER, OVER WHICH SUPPLIER HAS CONTROL, E.G., THE CUSTOMER'S GATEWAY*] [up to [*NUMBER*] [named] [concurrent] Customer users which, [at the Customer's option,] may be accessed at any time or times to up to [*NUMBER*] concurrent users] to the Web Server;

(b) [Internet e-mail accounts [with [*insert amount*] of storage capacity each, for up to *[NUMBER]* [named] Customer users [including the supply of a dedicated mail server exclusively for the use of Customer users]];

(c) *[SPEED E.G., T3]* [or better] connectivity from the Web Server to the [*INSERT NAME OF TELECOMMUNI-CATIONS COMPANY OR OTHER INTERNET BACK-BONE*] backbone, or to any other recognized Internet backbone;

(d) [access to the Supplier's Usenet news service by up to *[NUMBER]* named Customer users];

(e) [FTP download/upload facility from *[LOCATION, E.G., Internal Customer work stations]* to and from external vendors and other web sites];

(f) [telnet ability for remote technical login for up to *[NUMBER]* named Customer users];

(g) [*[FIREWALL NAME]* firewall technology at the Supplier's site [as described in the schedule attached] including without limitation, the capability for Customer Internet users to access secure web sites on the Internet; and]

(h) [tools to monitor Internet use by Customer Internet users, as agreed to in advance by the Supplier. If Customer requires network monitoring tools, including software, configuration and/or training, Supplier will provide subject to applicable charges.]

2.2 Hardware and Software. — [Except for any hardware leased or software licensed to Customer by the Supplier,] Customer shall provide and maintain [at its site] in good working order, [sufficient and adequate; or the following computer hardware, servers, peripherals, software, modems, communications equipment, access lines, routers and web browsers] necessary to allow its users, work stations and corporate computer network to access and utilize the ISP's services referred to in Section 2.1.

[The Parties shall enter into separate agreements for any hardware leased or software licensed to Customer by the Supplier.]

2.3 Security of Customer Systems. — [When acting for the Customer, the following clause should be inserted:

The Supplier shall use commercially reasonable efforts to prevent unauthorized access by other Internet users to the Customer's computer systems.

"Commercially reasonable efforts" shall mean the implementation of a *[NAME OF FIREWALL]* firewall server.]

[When acting for the Supplier, the following clause should be inserted:

Customer shall provide and be responsible for firewall security *[INSERT TECHNICAL REQUIREMENTS OR REFER TO SCHEDULE THAT DESCRIBES FIREWALL REQUIREMENTS]* to prevent unauthorized access by other Internet users to the Customer's computer systems.]

2.4 Implementation. — [The Supplier will provide project management necessary to ensure the installation by Customer of the *[SPEED AND TYPE OF CONNECTION, E.G., T1 LOCAL LOOP]*, the on-site installation by Customer of the required router and other hardware, to be supplied by Customer, the migration by Customer to a dedicated mail server, the transfer and configuration of e-mail addresses, the set-up and configuration of a Web Server, the upgrade to a *[NAME OR TYPE OF FIREWALL]* firewall server]

[The Supplier shall not provide the access referred to in Section 2.1 until the Web, e-mail and firewall servers and communications connections referred to in this Agreement have been installed, configured and tested to the Supplier's satisfaction.]

2.5 Other Customer Obligations. — Customer agrees and acknowledges that:

(a) it will follow appropriate Internet etiquette. In particular, Customer will comply with all Supplier's *[INTERNET AND PRIVACY POLICY NAMES]* and will not post inappropriate material or advertisements to the *[NAME/TYPE, E.G., USENET]* news groups not intended for such postings;

(b) it will adhere to the laws of [*province*] and Canada in using *[SUPPLIER'S ACCESS SERVICES NAME]*, including but not limited to those laws regarding:

(i) court ordered publication bans,

(ii) restrictions on publishing, printing, distributing, possessing, selling, advocating, promoting, or exposing, obscene material, child pornography, or hate propaganda and Customer understands that these situations could generate criminal liability;

(iii) restrictions on the use of trade-marks or trade names;

(iv) restrictions on the use of copyright work, including, without limitation, software;

(v) restrictions on defamation, libel, harm to reputation, violation of privacy, misuse or failure to protect personal information, violation of secrecy, unfair competition and other situations which could generate civil liability; and

(vi) export and import restrictions.

(b) it shall be responsible for any and all items or statements transmitted, posted or received through its account, and their content, even if transmitted, posted, received or created by another Person;

(c) it shall be responsible for ensuring that its directors, officers, employees, agents, contractors and affiliates are at all times in compliance with the Customer's obligations under this Agreement;

(d) any software which it receives from Supplier shall not be used and shall be returned to Supplier unless Customer agrees to accept and be bound by the applicable software license agreement; and

(e) it shall be responsible for maintaining the confidentiality of its passwords and shall be responsible for all activities and charges resulting from the use of the customer's account or passwords, including unauthorized use.

3. PROPRIETARY RIGHTS

3.1 Title to Internet Access Connectivity. — The Supplier shall have all ownership rights, title and interests including copyright, in and to the *[SUPPLIER'S HARDWARE, SOFTWARE, SERVERS, WEB SITES, TELECOMMUNICATIONS LINES AND OTHER MATERIALS]*.

4. FEES

4.1 Initial Charges. — The Customer shall pay to the Supplier a non-refundable one-time initial charge of *[AMOUNT]*.

4.2 Monthly Charges. — Customer shall pay the Supplier a monthly fee of *[AMOUNT]*, payable *[WHEN PAYMENT DUE, E.G., MONTHLY IN ADVANCE]*. [The Customer shall pay as a deposit the first and last month's charges upon execution of this Agreement.]

Customer agrees and acknowledges that:

(i) unused connection time cannot be transferred;

(ii) prepaid fees are non-refundable;

(iii) Supplier may modify the terms of this Agreement at any time, upon e-mail notice being sent to Customer;

(iv) Supplier may terminate this Agreement at any time and without notice or reason;

(v) invoices are due and payable *[WHEN PAYMENT DUE, E.G., WITHIN [NUMBER] DAYS OF INVOICE DATE OR RECEIPT]*; and

(vi) interest will be charged on outstanding balances at the lesser of: *[PERCENTAGE RATE]* per year or the maximum amount permitted by applicable law.

4.3 Additional Services. — Whenever the Customer adds users to the *[SERVICE E.G., MAIL SERVER]*, the Customer shall pay the Supplier a *[TIMING, E.G., ONE-TIME]* fee of:

(a) [*AMOUNT*] per user, if [*RANGE, E.G., 1-100*] users are added;

(b) [*AMOUNT*] per user, if [*RANGE, E.G., 101-200*] users are added; and

(c) [*AMOUNT*] per user, if [*AMOUNT, E.G., 201*] or more users are added.

For the provision of (*SERVICE, E.G., REMOTE DIAL-UP E-MAIL ONLY ACCESS, REMOTE FULL INTERNET ACCESS, ETC.*), the Customer shall pay the Supplier a [set-up] fee of (*AMOUNT*) per user, plus a[n*] (WHEN DUE, E.G., MONTHLY, ANNUAL, ETC.*) charge of (*AMOUNT*) per user.).

4.4. Payment of Invoices. — The Customer agrees to pay each invoice within *[TIMING, E.G., THIRTY (30) DAYS]* after the date of such invoice, except for initial charges listed in Section 4.1 and the payment of first and last month monthly charges as listed in Section 4.2, which are payable upon execution of this Agreement.

4.5 Taxes. — All prices, charges and other expenses payable hereunder are exclusive of GST, provincial sales tax or other applicable taxes, duties or withholding taxes.

5. OTHER SUPPLIER OBLIGATIONS

5.1 Customer Confidential Information. — The Parties acknowledge and agree that Supplier may, in its discretion, monitor, intercept, review, screen, edit, delete, remove, collect, use, store and disclose personal, proprietary or confidential information of the Customer, including without limitation e-mail messages, for any of the following purposes:

(a) providing Internet access services to the Customer;

(b) to determine and ensure compliance with this Agreement;

(c) for servicing or quality controls;

(d) to protect the Supplier and other customers from fraudulent, unlawful or abusive use of the Internet access services; or

(e) to comply with any legislation, regulation, or government, regulatory or investigative agency request.

Without limitation, information and data relating to Customer's Internet access usage, are considered the Customer's confidential information.

Supplier will not however be under any obligation to monitor, intercept, review, screen, edit, delete, remove, collect, use, store, disclose or otherwise control personal, proprietary or confidential information of the Customer. The Supplier agrees that except as provided in this Section 5.1, neither the Supplier nor its employees or agents shall disclose or otherwise make available any such personal, proprietary or confidential information to any third party without the Customer's prior written consent.

[The Supplier agrees to take the same precautions to safeguard such information as it does in protecting its own confidential or proprietary information by instruction, agreement or otherwise with its employees and consultants in respect to use, copying, modification and security of such information.]

[**5.2 Support.** — Throughout the Term, the Supplier shall provide the following support services without additional charge: [DESCRIPTION OF SUPPORT SERVICES, E.G., HELP DESK SUPPORT SHALL BE MADE AVAILABLE FROM 9.00 A.M. TO 12:00 MIDNIGHT ON ALL BUSINESS DAYS, AND FROM 12:00 NOON TO 12:00 MIDNIGHT ON SATURDAYS AND SUNDAYS EXCEPT ON STATUTORY HOLIDAYS. SUPPORT STAFF SHALL BE AVAILABLE AT ALL OTHER TIMES ON AN ON-CALL BASIS AT ADDITIONAL CHARGES. SUPPORT SERVICES MAY ALSO BE SET OUT IN A SEPARATE AGREEMENT OR SCHEDULE.]]

[**5.3 Training.** — Throughout the Term, the Supplier shall make training available to the Customer at its then current rates.]

[**5.4 Sole Supplier.** — During the term of this Agreement, the Customer agrees to use Supplier as its sole source to supply the services provided under this Agreement.]

6. CUSTOMER INDEMNITY

6.1 Customer Indemnity. — The Customer hereby agrees to defend, indemnify and to save harmless the Supplier and its affiliates and their respective directors, officers, employees and agents in respect of any claim, suit, proceeding, demand or action:

(a) that any [*insert description of materials delivered to Supplier under this Agreement*] infringe:

(i) a copyright in any country;

(ii) any valid patent registered as of the Effective Date in [*insert jurisdiction*]; or

(iii) any trade-mark in [*insert jurisdiction*]; or

(iv) results from the Customer's or any of its affiliates or their respective directors, officers, employees, agents or contractors breach of any of the terms of this Agreement.

The Customer shall pay settlement costs, court costs, damages and legal fees [including disbursements] incurred by the Supplier or its affiliates or their respective directors, officers, employees or agents in connection therewith.

The Supplier will:

(a) use reasonable efforts to give the Customer prompt written notice of any such claim, suit, proceeding, demand or action; and

(b) allow the Customer to control, and fully cooperate with the Customer in, the defence of the same and all related settlement negotiations.

7. REPRESENTATIONS AND WARRANTIES

7.1 Customer Representations and Warranties. — The Customer warrants and represents to the Supplier that:

(a) the entering into and performance of it obligations under this Agreement by the Customer have been duly authorized by the Customer and are not limited, restricted or in conflict with any other agreement by which the Customer is bound;

(b) it has the right to license to Supplier [*insert description of materials delivered to Supplier under this Agreement*] and such materials do not or will not infringe on:

(i) a copyright in any country;

(ii) any valid patent registered as of the Effective Date in [*insert jurisdiction*]; or

(iii) any trade-mark in [*insert jurisdiction*]; and

(c) [*Insert the following if Customer is an individual*: Customer is the end user of this account and has reached the age of majority.]

7.2 No Other Warranties. — EXCEPT AS SPECIFICALLY PROVIDED IN THIS AGREEMENT, ANY SERVICES PROVIDED BY THE SUPPLIER ARE PROVIDED "AS IS" AND NEITHER PARTY GIVES ANY OTHER EXPRESS OR IMPLIED WARRANTIES, REPRESENTATIONS, OR CONDITIONS OF ANY KIND, WHETHER STATUTORY OR OTHERWISE, INCLUDING BUT NOT LIMITED TO: WARRANTIES THAT THE SERVICES WILL BE UNITERRUPTED OR ERROR FREE; ACCESSIBILITY; PRIVACY; IMPLIED WARRANTIES OF MERCHANTABILITY, QUALITY OR FITNESS FOR A PARTICULAR PURPOSE; OR THOSE ARISING OUT OF A COURSE OF DEALING OR USAGE OF TRADE.

7.3 Limitation of Liability. — THE SUPPLIER SHALL NOT BE LIABLE FOR ANY LOSS SUFFERED BY THE CUSTOMER ARISING FROM OR CONNECTED WITH THE USE OR APPLICATION OF ANY SERVICES OR DELIVERABLES PROVIDED BY THE SUPPLIER. THE SUPPLIER SHALL NOT BE RESPONSIBLE OR LIABLE FOR ANY AND ALL ITEMS, STATEMENTS OR CONTENT TRANSMITTED, POSTED OR RECEIVED ON ITS SYSTEMS OR ANY OTHER SYSTEMS, OR FOR MONITORING THE SAME. THE SUPPLIER'S ENTIRE LIABILITY, REGARDLESS OF THE NUMBER OF CLAIMS, IN CONTRACT, TORT (INCLUDING WITHOUT LIMITATION FUNDAMENTAL BREACH, NEGLIGENCE AND GROSS NEGLIGENCE) OR OTHERWISE AND THE CUSTOMER'S EXCLUSIVE REMEDY SHALL BE: AT THE OPTION OF THE SUPPLIER TO EITHER REFUND THE AMOUNT THE CUSTOMER PAID TO THE SUPPLIER UNDER THIS AGREEMENT OR PROVIDE THE CUSTOMER WITH CORRECTED ITEMS PROVIDED THAT THE SUPPLIER IS NOTIFIED WITHIN NINETY (90) DAYS FROM THE DATE OF TERMINATION OF THIS AGREEMENT.

IN NO EVENT WILL THE SUPPLIER BE LIABLE FOR ANY DAMAGES, HOWSOEVER CAUSED, INCLUDING BUT NOT LIMITED TO, ANY LOST PROFITS, LOST SAVINGS, LOSS OF USE OR LACK OF AVAILABILITY OF FACILITIES INCLUDING COMPUTER RESOURCES, ROUTERS AND STORED DATA, INDIRECT, SPECIAL, INCIDENTAL, PUNITIVE, EXEMPLARY, AGGRAVATED, ECONOMIC OR CONSEQUENTIAL DAMAGES, CONTRIBUTION OR INDEMNITY, ARISING OUT OF THE USE, OR INABILITY TO USE THE SERVICES OR DELIVERABLES, IF ANY, PROVIDED UNDER THIS AGREEMENT, OR FOR CLAIM BY ANY OTHER PERSON, EVEN IF THE SUPPLIER OR ANY OF THEIR LAWFUL AGENTS, CONTRACTORS, OR EMPLOYEES HAVE BEEN ADVISED OF THE POSSIBILITY OF SUCH DAMAGES OR CLAIM. IN NO CASE WILL THE SUPPLIER'S TOTAL LIABILITY BE FOR MORE THAN THE AMOUNT PAID

BY THE CUSTOMER UNDER THIS AGREEMENT. IN NO EVENT WILL SUPPLIER, BE LIABLE TO THE CUSTOMER FOR DAMAGES OR LOSSES RESULTING FROM ANY THIRD PARTY, INCLUDING WITHOUT LIMITATION TELECOMMUNICATIONS SERVICE PROVIDERS, THE SUPPLIER'S CONTRACTORS, THE INTERNET BACKBONE, OR OTHER THIRD PARTY SUPPLIER OF PRODUCTS OR SERVICES, DAMAGES OR LOSSES CAUSED BY THE CUSTOMER, OR THEIR RESPECTIVE EMPLOYEES, AGENTS OR SUBCONTRACTORS, OR OTHER EVENTS BEYOND THE REASONABLE CONTROL OF THE SUPPLIER.

FOR THE PURPOSES OF THIS SECTION 7.3 AND 7.2, "SUPPLIER" SHALL INCLUDE THE SUPPLIER'S DIRECTORS, OFFICERS, EMPLOYEES, AGENTS, CONTRACTORS AND AFFILIATES.

THIS SECTION SHALL SURVIVE THE TERMINATION OF THIS AGREEMENT.

8. SUSPENSION, TERM AND TERMINATION

8.1 Initial Term. — The term of this Agreement shall begin on [*dd/mm/yr*] and shall expire on [*dd/mm/yr*] (the "Term").

8.2 Option to Renew. — The Customer shall have [two (2)] options to renew the Term, each for an additional [one (1)] year period, upon the same terms and conditions except for the fees in Article [ ] which the Parties shall renegotiate in good faith. The Customer may exercise each such option by giving the Supplier written notice of its election to exercise such option at least fifteen (15) days before the expiry of the then current term. If an agreement is not reached before the end of the current Term, the Agreement shall terminate.

8.3 Termination Without Notice. — Supplier may terminate this Agreement if:

(i) the Customer should fail to pay an amount when due hereunder;

(ii) the Customer shall file a voluntary petition in bankruptcy or insolvency or shall petition for reorganization under any bankruptcy law;

(iii) the Customer shall consent to involuntary petition in bankruptcy or if a receiving order is given against it under the *Bankruptcy and Insolvency Act* or the comparable law of any other jurisdiction;

(iv) there shall be entered an order, judgment or decree by a court of competent jurisdiction, upon the application of a creditor, approving a petition seeking reorganization or appointing a receiver, trustee or liquidator of all or a substantial part of the Customer's assets; or

(v) the Customer shall fail to perform any of the other material obligations set forth in this Agreement and such default in the case of a default which is remediable continues for a period of fifteen (15) days after written notice of such failure has been given by the Supplier.

8.4 Remedies Not Exclusive. — The remedies provided for in this Agreement, including without limitation those of termination, are neither exclusive nor mutually exclusive and either Party shall be entitled to resort to any such remedies, or any other remedy available to the Party at law or in equity, or some or all in any combination. No delay or failure of a Party to exercise any right or remedy will operate as a waiver thereof, except where specifically provided herein to the contrary.

8.5 Effect of Termination. — If this Agreement is terminated for any reason, the [*insert Party*] shall [*insert applicable Party's obligations, e.g., to return or destroy the other Party's software, confidential information or other proprietary materials*].

8.6 Suspension of Services. — The Supplier may, in its sole discretion, and from time to time, suspend Internet access services for routine repair or maintenance work. Supplier will give as much notice as reasonably practicable to customer in the circumstances and will endeavour to carry out such works during the scheduled maintenance periods as published by Supplier on [*insert web site address*] from time to time.

9. GENERAL

9.1 Non-Waiver. — The failure by either Party to exercise any right, power or option given under this Agreement, including without limitation the right of termination, or to insist upon the strict compliance with the terms and conditions of this Agreement by the other Party, shall not constitute a waiver of the terms and conditions of this Agreement with respect to any other or subsequent breach thereof, nor waiver by such Party of its right any time thereafter to require strict compliance with all terms and conditions hereof.

9.2 Assignment. — This Agreement shall be binding upon and inure to the benefit of the Parties and their respective successors and permitted assigns. Customer [shall not] assign this Agreement without first obtaining the written consent of the Supplier, which consent may [not] be unreasonably withheld. The Supplier shall have the right to assign and subcontract with others for the performance of any of its obligations under this Agreement.

9.3 Force Majeure. — Neither Party shall be liable to the other Party for any delay or failure to perform its obligations hereunder (other than an obligation to pay monies when due) due to strikes, labour disputes, inability to obtain labour, utilities or services, riots, storms, floods, explosions, act of God, war or any other cause or causes similar thereto which are beyond the reasonable control of such Party nor shall the Supplier be liable to the Customer for any delay or failure in the performance of any of Supplier's approved subcontractors or suppliers. The Parties hereto shall use their best efforts during the Term of this Agreement to avoid or, if unavoidable, minimize the effects of any force majeure upon the performance of their respective obligations under this Agreement.

9.4 Notices. — Any notice, demand or other communication (in this section, a "notice") required or permitted to be given or made under this Agreement shall be sufficiently given or made if:

(a) delivered in writing and in person during normal business hours on a Business Day and left with a receptionist or other responsible employee of the relevant Party at the applicable address set forth below;

(b) sent by prepaid first class mail; or

(c) sent by any electronic means of sending messages, including e-mail or facsimile transmission, which produces a hard copy confirmation ("Electronic Transmission") during normal business hours on a Business Day charges prepaid [and confirmed by prepaid first class mail];

in the case of a notice to Supplier, addressed to it at:

[Address]

Attention: ______________________

Fax No.: ______________________

E-mail: ______________________

with a copy to: ______________________

Address: ______________________

and in the case of a notice to Customer, addressed to it at:

[Address]

Attention: ______________________

Fax No.: ______________________

E-mail: ______________________

with a copy to: ______________________

Each notice sent in accordance with this section shall be deemed to have been received:

(a) if delivered, on the day it was delivered;

(b) if mailed on the fifth Business Day after it was mailed (excluding each Business Day during which there existed any general interruption of postal services due to strike, lockout or other cause); or

(c) on the same day that it was sent by Electronic Transmission, or on the first Business Day thereafter if the day on which it was sent by Electronic Transmission was not a Business Day.

Any Party may change its address for notice by giving notice to the other Party as provided in this section.

[9.5 Non-Solicitation of Employees. — During the term of this Agreement, and for a period of one (1) year thereafter, each of Supplier and the Customer agree not to hire or allow its respective affiliates to hire:

(i) any employee of the other Party; or

(ii) any person who was an employee of the other Party during the previous six (6) months, who was directly involved in the provision of the services provided hereunder unless otherwise mutually agreed to by the Parties.]

[**9.6 Arbitration.** — Any and all disputes, claims or controversies arising out of or in any way connected with or arising from this Agreement, its negotiation, performance, breach, enforcement, existence or validity, any failure of the Parties to reach agreement with respect to matters provided for in this Agreement and all matters of dispute relating to the rights and obligations of the Parties, which cannot be amicably resolved, even if only one of the Parties declares that there is a difference, will be referred to and finally settled by private and confidential binding arbitration held in (*insert location*) in English and governed by [*insert jurisdiction*] law pursuant to the *[insert name of applicable Arbitration's Act]* as amended, replaced or re-enacted from time to time.

The Arbitrator shall be a person who is legally trained and who has experience in the information technology field in Canada and is independent of either Party.]

9.7 Survival. — The following provisions shall survive termination or expiry of this Agreement:

(Insert article and section numbers for interpretation sections, ownership, confidentiality obligations, indemnities, representations and warranties as to title, right to license or non-infringement, limitations on liability and disclaimers, term and termination and general section.)

9.8 Governing Law. — This Agreement shall be governed by and construed in accordance with the laws of *[insert jurisdiction]* and federal laws of Canada applicable therein and shall be treated, in all respects, as an Ontario contract. The Parties submit to the [non-exclusive] jurisdiction of the courts of Ontario. The Parties hereby expressly exclude the application of the *United Nations Convention on Contracts for the International Sale of Goods* and the *International Sale of Goods Act* (Ontario), as amended, replaced or re-enacted from time to time. The Parties have required that this Agreement and all documents relating thereto be drawn up in English. Les Parties ont demandé que cette convention ainsi que tous les documents qui s'y rattachent soient rédigés en anglais.

9.9 Independent Contractors. — The Parties are separate and indepen-dent legal entities. Nothing contained in this Agreement shall be deemed to constitute either Party as agent, representative, partner, joint venturer or employee of the other Party for any purpose. Neither Party has the authority to bind the other Party or to incur any liability on behalf of the other Party, nor to direct the employees of the other Party.

9.10 Miscellaneous.—This Agreement, and any documents referred to herein, is the entire Agreement between the Customer and the Supplier and pertaining to Internet access [*insert other services*], and supersedes all prior or collateral oral or written representations or agreements related thereto. In the event that one or more of the provisions is found to be illegal or unenforceable, this Agreement shall not be rendered inoperative but the remaining provisions shall continue in full force and effect. Except as otherwise provided herein, no term or provision hereof shall be deemed waived and no breach excused unless such waiver or consent shall be in writing and signed by the Party claimed to have waived or consented. Any consent by any Party to, or waiver of, a breach by the other, whether expressed or implied, shall not constitute a consent to, waiver of, or excuse of any other different or subsequent breach.

IN WITNESS WHEREOF the Parties have executed this Agreement.

[NAME OF CUSTOMER]

Per: ______________________________

Name: ______________________________

Title: ______________________________

[NAME OF SUPPLIER]

Per: ______________________________

Name: ______________________________

Title: ______________________________

CHAPTER 4

INTERNET AND PRIVACY POLICIES

4.1 INTRODUCTION TO INTERNET AND PRIVACY POLICIES

Internet and privacy policies often exist as supplemental terms to contracts between ISPs, OSPs or content providers and their customers, and between employers and employees. Establishing and enforcing clear Internet and privacy policies in an e-commerce situation also helps to promote customer confidence and trust. Policies can also serve as tools to achieve legislative or regulatory compliance. For example, compliance with the federal *Personal Information Protection and Electronic Documents Act*[1] (in this Chapter, referred to as the "*Privacy Act*") or regulatory guidelines.

In order to ensure enforceability of Internet and privacy policies, it is important that they form part of an enforceable contract between the parties either by incorporating the policies into the terms of an agreement or by cross-referencing them in an agreement. The enforceability of on-line agreements and policies is dependent upon the contracting parties having had the opportunity to review the terms of such agreements and policies before accepting them (see Chapter 2) and there having been an exchange of consideration. However, in light of the rapidly changing Internet and e-commerce world, and the surrounding legal environment, Internet and privacy policies may need to be updated and changed on a regular basis. When drafting an agreement that refers to or incorporates the terms of a policy that may be unilaterally amended or replaced in the future, one needs to weigh the needs of the party creating the policy against the risks of unenforceability. As an alternative, the related agreement's term may be made shorter such that upon renewal of the agreement, both parties have the opportunity to review and agree to a new policy, for which additional consideration has been given and received.

4.2 PURPOSE OF INTERNET POLICIES

(i) Internet policies often supplement Internet access agreements (see Chapter 3 and Forms 3A and 3B) or web site terms and conditions, in that they provide additional guidelines for proper use of Internet services or web sites. (See Checklist 4A)

(ii) In an employment context, Internet and Intranet policies are drafted to provide guidelines as to the employees' proper use of the employer's resources, such as networks, hardware,

---

1 S.C. 2000, c. 5.

software, databases, files, web site, e-mail, telecommunications or other systems, including time spent surfing the Internet during the course of employment. Corporate Internet and Intranet policies also attempt to deal with the risks of leakage of corporate confidential information or trade secrets; vicarious liability by the employer for defamation, harassment, discrimination, intellectual property infringement and other acts of the employee; viruses entering the employer's systems; binding the corporation to contracts; breaches of security, and ensuring adequate record keeping and evidentiary requirements are met when business is conducted electronically.

(iii) Internet and Intranet policies also help to protect employers and employees from wrongful dismissal actions, by clarifying what type of conduct is cause for dismissal. The courts and administrative tribunals in Canada have held employers not to have wrongfully dismissed employees in violation of corporate policies.[2] As well, policies help to protect employers from violating employees' privacy rights. (For a discussion of privacy issues, see paragraph 2.2.3 and Section 4.4)

4.3 PRINCIPAL TERMS OF INTERNET POLICIES

In any event, the Internet policies should contain the following principle terms:

(i) **Access and Security**. The primary term of an Internet policy is describing what the user may have access to (e.g., the Internet, computer and communication systems, telephone network, voice mail, networks, databases, files, storage materials or devices, e-mail, etc.) and how access is to properly occur (e.g., through an approved firewall and not directly by modem). Virus detection or other security procedures should be set out clearly. (See also the ownership and licensing provisions in Chapter 3, paragraph 3.4.4)

---

2 *Bahmer Employment Insurance Claim Appeal* (September 28, 1998), CUB 42012A — Bahmer was dismissed by Imperial Oil for alleged misconduct including personal e-mail use and contravention of harassment-free work area policy (racist and sexist e-mail). Bahmer knew the e-mail was for business purposes and he willfully violated this policy. *Di Vito v. MacDonald Dettwiler & Associates Ltd.*, (1996) 21 C.C.E.L. (2d) 137 (B.C.S.C.) — Employees not wrongfully dismissed for circulating vulgar e-mail and lying about it.

(ii) **Purpose**. Internet policies also set out the purposes for which users may have the access described above. In an employment context, sometimes use of a company's systems is permitted for personal purposes provided that such use is minimal and not for an employee's personal financial gain.

(iii) **Prohibited Activities**. Access to computer systems or the Internet may result in certain risks or liabilities (see also Chapter 2 and paragraph 3.3) to the access provider, e.g., the employer, caused by the activities of the user, e.g., the employee. Therefore, as with Internet Access Services Agreements (see Chapter 3), prohibited activities should be clearly enunciated to draw to the attention of the user, prohibited and potentially illegal activities. Although an access provider, such as an employer, cannot by virtue of a contract with its user, contract out of statutory liability to third parties or criminal liability, the risks faced by the access provider will likely be reduced if the user is made aware of potential liabilities, if the user covenants not to engage in the activities that could create liability for the access provider and if the access provider has contractual or other legal remedies against the user for breach of the user's covenants.

Common prohibitions found in Internet policies are set out in Checklist 4A, below, and Form 4A. (See also Chapter 3, paragraph 3.4.2)

(i) **Communications**. Especially in the employment context, communications by e-mail, in chat groups, by posting items to newsgroups, require the exercise of care, given the ease of distributing messages electronically and the risk that the employee may be viewed as having the authority to make statements on behalf of the employer.

(ii) **Privacy**. In order to comply with any applicable legislation or regulations, to facilitate co-operation with law enforcement agencies (see paragraph 2.2.4), and to ensure that users are in compliance with the Internet policy, it is important that the policy permit (but not obligate) the access provider to monitor, audit, intercept and disclose the user's activities.[3] Consideration should also be given to including the privacy provisions discussed below in Section 4.4. By having users acknowledge that their use of the systems is not to be considered private, and agree not to send any private or

---

[3] Note that in Canada, interception, use or disclosure of private communications could be a criminal offence, unless consent has been obtained. See *Criminal Code*, R.S.C. 1985, c. C-46 as am., ss. 184 and 193.

personal information using these systems, the access provider can minimize the risk of privacy violations.

(iii) **Remedies**. The Internet policy (or related agreement, such as an employment contract that refers to the policy), should also set out the remedies that the access provider has if the user is in breach of the policy. Such remedies may include disciplinary action, such as suspension or termination of access rights or, in an employment context, the right for the employer to dismiss the employee. It may also be important to the access provider to impose an obligation on the user to report any violations, or suspected violations, of the policy by others.

4.4 PRINCIPAL TERMS OF PRIVACY POLICIES AND CONSENTS

(i) As discussed in Chapter 1 the Internet is an open network and privacy is becoming an increasingly important issue to Internet users. In addition, the *Privacy Act* contains obligations and restrictions on dealing with personal information (see Section 2.2.3). Privacy policies are becoming a common method to address these issues.

(ii) To be enforceable and in compliance with the *Privacy Act*, privacy policies should:

- not be separate documents or hidden in footnotes or web pages that are not immediately displayed to users at or before the time that their personal information is collected;
- be expressly consented to by users, and not merely presented to them; and
- not be unilaterally modifiable.

(iii) The *Privacy Act* requires an organization to identify in writing, and that the individual consent to, the specific purposes for which personal information is being collected, stored, used and disclosed, at or before the time that such information is collected. The collection, retention, use and disclosure of personal information must be limited to what is necessary for the purposes identified. This would include the purposes for which any third parties (including affiliates) to whom personal information will be disclosed, will use, store or disclose that information. If the purposes set out in the privacy policy are too vague, they might not be specific enough to comply with the *Privacy Act*.

(iv) As well, the *Privacy Act* requires that parties collecting, using or storing personal information have in place the following procedures, which are generally outlined in a privacy policy.

4.5 Limitations on Collection, Use, Retention and Disclosure

The privacy policy must describe the procedures for the collection, use, retention and destruction of personal information. Note that personal information that is no longer required for the purposes identified must be safely destroyed.

4.6 Accuracy

Personal information must be kept accurate, complete and up-to-date. The privacy policy must describe how the organization intends to ensure accuracy, completeness and up-to-dateness of information.

4.7 Safeguards

Every recipient of personal information must employ security safeguards such as appropriate firewall, encryption, and access security measures, to protect the personal information. Security safeguards must also extend to the disposal of personal information.

4.8 Individual Access, Challenging Compliance

Individuals have the right to be informed, within thirty (30) days after providing a written request, as to the use and disclosure of their personal information. The procedure for submitting such request to a recipient of personal information and having access to one's personal information, should be specified in the privacy policy as well as the procedures for correcting and deleting their personal information.

4.9 Openness

Privacy policies and procedures must be also made available to individuals.

Businesses should appoint a designated individual responsible for compliance with the *Privacy Act*. Staff should be trained about privacy policies, procedures and confidentiality obligations. It is also recommended that organizations ensure that the third parties to whom they disclose personal information have comparable policies and protections in place. Note that under the *Privacy Act*, the organization collecting personal information is responsible for information in its possession, including information that has been transferred to a third party. Businesses should, by contract or otherwise, ensure that any third party receiving the personal information uses the information only as authorized. The authorized purposes should be restricted to those for which consent was obtained. Further disclosure should be prohibited, unless consent is obtained. In case of related companies, internal company guidelines respecting privacy may be sufficient.

It is also important to note that the Ontario government has recently released a Consultation Paper on a proposed privacy Act for the use and exchange of personal information by businesses and organizations. The proposed provincial law, which will affect the private sector, would be based upon the same fair information practices contained in the federal *Privacy Act*. There will, however, be some significant differences, particularly with regard to the scope of the law's application, the means of compliance, and possibly the nature of consent. Draft legislation is expected in 2001. To the extent that it covers activities within Ontario in a substantially similar fashion as the *Privacy Act*, it will apply to business activities within Ontario. The *Privacy Act* will continue to apply to extra-provincial activities.

CHECKLIST 4A – FOR DRAFTING INTERNET USE POLICIES

- Ensure parties are clearly identified by their full legal names and for on-line agreements, see also checklist in Chapter 9;
- Specify ownership of systems and files and what facilities are covered, e.g., Internet, Intranet, e-mail, voice mail, hardware, software, networks, databases;
- Include trade-mark, copyright and other proprietary notices;
- If applicable, include assignments of intellectual property rights and waivers of moral rights;
- Identify purpose for using facilities, e.g., permitted uses (i.e., business purposes);
- Set out scope of a party's authority to bind the other party, e.g., requirement to insert disclaimers in personal e-mail or discussion groups;
- Draft security procedures, e.g., Internet access only through approved firewall, log out requirements, proper passwords, virus protection, e-mail attachments, permissions and acknowledgments regarding electronic transmission;
- Provide for record keeping, backup and purging obligations;
- Include disclaimers, e.g., regarding web site, hyper-links, content, liability (see Chapter 3);
- Specify specific prohibitions, such as:
  - sending, displaying, copying, reading, storing, receiving, printing, downloading, uploading, distributing or disseminating illegal, profane, obscene, pornographic, violent, hate, fraudulent, discriminatory, harassing, embarrassing, humiliating, degrading, intimidating, threatening or defamatory material, or material that is protected by intellectual property laws or is in violation of any laws,
  - infringing anyone's intellectual property rights,
  - installation, downloading, modification or copying of unauthorized software or hardware, including screen savers and "freeware",
  - criticism of company, staff or customers,
  - unauthorized interference, tampering, destruction, deletion, removal, concealment, copying or encryption,
  - unauthorized access, hacking, cracking, bugging or attempting to access systems, passwords, e-mail, voice mail, files or other data, whether internal to the system or external,

- virus distribution, whether internal to the system or external,
- disclosure of password and use of others' passwords,
- unauthorized posting of any material on the Internet, news groups, bulletin boards, chat rooms or other public forums,
- viewing, posting, sending or otherwise disclosing confidential, trade secret or proprietary material (may also be set out in a separate confidentiality policy),
- personal use, advertisements, solicitations, political material, spam, chain mail, or playing computer games;

• Obtain privacy consents and highlight when no expectation of privacy:
  - see Ontario's Information and Privacy Commissioner's paper on "*Privacy Protection Principles for Electronic Mail Systems*", **www.ipc.on.ca**,
  - reserve right to monitor, access and disclose,
  - no privacy over the Internet, unless using encryption;

• Outline implications of use of systems, e.g., that they may be susceptible to discovery (designate what is privileged), there is no such thing as permanent deletion, and there may or may not be regular backups;

• Cross-reference related policies, such as confidentiality, monitoring, harassment, discrimination;

• Inform of possible legislative sanctions, e.g., under the *Criminal Code* and *Copyright Act;*

• Clarify that ownership rights are to be respected;

• Obtain consent or acceptance by the party to the policy;

• Specify how the policy can be amended, e.g., when and by whom.

• Set out remedies for breach of policy, e.g., disciplinary measures and without limiting other remedies available under contract, at law, in equity, or for breach of other policies.

CHECKLIST 4B – PRIVACY POLICIES

- Ensure parties are clearly identified by their full legal names and for on-line agreements, see also checklist in Chapter 9;
- Identify the specific purposes for which personal information is being collected, stored, used and disclosed;
- Include the purposes for which any third parties (including affiliates) to whom personal information will be disclosed, will use, store or disclose that information;
- Describe the procedures for the collection, use, retention and destruction of personal information;
- Describe how the organization intends to ensure accuracy, completeness and up-to-dateness of information;
- Specify security safeguards such as firewall, encryption, and access security measures, to protect the personal information;
- Outline the procedure for individuals to submit written requests about the use and disclosure of personal information as well as the procedures for correcting and deleting their personal information;
- Provide business contact information, i.e., names, addresses, e-mail addresses, telephone numbers and fax numbers, at which individuals can make inquiries;
- Ensure each individual consents to the policy.

FORM 4A – COMPANY INTERNET AND SYSTEMS USE POLICY

This policy establishes guidelines for proper use of the hardware, software, networks, databases, files, storage devices and materials, web site, e-mail, telecommunications or other systems, including without limitation those systems that support and host the network (all of which are referred to herein as the "Facilities") of ABC Incorporated (the "Company") by all employees, contractors, customers and other users (the "Users") of the Facilities.

(i) **Ownership of Facilities.** The Facilities belong to the Company. Users are given access to the Facilities to help them perform their job duties and further the Company's interests.

(ii) **Use of Facilities.** Except for occasional personal use, the Facilities are to be used for authorized business purposes only. Company will determine in its sole discretion the scope of permissible "occasional personal use".

(iii) **Access.** Users may access the Facilities only through an approved Facilities firewall. Direct access by modem is strictly prohibited unless the accessing computer is not connected to the Company's network. Users shall always log out completely when finished accessing the Facilities. Users shall keep passwords confidential. Users shall run Company approved virus protection software before opening any e-mail attachments or running or installing any software programs on the Facilities.

(iv) **Prohibited Activities.** Users shall not use the Facilities:

- for commercial advertisements, solicitations, or promotions other than on behalf of the Company and to further the Company's interest
- for spam, chain mail, or playing computer games
- to disseminate virus software or political material
- to further any unlawful purpose
- to send, display, copy, read, store, receive, print, download, upload, distribute or disseminate illegal, profane, obscene, pornographic, violent, hate, fraudulent, discriminatory, harassing, embarrassing, humiliating, degrading, intimidating, threatening or defamatory material, or material that is protected by intellectual property laws or is in violation of any laws
- to infringe anyone's intellectual property rights

- to install, download, modify or copy unauthorized software or hardware, including screen savers and "freeware"
- to criticize the company, staff or customers

Users shall not engage in:

- unauthorized interference, tampering, destruction, deletion, removal, concealment, copying or encryption
- unauthorized access, hacking, cracking, bugging or attempting to access systems, passwords, e-mail, voice mail, files or other data, whether internal to the Facilities, or external
- virus distribution whether internal to the Facilities or external
- disclose passwords or use others' passwords
- posting any material on the Internet, newsgroups, bulletin boards, chat rooms or other public forums, except as expressly authorized by Company management
- view, post, send or otherwise disclose confidential, trade secret or proprietary material (refer also to Company's Confidentiality Policy)

Users shall insert the following disclaimers in any personal e-mail or discussion groups: (*insert disclaimer*).

(i) **Passwords.** Passwords may not be disclosed by Users to any third party.

(ii) **Trade Secrets Disclosure.** In communicating with others, Users must exercise at least the same level of care in what they reveal as they do when using other forms of communication. The Facilities are not a secure medium unless encryption or other similar measures are taken. Sensitive or confidential information should not be communicated over the Facilities unless security safeguards are in place.

(iii) **Sexual Harassment and Non-Discrimination Policy.** Company's policy prohibiting sexual harassment and discrimination applies to the Facilities and Users.

(iv) **No Expectation of Privacy.** The Company may (but is not obligated to) monitor, audit, intercept, review, screen, edit, delete, remove, collect, use, store and disclose any information or materials relating to users' activities on or through the Facilities. Users' use of the Facilities are not to be considered private, and Users shall not send, store, collect or otherwise use any private or personal information on or through the Facilities.

In any event, each user consents to the Company monitoring, auditing, intercepting, reviewing, screening, editing, deleting, removing, collecting, using, storing and disclosing personal, proprietary or confidential information of the user, including without limitation e-mail messages, to determine and ensure compliance with this policy; to protect the Company, its customers, other users and third parties from fraudulent, unlawful or abusive use of the Facilities; or to comply with any legislation, regulation, or government, regulatory or investigative agency request. I have read this Policy and agree to comply with it in consideration of my being granted access to the Facilities. I understand that violation of this Policy may result in disciplinary action, including without limitation possible termination of my Facilities' access rights, termination, dismissal and other legal action.

Signed: ______________________________

Printed Name:

Date:

FORM 4B – CREDIT INVESTIGATION AND PRIVACY CONSENT

TO: [*Insert full legal name of data collector*] ("[*Insert name of data collector*]")

AND TO: Each [*Insert full legal name of supplier*] that from time to time participates in the Portal, as defined below (each, a "[*Insert name of supplier*]")

AND TO: Each lessor or lendor that from time to time participates in the Portal or is selected by any [*Insert full legal name of supplier*] to provide me with a proposed or computed [*insert name of product*] lease, loan, or other financing (each, a "Financial Institution")

1. In this consent:

   (a) the words "I", "my" and "me" refer to each applicant and co-applicant who signs this consent;

   (b) the word "Personal Information" refers to information regarding my name, address, telephone number, date of birth, credit information and any other information obtained through a credit reporting agency, credit investigation, credit bureau, financial institution or other person or entity, my social insurance number, driver's license number, mother's maiden name, employment history, income, housing cost details, and pre-authorized payment facilities and all information provided by me in any credit application;

   (c) the word "Portal" refers to the Internet web site known as "[*insert name of Portal*]" on the Internet currently located at [*insert www. Address*];

   (d) the word "Transaction" refers to any proposed, completed or future credit application, quote, purchase, lease, financing and/or service of any [*Insert name of product*] by or for me, whether in my own name or on behalf of another person or entity;

   (e) the words "use" and "used" include the rights to collect, use, copy, store, maintain, update, share, disclose and provide access to;

(f) the word "you" refers to [*Insert name of data collector*], each [*Insert name of supplier*], each Financial Institution and their respective successors and assigns.

2. I certify that all information provided by me in any credit application or other documentation given in connection with any Transaction is true, accurate and complete in all respects.

3. I authorize you to use any Personal Information for any reasonable purpose related to the Transaction.

4. I authorize you to use Personal Information regarding my name, address, telephone number, date of birth, driver's license number and mother's maiden name to avoid duplicating database information, and for any other reasonable purpose related to any Transaction.

5. I understand that:

(a) Personal Information regarding my employment history, income, housing cost details, social insurance number and pre-authorized payment facilities will be disclosed to or accessed only by any of you that is directly or indirectly involved in any Transaction; and

(b) I may update my Personal Information as necessary by contacting [*Insert name of data collector*] at [*insert phone number and/or address*], by sending an e-mail to [*insert e-mail address*] or by writing [*Insert name of data collector*] at [*insert address*].

6. I AUTHORIZE AND CONSENT TO THE CONDUCTING OF CREDIT INVESTIGATIONS ON ME BY ANY OF YOU FROM TIME TO TIME AND TO THE RECEIPT AND EXCHANGE OF CREDIT OR OTHER PERSONAL INFORMATION ON ME BY ANY OF YOU FROM TIME TO TIME, INCLUDING THE RECEIPT AND EXCHANGE OF CREDIT OR OTHER PERSONAL INFORMATION WITH ANY CREDIT REPORTING AGENCY, CREDIT BUREAU, FINANCIAL INSTITUTION OR OTHER PERSON OR ENTITY.

Date Applicant Co-Applicant

CHAPTER 5

WEB SITE AND CONTENT DEVELOPMENT CONTRACTS

5.1 INTRODUCTION TO WEB SITE AND CONTENT DEVELOPMENT

As discussed in Chapter 1 (see paragraph 1.2.2), a *Web Site* is merely a computer program or software, written in a programming language such as *HTML*. Therefore web site development contracts are not unlike software development contracts with many similar issues. However, the main difference between a web site and traditional software is that a web site also contains *content*, such as data and files that may contain text, video, pictures (e.g., gif files), sound or other multimedia. The *content* may be embedded directly into the *Web Site*, or it may be retrieved indirectly from a *hyper-link* to another *Web Site*, *Web Page*, data or file source. Therefore, when drafting and negotiating web site development agreements, one must also give consideration to development, ownership and intellectual property issues surrounding the content.

5.2 PRINCIPAL TERMS OF WEB SITE AND CONTENT DEVELOPMENT AGREEMENTS

5.2.1 Development Services

The web site development agreement must clearly describe the development services being provided. If the services to be provided include more than mere development services (such as the hosting or maintenance of the customer's web site), then the terms of the web site development agreement should also include the terms of other agreements (see web site hosting terms or support terms in Chapter 7 and Form 7A).

The agreement should adequately describe:

(i) what is to be developed (e.g., only the underlying software or the content as well) and by whom (e.g., by the developer or jointly with the customer);

(ii) the look and feel and format of the development (usually set out in the specifications);

(iii) what is to be delivered by each of the parties and when (e.g., the customer may be required to provide certain content for the developer to include in the items to be developed); and

(iv) any additional obligations on the parties, such as acceptance testing (see paragraph 5.2.6, below).

In the fast-paced Internet and e-commerce industry, parties often want to conclude contracts before the details of the services to be performed have been agreed upon. There is a great risk that an agreement which is concluded prior to sorting out the scope of the services, may later be disputed by the parties, or even held to be unenforceable if the material terms were not agreed to at the time of contract signing. It is therefore recommended that all functional and technical specifications, delivery timetables, testing criteria and scope of services be agreed upon prior to the execution of a web site development agreement.

However, the reality in this industry is that development work is sometimes an evolution, and it is not always easy for parties to agree in advance to the detailed technical specifications, or even delivery milestones, acceptance testing criteria and procedures or time schedules for testing and delivery. The next best thing is for the parties to at least agree to the basic functional requirements of the web site to be developed (which should be attached as a schedule to the agreement), and to provide for a procedure in the agreement to deal with the development of missing items such as testing criteria, technical specifications, milestones and time schedules. In other words, the technical specifications and delivery schedules for the web site, if not attached as schedules to the agreement, should be part of the deliverables to be developed under the agreement or should be included in statements of work to be agreed upon by the parties (see Form 5A, Section 1).

It is also important in a web site development agreement to clearly distinguish each party's obligations. When acting for the developer, any dependencies on the customer (e.g., for content) or third-party suppliers, could affect delivery schedules and the developer's performance obligations.

Where the customer has obligations to supply any materials such as content, the agreement should specify the format in which the materials are to be supplied (i.e., file format and delivery format).

Where web site content is to be supplied by a hyper-link, the agreement should specify the details of the hyper-link and that it is to be programmed by the developer into the web site. (See also Intellectual Property Issues in Chapter 2, paragraph 2.2.1 and hyper-linking agreements in Chapter 12)

5.2.2 Specifications

In drafting specifications, assistance may be required from technical advisors. Common web site specifications include:

- compatibility with certain web browsers;
- software code that the web site is written in, e.g., HTML;
- placement of content (including legal notices – see Chapter 9) and what the look and feel of the web site will be;
- size of content and embedded files and extent to which compression or caching technology is used, which affects the speed at which the web site will be viewable by Internet surfers;
- compliance with TCP/IP and other Internet protocols or standards.

For an example of web site specifications, see Form 5A, Schedule "C".

5.2.3 Changes to the Web Site or the Content

The web site development agreement may contain a change order procedure to address changes required by the customer to the work in process or specifications. The ability to request changes is particularly important to the customer if they are not jointly involved with the developer in the development of the web site, content or specifications. On the other hand, from the developer's perspective, one would be concerned about the customer having the unilateral ability to request changes to the project scope, unless the delivery timetables and fees could also be adjusted.

Often, web site and content development agreements permit customers to request changes pursuant to a change order process, whereby they submit the request to the developer who then has the opportunity to review and submit an amended price, specifications and delivery schedule back to the customer for its consideration. Sometimes, customers are permitted to unilaterally request minor changes that do not affect the previously agreed upon functional or technical specifications.

If the developer is given permission under the agreement to modify any materials provided or owned by the customer, such as prior existing software or content, the ownership section of the agreement should address who owns such modifications. (See also discussion in paragraph 5.2.4, below, regarding ownership)

5.2.4 Ownership and Licensing

It is important that the agreement distinguish ownership of the developed works from ownership of any pre-existing works that were supplied by the customer, the developer or third-parties. Generally speaking, if the customer is supplying its own content for the web site, then it or its licensors would likely want to remain the owners of the content and to license the same to the developer for the purposes of the development services. On the other hand, the developer may want to retain ownership of the developed works, such as the underlying software of a web site. From a developer's perspective, ownership of its work (either as the sole owner or joint owner) becomes important when it needs the unfettered ability to re-use the work in subsequent development projects for other customers. If the developer is to retain sole ownership of the work, a license to the customer would be required to grant permission to the customer to use the work.

However, customers are often concerned about paying for a custom web site that may be re-used by the developer in a project for one of the customer's competitors. Therefore, a customer is likely to request that it obtain ownership of any developments by the developer through an assignment of all intellectual property rights and a waiver of any authors' moral rights.

Often, the parties can negotiate a compromise by allowing the customer to own the developments and by giving a limited license back to the developer of certain restricted rights. The scope of any license granted should be carefully drafted. Consideration should be given as to what specific rights are required to be licensed (e.g., the right to run, copy, modify, sublicense, distribute, etc.), whether the license is exclusive, sole or non-exclusive[1] and whether there are any territorial, usage or other restrictions or limitations. In negotiating license rights, one must ensure that the party one represents will obtain all of the rights it needs. Familiarity with intellectual property law is essential for an understanding of the rights that intellectual property owners have and the scope of rights that may be granted.[2]

---

1 An "exclusive" license means only the licensee can exercise the rights granted, even to the exclusion of the licensor. A "sole" license means no one other than the licensee and licensor can exercise the rights granted.

2 It is not sufficient to simply grant or obtain a license to "use" the web site, as this term is extremely vague and is not one of the enunciated rights that a copyright owner has under the *Copyright Act*, R.S.C. 1985, c. C-42. Most of the intellectual property in a web site (e.g., underlying rights in the software and content) will consist of copyrights; however, other rights, such as trade-mark and patent rights, should be analyzed and the applicable rights of any copyright, trade-mark, patent or other intellectual property owners, should be reflected in the agreement.

A non-compete clause that prohibits the developer from creating similar work for one of the customer's competitors, or a confidentiality covenant, may also be a means of addressing the customer's concerns.[3]

Consideration should also be given to ownership of work in process, which is not complete and is still in the possession of the developer.

5.2.5 Fees and Reporting

There are many different ways to structure fees for web site and content development projects. Some of the possibilities upon which fees can be based include each of the following or a combination of the following:

(i) one-time charge, e.g., for delivery of the completed and tested web site;

(ii) fixed rates over time, e.g., a percentage of the total fee upon successful acceptance testing of each deliverable; or

(iii) variable rates based on development time spent (similar to consulting agreements where hourly, daily or weekly rates are charged for work done).

The agreement should specify when fees are due and payable. One may reasonably argue that fees should be invoiced and paid upon the achievement of a particular milestone, such as the successful acceptance test of a deliverable. From a customer's perspective however, it is not reasonable to have to pay for any undelivered items or items which have not passed agreed upon acceptance tests.

The agreement should also specify whether the fees are inclusive or exclusive of applicable taxes and duties.

As discussed in paragraph 5.2.3 on Changes above, the parties should also address whether additional fees for changing the scope of the development work will be charged.

It may also be reasonable to impose an obligation on a party to provide regular reports as to the criteria upon which the fees are based and to allow audits of a party's records to verify fees.

---

[3] One must be careful when drafting non-compete clauses to ensure that they are not in restraint of trade or anti-competitive.

5.2.6 Acceptance Testing

As with traditional software development agreements, a Web Site and Content Development Agreement should contain acceptance testing criteria and procedures. It is important that:

(i) the parties mutually agree upon these criteria to be set out in the agreement;

(ii) set out which of them (if not both parties jointly) will conduct the tests; and

(iii) the agreement specify when the tests need to be completed.

Also, the procedures and remedies for failure to meet acceptance tests need to be negotiated and drafted into the agreement. It is important to consider whether the remedies that a customer would want for failure of an acceptance test early on in the development process, will be different from the remedies needed if the failed acceptance occurs after most of the deliverables have been provided and accepted.

As discussed above in paragraph 5.2.1, it is possible, although somewhat risky, for the acceptance testing criteria and procedures to be developed as part of the deliverables under the development agreement. If such is the case, the customer would generally want to be involved in the development of the testing terms, as the developer's performance obligations and the customer's payment obligations are often tied to successful acceptance testing of deliverables.

5.2.7 Confidentiality

In the situation where the parties to the agreement are exchanging confidential information, such as trade secrets or other proprietary material, it is recommended that the agreement contain a confidentiality clause.

5.2.8 Representations and Warranties

In addition to the usual representations and warranties given by parties to a contract, such as that each party has the right to enter into the agreement and that the agreement does not and will not conflict with any other agreement or obligation that a party may have, web site and content development agreements require some additional representations and warranties to minimize the risk of unique liabilities that arise in the development context.

When acting for the developer, it is recommended that the following warranties be obtained from the customer:

- if applicable, that the customer has the right to license or provide a hyper-link to (as the case may be) any content or other materials provided to or accessible by the developer;
- that such materials provided to or accessible by the developer do not and will not infringe on any copyright or any trade-mark, patent, trade secret or other intellectual property right of any third-party, in countries where the developer will be using or accessing the materials or where the developer is at risk of being sued for infringement. However, customers will be relatively reluctant to give representations or warranties for any third-party items which were not created by the customer (such as third-party content or software); which the customer does not own; or over which the customer has no control or has not received similar representations or warranties from the customer's suppliers or licensors.

When acting for the customer, it is recommended that the following warranties be obtained from the developer:

- that the deliverables meet the functional and technical specifications or other performance criteria;
- the deliverables are free of disabling mechanisms and viruses and that they do not contain any content or metatags that were not identified in the specifications;
- if applicable, that the deliverables are original works of the developer;
- if the developer is assigning ownership in the deliverables to the customer, that the developer has the right to make the assignment and has obtained assignments and waivers of moral rights from its employees and subcontractors, in favour of the customer and its assignees;
- if the developer retains ownership rights in the web site or content, which is being licensed to the customer, that the developer is the owner of the deliverables and has the right to license;
- that the deliverables do not infringe on any copyright or any trade-mark, patent, trade secret or other intellectual property right of any third-party, in countries where the customer will be using or accessing the materials or where the customer is at risk of being sued for infringement. However, developers will be relatively reluctant to give representations or warranties for any third-party items which were not created by the developer (such as software or content supplied by the customer); which the developer does not own; or over which the developer has no control or has not received

similar representations or warranties from the developer's suppliers, subcontractors or licensors;

- where other services such as web site hosting are being provided by the developer, warranties pertaining to such services (see Chapter 7); and
- that performance of the services under the agreement will be done in a competent manner by qualified personnel.

5.2.9 Indemnities

See the discussion in respect of indemnities in Chapter 3, paragraph 3.4.10.

5.2.10 Limitations on Liability and Disclaimers

See the discussion in respect of limitations on liability and disclaimers in Chapter 3, paragraph 3.4.11.

5.2.11 Remedies

The web site and content development agreement should also set out the remedies that each party has if the other party is in breach of the agreement. Such remedies may include the right for the non-breaching party to terminate the agreement, to receive liquidated damages and to be indemnified for any third-party claims or damages. (See paragraph 5.2.9 and Form 5A Section 10)

As discussed in paragraph 5.2.6, the remedies for failure to meet acceptance tests need to be negotiated and drafted into the agreement. The remedies for failure of an acceptance test early on in the development process, are usually different from the remedies needed if the failed acceptance occurs after most of the deliverables have been provided and accepted. If the agreement is breached, or an acceptance test fails, in the early part of the term of the agreement when the parties have not invested a lot of time or money, it may be adequate to draft a remedy that requires return of all fees paid and deliverables to the respective parties. On the other hand, if the development is nearly complete and paid for, one may reasonably argue that a breach or failure that is not cured within a reasonable period of time should require the developer to deliver up all work in process to allow the customer to finish the development and the customer should be entitled to liquidated damages for the additional costs it incurs in the completion of the web site or content development.

As well, it may be important to distinguish suspension of services from termination of the entire agreement, in the event of a breach. For example, if the customer has obligations under the agreement to supply content or provide other input to the developer, the appropriate remedy may be for the developer to have the right to suspend services and extend delivery and testing schedules, as opposed to terminate the agreement.

5.2.12 Term

See the discussion in respect of the term in Chapter 3, paragraph 3.4.8.

5.2.13 General Clauses

As with other commercial agreements, in Internet and e-commerce agreements, one should consider including notice clauses, further assurances, non-waiver, severability, currency, assignability, entire agreement, force majeure, time of the essence, interpretation, independent contractors, binding on successors, survival, governing law and choice of language clauses.

CHECKLIST 5 – FOR DRAFTING WEB SITE AND CONTENT DEVELOPMENT AGREEMENTS

- Ensure parties are clearly identified by their full legal names and for on-line agreements, see also checklist in Chapter 9;
- Clearly describe the development services;
- Specify what is to be developed and by whom;
- Describe the web site to be developed;
- If available, attach functional and technical specifications including:
  - requirements for compatibility with common web browsers,
  - details about the software code that the web site is to be written in,
  - specifying placement of content (including legal notices: see Chapter 9) and what the look and feel of the web site will be,
  - size of content and embedded files and extent to which compression or caching technology is used, which affects the speed at which the web site will be viewable by Internet surfers,
  - requirements as to compliance with TCP/IP and other Internet protocols or standards;
- Set out deliverables/milestones by each party and time schedules;
- If not available at the time of signing, provide procedure for the development of technical specifications, milestones and time schedules;
- Include terms for related services, such as the hosting or maintenance of the web site;
- Add customer obligations and third-party dependencies and consider implications on delivery schedules and the developers performance obligations if such obligations or dependencies are not met;
- Specify the format in which the materials are to be supplied;
- Insert details of any hyper-links and obligation on the developer to program same into the web site;
- Draft a change order procedure;
- Clarify ownership of the developed works, works in process, ownership of any pre-existing works that were supplied by the customer, the developer or third-parties and ownership of any modifications;

- If developer to retain ownership of web site and/or content, draft license to the customer;
- If customer to retain ownership of web site and/or content, draft assignment of all intellectual property rights by developer and obtain waiver of moral rights;
- If customer to retain ownership of web site and/or content, consider giving a limited license back to the developer;
- Consider non-compete clause;
- Consider confidentiality covenants;
- Include fee and payment terms, when due and whether taxes are extra;
- Include acceptance testing criteria and procedures or procedure for developing acceptance testing terms;
- Add remedies for failure to meet acceptance tests;
- Add developer's representations, warranties and indemnities, such as:
    - the right to enter into the agreement ,
    - that the agreement does not and will not conflict with any other agreement or obligation,
    - that the deliverables meet the functional and technical specifications or other performance criteria,
    - the deliverables are free of disabling mechanisms and viruses and that they do not contain any content or metatags that were not identified in the specifications,
    - if applicable, that the deliverables are original works of the developer,
    - if the developer is assigning ownership in the deliverables to the customer, that the developer has the right to make the assignment and has obtained assignments and waivers of moral rights from its employees and subcontractors, in favour of the customer and its assignees,
    - if the developer retains ownership rights in the web site or content, which is being licensed to the customer, that the developer is the owner of the deliverables and has the right to license,

- that the deliverables do not infringe on any copyright or any trade-mark, patent, trade secret or other intellectual property right of any third-party, in countries where the customer will be using or accessing the materials or where the customer is at risk of being sued for infringement. Consider exclusions for any third-party items which were not created by the developer (such as software or content supplied by the customer); which the developer does not own; or over which the developer has no control or has not received similar representations or warranties from the developer's suppliers, subcontractors or licensors,
- indemnities for losses resulting from intellectual property infringement or trade secret misappropriation claims (and consider exceptions and limitations on indemnities),
- where ancillary services such as web site hosting are being provided by the developer, warranties pertaining to such services (see Chapter 7),
- that performance of the services under the agreement will be done in a competent manner by qualified personnel;

• Add customer's representations, warranties and indemnities, such as:
  - the right to enter into the agreement,
  - that the agreement does not and will not conflict with any other agreement or obligation,
  - if applicable, that the customer has the right to license or provide a hyper-link to any content or other materials provided to or accessible by the developer,
  - that materials provided to or accessible by the developer do not and will not infringe on any copyright or any trade-mark, patent, trade secret or other intellectual property right of any third-party, in countries where the developer will be using or accessing the materials or where the developer is at risk of being sued for infringement. Consider exclusions for any third-party items which were not created by the customer (such as third-party content or software); which the customer does not own; or over which the customer has no control or has not received similar representations or warranties from the customer's suppliers or licensors,
  - indemnities for losses resulting from intellectual property infringement or trade secret misappropriation claims (and consider exceptions and limitations on indemnities);

- Disclaimers and limitations on liability to consider:
  - as applicable to indemnities,
  - for performance,
  - disclaimer of implied warranties,
  - force majeure events,
  - third-party products, acts or omissions,
  - liability by developer for problems with customer-supplied content or materials,
  - indirect damages (should be described);
- Draft the term, termination and suspension provisions and consider which terms of the agreement survive termination or expiry;
- Consider post-termination or expiry provisions, e.g., return of software or materials and transitional services;
- Set out the remedies that each party has if the other party is in breach of the agreement, e.g., to receive liquidated damages and to be indemnified for any third-party claims or damages;
- Boilerplate provisions, e.g., notice clauses, further assurances, non-waiver, currency, severability, assignability, entire agreement, force majeure, time of the essence, interpretation, independent contractors, binding on successors, survival, governing law and choice of language clauses.

FORM 5A – WEB SITE DEVELOPMENT AGREEMENT

BETWEEN:

[*INSERT FULL LEGAL NAME AND ADDRESS OF DEVELOPER*]

(the "Developer"),

and

[*INSERT FULL LEGAL NAME AND ADDRESS OF CUSTOMER*]

(the "Client")

1. DEVELOPMENT SERVICES

1.1 Services. Developer shall use commercially reasonable efforts to develop Client's web site (the "Deliverables") materially in conformance with each statement of work agreed to and signed by the parties from time to time and attached as a schedule to this Agreement (the "Statement of Work"). This Agreement does not include any obligation on Developer to register, link, host or maintain Client's Web Site and the parties may enter into separate agreements for such additional services.

1.2 Changes. Additions or modifications to the Statement of Work may be accomplished through the use of a "Change Order". A Change Order must be in writing and signed by both parties in order to be effective. The Change Order as submitted by Developer, the Change Order will become part of the Statement of Work. For greater clarification, a Change Order is not required for minor changes which do not result in an addition or modification to the Statement of Work. However, Developer shall be obligated to make no more than two such minor changes.

1.3 Personnel. Developer shall have the exclusive authority to make staffing decisions with respect to use of its personnel or subcontractors in the provision of the Work.

1.4 Project Coordinators. Each party shall designate a Project Coordinator to be listed on Schedule "B". The Project Coordinator of each party shall be responsible for arranging all meetings between the parties, and for the transmission and receipt of Deliverables, Client Materials, any information and notices between the parties. The Project Coordinators shall also be responsible for all administrative matters such as invoices, payments, and amendments.

1.5 Risk of Loss. Risk of loss of any Deliverables shall pass to Client upon delivery.

1.6 [Optional – **Exclusive Developer**. Throughout the Term of this Agreement, Client agrees to use Developer as its exclusive web site designer and developer].

2. OWNERSHIP

2.1 Ownership of Deliverables. [*Insert name of party obtaining ownership*], its licensors or suppliers as the case may be, shall at all times be and remain the sole and exclusive owners of any work in process, the Deliverables and any Work.

2.2 Assignment. To the extent that any work performed *by [Insert name of party transferring ownership*] under this Agreement may be covered by the definition of "Deliverables", [*Insert name of party transferring ownership*] hereby assigns and conveys its entire right, title and interest therein and all copies thereof, and all copyright and other proprietary rights therein, without further consideration, free from any claim or lien or retention of rights, to [*Insert name of party obtaining ownership*] and the [*Insert name of party transferring ownership*] hereby waives in whole any and all moral and other rights it may have in such deliverables, or agrees to cause all authors of the Deliverables to waive in whole any and all moral and other rights they may have in the Deliverables, including but not limited to: the right to restrain or claim damages for any distortion, mutilation or other modification of; the right to restrain use or reproduction of; the right to the integrity of; and the right to be associated with; the Deliverables in any context and in connection with any product, service, cause or institution, to and in favour of [*Insert name of party obtaining ownership*] and its assignees and licensees.

2.3 Ownership of Client Materials. The parties agree that Client will at all times be and remain the sole and exclusive owner of the Client Materials or any modifications thereto.

2.4 License to Client. Developer agrees to grant to Client, upon the date that all Fees in any Statement of Work have been paid by Client, a [non] exclusive, [non-]sublicenseable, [worldwide] license to [execute, perform, display, operate, copy and modify] the Deliverables in any such Statement of Work, on the Internet in accordance with the terms of this Agreement, except for any Third-Party Products forming part of the Deliverables.

2.5 Third-Party Product License Assignment. Developer agrees to assign upon the date that all Fees in any Statement of Work have been paid by Client, to Client, and only to the extent Developer has the right to assign, any and all

Developer's rights in any Third-Party Product licenses, including without limitation software and files, forming part of the Deliverables on an as-is basis, under such Statement of Work, and Client agrees to assume all of Developer's obligations for such Third-Party Products.

2.6 Restrictions. Developer grants no rights other than those explicitly granted herein, and Client shall not exceed the scope of any licenses granted or assigned by Developer hereunder. Except as expressly authorized in this Agreement, Client will not, distribute or transfer (by any means), sublicense or rent the Deliverables.

2.7 License to Developer. Client grants to Developer and Developer accepts a non-exclusive, royalty-free, worldwide license to use Client Materials as Developer deems necessary to perform its obligations under this Agreement [and for the marketing and promoting of Developer's business.] [The parties agree that any modifications to the Client Materials shall be owned by the Client.]

3. CLIENT OBLIGATIONS

3.1 Client Obligations. Client shall cooperate with and assist Developer by providing to Developer such information and such access to Client's personnel, facilities, equipment, databases, software, Client Materials or resources as are described in the Statement of Work, or as Developer may reasonably request in the format to be agreed upon by the parties. All such information and access will be considered Client Materials, the timely, complete, and accurate provision of which is a condition precedent to Developer meeting its delivery dates described in each Statement of Work.

4. ACCEPTANCE TESTING

4.1 Acceptance Testing. Immediately upon completion of each Statement of Work and delivery of all Deliverables by Developer to Client, Client shall have *(insert number)* days to test the general function and operation of such Deliverables using the Web Browsers referred to in Schedule "A" and evaluate the same to determine whether the Deliverables materially comply with the acceptance criteria set forth in the applicable Statement of Work. Within such *(insert number)* day period, Client shall give Developer written notice stating why any Deliverables are unacceptable. Upon receipt of such notice, Developer shall use commercially reasonable efforts to correct the material deficiencies as soon as practical. Client shall then have another *(insert number)* days to test and re-evaluate the corrected Deliverables. This procedure of acceptance testing and correction shall be repeated until Client, acting reasonably accepts the Deliverables in accordance with the terms above. Client acknowledges and agrees that material compliance with the acceptance criteria set forth in the applicable Statement of Work shall be deemed acceptance. If Client does not give written notice to Developer within the *(insert number)* day testing period that the Deliverables do not satisfy the acceptance criteria, Client shall be deemed to have accepted the Deliverables upon expiration of such period.

5. FEES

Client agrees to pay the fees as listed in each Statement of Work plus all applicable taxes and duties, and reasonable expenses and disbursements, if any, for Developer's Work (the "Fees").

5.1 Payment Schedule. When both parties have signed a Statement of Work, Client will pay to Developer the non-refundable amount of *(insert amount)*% of the Fees set out in such Statement of Work. Client will forward to Developer further non-refundable payments in the amounts of *(insert amount)*% of the Fees each month until all Deliverables under such Statement of Work have been delivered, at which time all Fees, except for *(insert amount of hold-back)*%, shall be paid. Client shall be able to hold back *(insert amount)*% of the Fees set out in a Statement of Work until final acceptance of the Deliverables in accordance with Section 5.1. All Fees are due within *(insert number)* days of receipt of invoice from Developer and payable in cash or cheque made payable to Developer.

5.2 Late Payment. Without limiting Developer's other rights or remedies, any late payment shall be subject to interest at *(insert amount)*% per month or the maximum amount permitted by law and Developer shall be entitled to stop the Work and not deliver any Deliverables until payment in full of all outstanding amounts is received.

6. CONFIDENTIALITY AND NON-DISCLOSURE

6.1 Confidential Information. The parties acknowledge that it will be necessary for each of them to disclose or make available to each other information and materials (collectively the "Confidential Information") that may be confidential or proprietary or may contain valuable trade secrets, [and that some such information may already have been disclosed prior to the Effective Date]. [Prior to disclosure, the disclosing party shall use reasonable efforts to designate all Confidential Information by marking the information with the word "Confidential" or similar legend]. The Parties agree that the Client Materials and the Deliverables are Confidential Information, as are any passwords, server logs, and all documentation or other materials provided in connection therewith.

6.2 Non-Disclosure. Both during and after the term of this Agreement, each of the parties agrees:

(a) to use commercially reasonable efforts to protect the Confidential Information of the other party from unauthorized use or disclosure and to use at least the same degree of care with regard thereto as it uses to protect its own Confidential Information of a like nature;

(b) to use and reproduce the Confidential Information of the other party only as permitted under this Agreement or as needed to perform its duties hereunder; and

(c) not to disclose or otherwise permit access to the Confidential Information of the other party to any third-party, without the other party's prior written consent.

6.3 Exceptions. Information will not be considered to be Confidential Information if it:

(a) becomes publicly available through no fault of the disclosing party;

(b) is lawfully received from a third-party having the right to disclose the information without restriction; or

(c) has been independently developed.

Furthermore, it is understood that each party shall be free to use any ideas, concepts, know-how and techniques related to the scope of its business, provided they contain no specific or identifiable elements unique to the other party hereto or its property.

7. REPRESENTATIONS AND WARRANTIES

7.1 Client Representations and Warranties. Client warrants and represents to Developer that:

(a) the entering into and performance of this Agreement by Client has been duly authorized by Client and such performance is not limited, restricted or in conflict with any other agreement by which Client is bound;

(b) any Client Materials provided by Client to Developer under this Agreement are owned or licensed by Client and Client has the authority to provide them to Developer to allow Developer to do the Work; and

(c) it has the right to grant the licenses herein.

7.2 Developer's Limited Warranty. Developer warrants that, for a period of thirty (30) days from the date of acceptance of the Deliverables under a Statement of Work by Client, the Deliverables (excluding any Third-Party Products), provided that they have been properly installed and have not been altered or modified by anyone other than Developer, will perform substantially in accordance with the applicable Statement of Work. If any such Deliverables do not so perform during such period, Developer will use reasonable efforts to correct, at no cost to Client (other than reasonable travel expenses to Client's site, if necessary), programming errors in such Deliverables to make such Deliverables so perform provided that:

(a) the Deliverables have been properly used by Client in accordance with any documentation or instructions given by Developer to Client in connection therewith;

(b) Client notifies Developer forthwith and describes with specificity the nature of the suspected errors and of the circumstances in which they occur;

(c) Client or any third-party, other than Developer, has not changed or modified the respective Deliverables; and

(d) the error relates to material developed solely by or on behalf of Developer.

Upon assignment of Developer's rights in any Third-Party Products in accordance with Section 2.5, Client shall obtain from such third parties the benefit of any such Third-Party Product warranties to which Developer was entitled provided that such warranties, if any, are assignable by Developer and Client is in compliance with all such Third-Party Product licenses.

8. DISCLAIMERS AND LIMITATIONS ON LIABILITY

8.1 DISCLAIMER OF OTHER WARRANTIES. EXCEPT AS EXPRESSLY PROVIDED IN THIS AGREEMENT THERE ARE NO OTHER REPRESENTATIONS, WARRANTIES OR CONDITIONS, EXPRESS OR IMPLIED, IN FACT OR IN LAW, OR THOSE ARISING BY STATUTE OR OTHERWISE IN LAW OR FROM A COURSE OF DEALING OR USAGE OF TRADE), INCLUDING BUT NOT LIMITED TO WARRANTIES OR CONDITIONS OF MERCHANTABILITY, DESCRIPTION, QUALITY OR FITNESS FOR A PARTICULAR PURPOSE.

8.2 Limitation Period. Should Developer be in breach of any obligation under this Agreement, Client agrees that Client's remedies will be limited to those set forth in this Agreement and no action may be brought by Client more than *(insert number)* months after the facts giving rise to the cause of action have occurred, regardless of whether those facts by that time are known to, or reasonably ought to have been discovered by, Client.

8.3 NO INDIRECT DAMAGES. IN NO EVENT SHALL EITHER PARTY [ITS DIRECTORS, OFFICERS, EMPLOYEES, AGENTS, CONTRACTORS OR AFFILIATES], BE LIABLE FOR ANY CLAIM FOR: (A) INDIRECT, CONSEQUENTIAL OR PUNITIVE DAMAGES; (B) DAMAGES FOR LOSS OF PROFITS OR REVENUE, FAILURE TO REALIZE EXPECTED SAVINGS, LOSS OF USE OF CLIENT MATERIALS, COMPUTER HARDWARE, SOFTWARE, WEB SITE AND ANY STORED DATA; (C) CONTRIBUTION, INDEMNITY OR SET-OFF IN RESPECT OF ANY CLAIMS AGAINST CLIENT; OR (D) ANY DAMAGES WHATSOEVER RELATING TO THIRD-PARTY PRODUCTS, OR MATERIALS OR ANY GOODS OR SERVICES NOT DEVELOPED OR PROVIDED BY THAT PARTY.

8.4 LIMITATION ON LIABILITY. EXCEPT FOR BREACH OF WARRANTIES AS TO NON-INFRINGEMENT, BREACH OF CONFIDENCE OR WITH RESPECT TO ANY INDEMNITIES IN THIS AGREEMENT, EACH PARTY'S, [ITS DIRECTORS', OFFICERS', EMPLOYEES', AGENTS', CONTRACTORS' AND AFFILIATES',] MAXIMUM TOTAL LIABILITY FOR ANY CLAIM WHATSOEVER, INCLUDING WITHOUT LIMITATION CLAIMS FOR BREACH OF CONTRACT, TORT (INCLUDING, WITHOUT LIMITATION, NEGLIGENCE) OR OTHERWISE, AND THE OTHER PARTY'S SOLE REMEDY, SHALL BE AN AWARD FOR DIRECT, PROVABLE DAMAGES NOT TO EXCEED THE AMOUNTS PAID HEREUNDER BY CLIENT TO DEVELOPER UNDER THE APPLICABLE STATEMENT OF WORK DURING THE CURRENT TERM, LESS THE AMOUNT OF ANY DAMAGES ALREADY PAID.

9. INDEMNITIES

9.1 Developer Indemnity. Developer shall indemnify, defend and hold Client harmless in respect of any and all claims, demands or actions of any other person and resulting costs (including reasonable legal fees) that any Deliverables (except for Client Materials and Third-Party Products) supplied under this Agreement infringe a presently existing copyright or trade-mark of any other person enforceable in Canada, provided that:

(a) Client gives Developer prompt written notice of any such claim, demand or action;

(b) Client allows Developer to control and fully cooperates with Developer in the defence of the same and all related settlement negotiations; and

(c) the Deliverables have not been modified or altered by anyone other than Developer. If such Deliverable or any portion thereof is held to constitute such an infringement, and use thereof is enjoined, Developer may, at its option, either:

  (i) procure the right to use the infringing element of such Deliverable; or

  (ii) replace or modify the element of such Deliverable so that the infringing portion is no longer infringing.

The foregoing states the entire obligations of Developer and Client's sole and exclusive remedy with respect to infringement of proprietary or intellectual property rights of third-parties.

9.2 Client Indemnity. Client shall indemnify, defend and hold Developer, its officers, directors, subcontractors, agents or affiliates, harmless from any and all claims, demands, actions, resulting costs, expenses, damages, losses, consequences, awards and judgments (including without limitation, punitive damages, court costs, arbitration fees, penalties, fines, amounts paid in settlement of claims and reasonable legal fees, disbursements and expenses of investigation) relating to any Client Materials including without limitation patent, copyright, trade secret or other intellectual property infringement claims.

10. TERM AND TERMINATION

10.1 Initial Term. The term of this Agreement shall begin on the date it is signed and shall expire on completion of the Work and acceptance by Client of all Deliverables, in accordance with Section 5.1 unless terminated earlier in accordance with the terms herein (the "Term").

10.2 Termination on Default with Notice. [Either party may terminate this Agreement or a Statement of Work upon the occurrence of a material breach by the other party, which material breach has not been cured within sixty (60) days after receipt of written notice thereof by the breaching party from the other,] unless the cause for termination is a failure to pay, in which event this Agreement may be terminated upon five (5) calendar days' notice by Developer.

10.3 Termination without Notice. [Either party] may at its option, terminate this Agreement or a Statement of Work, effective immediately without notice or prior opportunity to cure the default if the [other party] makes a general assignment for the benefit of its creditors or a proposal or arrangement under the *Bankruptcy and Insolvency Act* (or any similar statute), or a petition is filed against the [other party] under the *Bankruptcy and Insolvency Act*, or if the [other party] shall be declared or adjudicated bankrupt or if a liquidator, trustee in bankruptcy, custodian, receiver, manager, or any other officer with similar power shall be appointed of or for the [other party] or if the [other party] shall commit an act of bankruptcy or shall propose a compromise or arrangement or institute proceedings to be adjudged bankrupt or insolvent or consents to the initiation of such appointment or proceedings or admits in writing its inability to pay debts generally as they become due.

10.4 Effect of Termination. Except as provided in this Agreement, termination by either party in accordance with the terms of this Agreement shall not be exclusive nor limit the terminating party's other rights or remedies available at law or in equity, or under this Agreement. Also, if this Agreement terminates prior to the payment in full of all Fees under any particular Statement of Work, the license and assignment under Sections 2.2 and 2.4 shall not be granted with respect to any Deliverables and Third-Party Products under such unpaid Statement of Work and all such Deliverables and Third-Party Products shall be returned to Developer.

10.5 Survival. Articles *(insert numbers)* and Sections *(insert numbers)* shall survive termination or expiry of this Agreement.

11. GENERAL

11.1 Interpretation. In the event of any conflict between the provisions of this Agreement or any schedule, the provisions of this Agreement shall prevail.

11.2 Number and Gender. Words importing the singular include the plural and vice versa; and words importing gender include all genders.

11.3 Headings. The Section headings contained herein are included solely for convenience, and are not intended to be full or accurate descriptions of the content thereof and shall not be considered part of this Agreement or to affect the interpretation hereof.

11.4 Currency. Unless otherwise indicated, all dollar amounts referred to in this Agreement are in Canadian funds.

11.5 Entire Agreement. This Agreement, including any and all schedules, is the complete and exclusive statement of the agreement of the parties with respect to the subject matter hereof and supersedes all prior agreements, negotiations and representations, oral or written, between the parties with respect to the subject matter hereof. This Agreement may not be modified except by a written instrument duly executed by the parties hereto.

11.6 Severability; No Waiver. If any provision of this Agreement is held to be invalid or unenforceable for any reason, the remaining provisions will continue in full force. The waiver by either party of a breach of any provision of this Agreement will not operate as a waiver of any other breach. No delay or failure of Client or Developer to exercise any right or remedy will operate as a waiver, except where specifically provided to the contrary.

11.7 Assignment. Client may not assign or transfer any or all of its rights or its duties or obligations hereunder without the consent of Developer, which consent shall not be unreasonably withheld. Client may assign this Agreement, without the need to obtain consent of Developer, to an affiliate of Client or to a successor in interest to substantially all of the business of Client to which this Agreement relates, who has agreed to be bound by the terms of this Agreement. Developer may assign this Agreement or any part thereof without Client's consent upon notice to the Client.

11.8 Independent Contractors. The parties to this Agreement are independent contractors, and not agents, partners, joint ventures or employees of one another.

11.9 Counterparts. This Agreement may be executed in one or more counterparts, each of which shall be deemed an original and all of which shall be taken together and deemed to be one instrument.

11.10 Force Majeure. Neither party shall be liable to the other party for any delay or failure to perform its obligations hereunder due to strikes, labour disputes, riots, storms, floods, explosions, act of God, war or other cause beyond the reasonable control of such party nor shall Developer be liable to Client for any delay or failure caused by the performance of any of Developer's subcontractors, suppliers or shortage of labour or materials.

11.12 Notice. Any notice, request, demand, consent or other communication provided or permitted hereunder shall be in writing and given by personal delivery, or sent by registered mail, postage prepaid, or transmitted by fax or e-mail addressed to the receiving party's Project Coordinator at its address in the schedules hereto. Any notice so given shall be deemed to have been received on the date on which it was delivered or transmitted by fax or e-mail, or five days following the mailing thereof. In the event of actual or threatened disruption of postal services notice shall not be sent by mail.

11.13 [Optional – **Non-Solicitation of Employees.** During the term of this Agreement, and for a period of one (1) year thereafter, each of Developer and the Client agree not to hire or allow its respective affiliates to hire:

(i) any employee of the other party; or

(ii) any person who was an employee of the other party during the previous six (6) months, who was directly involved in the provision of the services provided hereunder unless otherwise mutually agreed to by the parties.]

11.14 [Optional – **Arbitration.** Any and all disputes arising out of this Agreement, its performance, breach, enforcement, existence or validity, any failure of the parties to reach agreement with respect to matters provided for in this Agreement and all matters of dispute relating to the rights and obligations of the parties, which cannot be amicably resolved, even if only one of the parties declares that there is a difference, will be referred to and finally settled by private and confidential binding arbitration held in Ontario in English and governed by Ontario law pursuant to the Ontario *Arbitration Act, 1991*, as amended, replaced or re-enacted from time to time. The Arbitrator shall be a person who is legally trained and who has experience in the information technology field in Canada and is independent of either party.]

11.15 Governing Law. This Agreement shall be governed by and construed in accordance with the laws of Ontario and federal laws of Canada applicable therein and shall be treated in all respects, as an Ontario contract. The parties submit to the non-exclusive jurisdiction of the courts of Ontario. The parties have required that this Agreement and all documents relating thereto be drawn-up in English. Les parties ont demandé que cette convention ainsi que tous les documents qui s'y rattachent soient rédigés en anglais.

SIGNED THIS __________ DAY OF ______________________, 200___.

[*INSERT NAME OF CLIENT*]

Per: ____________________________________

Name: ____________________________________

Title: ____________________________________

[*DEVELOPER*]

Per: ____

Name: ____

Title: ____

SCHEDULE "A"

STATEMENT OF WORK

Description of Work: ______________________

Specifications (if any): ______________________

Deliverables: beta test, final, format, etc.

Estimated Delivery Schedule: ______________________

Acceptance Criteria (if any): Material conformance with the following:

Required Client Materials:

Fees: plus applicable taxes, duties withholding taxes, expenses and disbursements.

Web Browsers to be acquired by Client: ______________________

SCHEDULE "B"

PROJECT COORDINATORS

Client's Project Coordinator: ______________________

Name: ______________________

Address: ______________________

Telephone: ______________________

Facsimile: ______________________

E-mail: ______________________

Developer's Project Coordinator: ______________________

Name: ______________________

Address: ______________________

Telephone: ______________________

Facsimile: ______________________

E-mail: ______________________

The parties' Project Coordinators will be available Monday through Friday, 9:00 a.m. EST to 5:00 p.m. EST, and will endeavour to respond within one business day of receipt of any requests for information or requests for decisions that are communicated "live" by telephone between the Project Coordinators (not over voice mail) or that are communicated by e-mail received and read by the party's Project Coordinator during those hours.

SCHEDULE "C"

SPECIFICATIONS

(i) All graphics used in Client's Web Site shall be in interlaced [GIF] format.

(ii) No items in the Web Site shall exceed [640 pixels] in width unless otherwise specified herein or agreed in writing by the managing partner of Client.

(iii) Each page of the Web Site will have the following initial "body" statement:

BODY BACKGROUND="marble.jpg" link="#0000ff" vlink="#9932cd".

(iv) With the exception of the first page of the Web Site, each page of the Web Site will have the transparent graphic "•.gif" centred at the top of the page (the HTML command to display the graphic will use the "alt" feature of HTML to display the text "•" if the graphic cannot be viewed with the user's Web Browser), followed by a Derivative Work of the graphic "•.gif" used as a horizontal rule (which shall either span the entire width of the user's page no matter how wide or narrow, if this is possible, or, if this is not possible, which shall be displayed using the "centre" command, and which shall use dashes as "alt" text to simulate the horizontal rule if graphics are not displayed), followed by the subject matter of the particular page, followed by a Derivative Work of the graphic "•.gif" used as a horizontal rule (spanning the width of the page or centred, as specified above, and using dashes as "alt" text as specified above), followed by a graphical and then textual button bar to be designed and agreed upon by Client and Developer, each of which shall be centred at the bottom of each page.

(v) The graphical button bar that is to appear at the bottom of each page (except the first page) will be a functioning HTML image map with the "alt" text "Navigational button bar". Below the graphical button bar there will appear a centred textual button bar that will read as follows: [Web Site specifications]. The words, but not the brackets, in the textual button bar will constitute links to the appropriate portions of Client's Web Site.

(vi) All non-transparent graphics (including image maps) used in Client's Web Site shall be displayed with the image's width and height specified in the HTML code.

(vii) The title for each page will identify the page, and will in most cases also be the first text that appears on the page beneath Client's logo.

CHAPTER 6

DOMAIN NAME TRANSFER AGREEMENTS

6.1 INTRODUCTION TO DOMAIN NAME TRANSFERS

Domain names are becoming increasingly important business assets. As discussed in Chapter 1, paragraph 1.2.1, domain names give each computer on the *Internet* an alphanumeric address, which is easier to remember than a numerical address and is therefore better for marketing purposes. Domain Names are organized in a hierarchy of levels and different countries have their own domain name registration systems and authorities. In Canada, the .ca domain name system is operated by the *Canadian Internet Registration Authority* or *CIRA*. *CIRA* has its own rules that deal with the registration, transfer, renewal and modification of .ca domain names. For other domain names, one must look to the rules of the applicable domain name registry.

Under the CIRA system, persons who have registered domain names are known as registrants. Registrants must enter into agreements with CIRA for the service of a domain name.[1] The domain name registration agreement with CIRA is, in effect, a service agreement for a limited time period of one to ten years. It does not convey, and expressly excludes, any ownership rights in the domain name to the registrant. However, domain names may acquire trade-mark rights if they meet the common law or statutory requirement for trade-marks.

To transfer a domain name, one must comply with the rules and procedures of the applicable domain name registry. For example, to transfer a .com domain name, one must file a Registrant Name Change Agreement with Network Solutions, Inc., the current .com domain name registrar. However, these domain name transfer agreements are merely forms for processing by the registrar, and do not contain the necessary representations, warranties and indemnities, as well as other terms, which should be considered in a domain name acquisition transaction. Therefore, parties to a domain name transfer often enter into a separate agreement (see Forms 6A and 6B) to deal with the additional risks that arise in such a transaction.

---

[1] Registrants must satisfy the Canadian Presence Requirements for Registrants, set out on CIRA's web site at www.cira.ca and summarized in the *Blakes Report* referred to in Chapter 1, footnote 4.

6.2 WHAT RISKS DOES A DOMAIN NAME TRANSFEREE FACE IN ACQUIRING A DOMAIN NAME AND HOW TO AVOID THEM?

A transferee of a domain name would primarily be concerned with ensuring that it is contracting with the right party (i.e., that the transferor is the registrant of the domain name) and that the domain name services agreement has not been terminated or has not expired. To address this risk, one should conduct a domain name search (a "whois search") to review the registration information recorded in the applicable domain name registry for the proposed domain name. The recorded registration information should specify who the current registrant is and whether the domain name service agreement is still effective. Since there will likely be a delay between the execution of the agreement and the transfer of the domain name, the name search should be updated upon closing, and any monies payable to the transferor should be placed into escrow until the transfer is completed.

The agreement should also contain a warranty that the transferor is the registrant and has not assigned, secured, pledged or licensed the domain name services agreement or any rights it may have in the domain name or related trade-marks, to any person or entity.

A domain name transferee would also be concerned that the transferor file the requisite transfer forms with the applicable domain name registry and that the transferee is recorded in the registry's database as the registrant, before money exchanges hands. As discussed above, the parties should consider placing any amounts payable to the transferor into escrow until the domain name transfer is complete (i.e., the registry recognizes the new registrant as the transferee).

As well, a transferee would be concerned about the risk of the domain name infringing a third-party's trade-mark. This risk can be dealt with by making enquiries with the applicable domain name registry as to any disputes or arbitration proceedings; conducting trade-mark searches; and obtaining from the transferor representations, warranties and indemnities for no claims, disputes or infringement, especially in the jurisdictions where the domain name is registered, where the transferor conducts its business, where the transferor's web site resides; where the transferee intends to use the domain name or in any other jurisdiction where either of the parties may be at risk.

Although a domain name is likely not considered property under Canadian law, it would be prudent for a transferee to conduct standard due diligence, as one would do when acquiring any other property, such as a *Personal Property Security Act* ("PPSA") search.

If the transferor does not have a lot of assets, the representations, warranties and indemnities might not offer much protection to the transferee. Therefore, the parties should consider obtaining third-party guarantees (such as from a parent company), hold-backs or reduction of the fees in the agreement, or other forms of security (such as letters of credit) for breach of any warranty or for failure to indemnify.

6.3 WHAT RISKS DOES A DOMAIN NAME TRANSFEROR FACE IN TRANSFERRING A DOMAIN NAME AND HOW TO AVOID THEM?

Since there will likely be a delay between the execution of the agreement, the transfer of the domain name and receipt of consideration, a transferor would be concerned about receiving consideration for the domain name. To address this concern and as discussed in Section 6.2 above, the parties should consider placing funds into escrow until the domain name transfer is complete (i.e., the registry recognizes the new registrant as the transferee).

The transferor would also be concerned about the scope of any representations, warranties and indemnities given by it under a domain name transfer agreement. The transferor would not want to give an unlimited indemnity for any claims, in any jurisdiction, for an unlimited time period. However, it is reasonable to negotiate limitations on the scope of the warranty and indemnity to jurisdictions where the transferor could be expected to have conducted trade-mark searches and registrations, and for a limited time period following the transfer.

6.4 PRINCIPAL TERMS OF DOMAIN NAME TRANSFER AGREEMENTS

6.4.1 Transferor's Obligations

The agreement should clearly describe the exact domain name, how and when it is to be transferred. The procedures required by the applicable domain name registry (e.g., completion and delivery by the transferor of a registrant name change agreement) may be specified and copies of any forms may be attached as schedules to the agreement. (See Form 6A, Section 1)

The agreement should also contain a further assurance clause, that the transferor will take all other steps reasonably necessary to effect the transfer of the domain name to the transferee.

From the transferee's perspective, the transferor should be obligated to not take any action to withdraw, suspend or otherwise terminate the registrant name change with the registry and should be obligated to cease all use of the domain name upon completion of the transaction.

Consideration should be given as to non-disclosure of the terms of this agreement and restrictions on the transferor to register, license, transfer, own or otherwise use any domain name confusingly similar to the domain name that was transferred to the transferee.

6.4.2 Assignment Clauses

The agreement should contain an assignment by the transferor of all of the rights, title and interest in the domain name and the domain name services agreement dated (*insert date*) with (*insert registry*). There is also the possibility that the transferor may have acquired trade-mark rights in the domain name under common law or by registration with the applicable trade-marks office. Therefore, the agreement should also contain an assignment of all trade-mark rights in the domain name.

6.4.3 Transferee's Obligations

The transferee's main obligation under the agreement is to give some consideration for the domain name transfer. This is often in the form of a fixed payment, which may be made to an escrow agent to be released upon the transferee having been registered with the applicable domain name registry as the registrant of the domain name. Consideration should also be given as to which party will pay any fees levied by third parties, such as escrow agents or domain name registrars, in the course of the transfer.

6.4.4 Representations and Warranties

The following representations and warranties are commonly given by transferors to transferees of domain names:

- that the transferor has the authority and right to enter into this agreement, perform its obligations, and in particular, to transfer any and all title and ownership of the domain name (including trade-marks) to the transferee;

- that the domain name is free and clear of all encumbrances;
- that the domain name has not been assigned or licensed previously;
- that the transferor is the sole registrant of the domain name and sole owner of any trade-mark rights in it; and
- that all domain name registration and renewal fees have been paid in full.

6.4.5 Indemnities

See the discussion in respect of indemnities in Chapter 3, paragraph 3.4.10.

6.4.6 Limitations on Liability and Disclaimers

See the discussion in respect of limitations on liability and disclaimers in Chapter 3, paragraph 3.4.11.

6.4.7 Remedies

The agreement should also set out the remedies that each party has if the other party is in breach of the agreement. Such remedies may include the right for the non-breaching party to terminate the agreement, to receive liquidated damages and to be indemnified for any third-party claims or damages. (See paragraph 6.4.5 and Form 6B, Section 4.2)

6.4.8 General Clauses

As with other commercial agreements, in domain name transfer agreements, one should consider including notice clauses, further assurances, non-waiver, severability, currency, assignability, entire agreement, survival, force majeure, time of the essence, interpretation, independent contractors, binding on successors, governing law and choice of language clauses.

CHECKLIST 6 – FOR DRAFTING DOMAIN NAME TRANSFER AGREEMENTS

- Ensure parties are clearly identified by their full legal names and for on-line agreements, see also checklist in Chapter 9;
- Clearly describe the exact domain name, how and when it is to be transferred;
- Set out transferor's obligations, in particular:
    - to comply with the procedures required by the applicable domain name registry,
    - assignment of any and all rights in the domain name, related trade-mark and domain name services agreement,
    - to not take any action to withdraw, suspend or otherwise terminate the registrant name change with the registry,
    - to cease all use of the domain name upon completion of the transaction;
- Consider non-compete clause, e.g., restrictions on the transferor to register, license, transfer, own or otherwise use any domain name confusingly similar to the domain name that was transferred to the transferee;
- Consider confidentiality covenants, e.g., non-disclosure of the terms of this agreement;
- Set out transferee's obligations, in particular fee and payment terms, when due and whether taxes are extra;
- Set out which party will pay any fees levied by the domain name registrar or any escrow agent;
- Consider escrow of fees until transferee has been registered as new domain name registrant;
- Add transferor's representations, warranties and indemnities, such as:
    - the authority and right to enter into this agreement, perform its obligations, and in particular, to transfer any and all title and ownership of the domain name (including trade-marks) to the transferee,
    - that the agreement does not and will not conflict with any other agreement or obligation,

  - that the domain name does not infringe on the trade-mark or other intellectual property rights of any third-party, in countries where the transferor has used or the transferee will be using the domain name or where the transferee is at risk of being sued for infringement,
  - that the domain name is free and clear of all encumbrances,
  - that the domain name has not been assigned or licensed previously,
  - that the transferor is the sole registrant of the domain name and sole owner of any trade-mark rights in it,
  - that all domain name registration and renewal fees have been paid in full,
  - indemnities for losses resulting from intellectual property infringement or breach of this agreement (and consider exceptions and limitations on indemnities);
- Disclaimers and limitations on liability to consider:
  - as applicable to indemnities,
  - consider disclaimer of implied warranties,
  - force majeure events,
  - indirect damages (should be described);
- If applicable, draft the termination provisions and consider which terms of the agreement survive termination or expiry;
- Set out the remedies that each party has if the other party is in breach of the agreement, e.g., to receive liquidated damages and to be indemnified for any third-party claims or damages;
- Boilerplate provisions, e.g., further assurances, non-waiver, currency, severability, assignability, entire agreement, force majeure, time of the essence, interpretation, independent contractors, binding on successors, survival, and governing law and choice of language clauses.

FORM 6A – DOMAIN NAME TRANSFER AGREEMENT – SHORT FORM

THIS DOMAIN NAME TRANSFER AGREEMENT MADE AS OF THE *(INSERT DAY)* DAY OF *(INSERT MONTH AND YEAR)*

BETWEEN:

[*Insert full legal name and address*]

("Purchaser")

-and-

[*Insert full legal name and address*]

("Vendor")

WHEREAS Vendor is the registrant of the Internet the domain name [*insert domain name*] (the "Domain Name");

AND WHEREAS Vendor has agreed to sell and Purchaser has agreed to purchase the Domain Name;

NOW THEREFORE THIS AGREEMENT WITNESSES that, in consideration of the mutual agreements contained in this Agreement, the receipt and sufficiency of which is hereby acknowledged, THE PARTIES HEREBY AGREE AS FOLLOWS:

1. Purchase and Sale. Vendor hereby assigns to Purchaser all of the right, title and interest in the Domain Name, the trade-mark *(insert domain name)* and the Domain Name services agreement dated *(insert date)* with *(insert registry)*. Immediately upon execution of this Agreement, Vendor shall cause to be transmitted to *(insert domain name registry)*, a *(insert name of domain name registry's Name Change Agreement)*, substantially in the form of Schedule "A" hereto (the "RNCA") and take all other steps reasonably necessary to effect the transfer of the Domain Name to Purchaser.

2. Purchase Price. The purchase price payable by Purchaser to Vendor upon registration of the Domain Name in Purchaser's name shall be $*(insert amount)* (the "Purchase Price") inclusive of all taxes of any sort.

3. Delivery of Purchase Price. Upon execution of this Agreement by Purchaser, Purchaser shall deliver to *(insert name of escrow agent)* ("Purchaser's Solicitors"), the Purchase Price. The Purchase Price shall be kept in trust and held by Purchaser's Solicitors in a non-interest bearing account. Once Purchaser has received confirmation from *(insert domain name registry)* that it has modified the existing registration for the Domain Name in accordance with the RNCA, and that Purchaser is, as a consequence, listed as the owner of the Domain Name in *(insert domain name database name, e.g., WHOIS database)*, Purchaser's Solicitor shall forthwith forward to *(insert name)* ("Vendor's Solicitors") a cheque payable to Vendor in the amount of the Purchase Price.

4. Cessation of Use of Domain Name. Immediately upon the release of the Purchase Price by Purchaser's Solicitors to Vendor's Solicitors, Vendor shall cease all use of the Domain Name. The parties acknowledge that no domain name other than the Domain Name owned by the Vendor is subject to this section. This section shall survive the termination or expiry of this Agreement.

5. Representations and Warranties of Vendor. Vendor represents and warrants to Purchaser as follows and acknowledges that Purchaser is relying on these representations and warranties in connection with the entering into of this Agreement and the purchase of the Domain Name:

(a) Vendor has sufficient authority and right to enter into this Agreement and perform his obligations hereunder, and in particular, to transfer all title and ownership of the Domain Name to Purchaser as provided in this Agreement, free and clear of all encumbrances;

(b) There is no contract, option or any other right of any person binding upon Vendor, or which at any time may become binding upon Vendor, to sell, transfer, assign, license or in any other way dispose of or encumber the Domain Name other than pursuant to the provisions of this Agreement;

(c) Vendor is the sole registrant of the Domain Name, with good and marketable title to the trade-marks in the domain name, free and clear of any encumbrances and Vendor has the right to transfer the Domain Name to Purchaser;

(d) To the best of Vendor's knowledge, the use of the Domain Name by Vendor does not infringe upon or otherwise violate any rights of any other person;

(e) The RNCA is the only filing necessary to transfer to Purchaser all of Vendor's right, title and interest in the Domain Name and upon receipt of the confirmation from *(insert name of domain name registry)* that the RNCA has been made, Purchaser shall be the registrant of the Domain Name and shall possess all rights (including without limitation ownership rights if any) in the Domain Name; and

(f) Vendor has not knowingly withheld from the Purchaser, knowledge of any circumstance that has caused or might cause the registration of the transfer of ownership of the Domain Name to be objected to by any person.

This Section 5 shall survive the termination or expiry of this Agreement.

6. Non-termination. After submitting the RNCA, Vendor shall not take any action to withdraw, suspend or otherwise terminate the RNCA and that, if queried by *(insert domain name registry)*, shall confirm that the RNCA is genuine and reflects his intentions.

7. Confidentiality. With the exception of the RNCA, which shall be filed with *(insert name of registry)*, Vendor shall not disclose the terms of this agreement to any person except:

(i) to Vendor's legal and business advisors, in confidence;

(ii) unless compelled to do so by any Court of competent jurisdiction; or

(iii) in an action to enforce its terms. This section shall survive the termination or expiry of this Agreement.

8. Further Assurances. Each of Vendor and Purchaser shall execute and deliver such further and other documents as may be necessary to give effect to this Agreement and to carry out its provisions. This section shall survive the termination or expiry of this Agreement.

9. Fees and Taxes. Each of Purchaser and Vendor shall be responsible for payment of their own fees, costs and expenses incurred in connection with the transfer of the Domain Name and the payment of any applicable taxes.

10. Successors and Assigns. This Agreement shall inure to the benefit of and be binding on the parties and the respective successors and assigns.

11. Governing Law. This Agreement shall be governed by the laws of the Province of *(insert province)* and the laws of Canada applicable therein. This section shall survive the termination or expiry of this Agreement.

EXECUTED at *(insert location)* as of the date first written above.

FORM 6B – TRANSFER OF DOMAIN NAME AGREEMENT – LONG FORM

THIS DOMAIN NAME TRANSFER AGREEMENT IS MADE AS OF THE *(INSERT DATE)* DAY OF *(INSERT MONTH, YEAR)*.

BETWEEN:

[Insert Name of Purchaser]

("Purchaser")

-and-

[Insert Name of Vendor]

("Vendor")

WHEREAS:

A. Internet-related services in the (*insert jurisdiction*) area and is, operating as "(*insert registrant's name*)", the registrant of the Domain Name.

B. The Domain Name was registered under the name (*insert registrant's name*) on or about (*insert date*).

C. The Vendor asserts that he owns all right, title and interest in, and all rights necessary to use on the Internet the Domain Name, as defined below.

D. The Vendor has agreed to sell and Purchaser has agreed to purchase the Domain Name and Vendor's right, title and interest in the Domain Name if any, subject to the terms and conditions set out below.

NOW THEREFORE THIS AGREEMENT WITNESSES that, in consideration of the mutual agreements contained in this Agreement, the receipt and sufficiency of which is hereby acknowledged, **THE PARTIES HEREBY AGREE AS FOLLOWS**:

1. DEFINITIONS

1.1 In this Agreement, the following terms and phrases shall have the following meanings:

"**Agreement**" means this Domain Name Transfer Agreement and any schedules referred to herein;

"**Domain Name**" means the domain name (*insert domain name*);

"**InterNIC**" means InterNIC, Network Solutions, Inc. or any other entity responsible for recording ownership of the Domain Name;

"**Notice**" means notice from InterNIC that it has modified the existing registration for the Domain Name in accordance with the RNCA, and that, as a consequence, the Purchaser is listed as owner of the Domain Name in WHOIS;

"**Parties**" means the parties to this Agreement, namely the Vendor and the Purchaser;

"**Purchase Price**" means the sum of $x *(insert currency)* payable by the Purchaser to the Vendor inclusive of all taxes of any sort;

"**Purchaser's Solicitors**" means (*insert legal counsel name and address*);

"**RNCA**" means the Registrant Name Change Agreement or similar documents necessary to be completed and filed with InterNIC to effect the transfer of the Domain Name from Vendor to Purchaser; and

"**WHOIS**" means the web site accessible on the Internet which advises who is recorded as the owner of and provides pertinent contact information in respect of a given domain name.

2. VENDOR'S OBLIGATIONS

2.1 Vendor hereby assigns to Purchaser all of Vendor's right, title and interest in the Domain Name and the domain name services agreement with InterNIC. Vendor shall, immediately upon execution of this Agreement, transmit to InterNIC the RNCA, substantially in the form of Schedule "A" hereto and take all other steps reasonably necessary, including without limitation, providing to InterNIC all information necessary to effect the transfer of the Domain Name to Purchaser.

2.2 Vendor shall take such steps as are reasonably required to allow Purchaser's Solicitors to satisfy themselves that transfer of the Domain Name from Vendor to Purchaser and to receive the Notice from InterNIC.

2.3 Immediately upon release of the Purchase Price by the Purchaser's Solicitors to the Vendor, the Vendor shall cease all use of the Domain Name and shall not use any Internet domain name that contains the word "*(insert sample)*" as a separate term (e.g., (*insert sample domain name*)). This section shall survive the termination or expiry of this Agreement.

2.4 The Vendor acknowledges that any unauthorized use of the Domain Name by the Vendor or any third parties under Vendor's control or with Vendor's authorization constitutes a breach of this Agreement and an infringement of the Purchaser's intellectual property rights.

2.5 The Vendor shall not register, license, transfer, own or otherwise use any domain name confusingly similar to the Domain Name. This section shall survive the termination or expiry of this Agreement.

2.6 Vendor shall, at its expense, execute any further document that Purchaser may reasonably require to enable Purchaser to become the registrant of the Domain Name at the direction of the Purchaser. This section shall survive the termination or expiry of this Agreement.

2.7 After submitting the RNCA, Vendor shall not take any action to withdraw, suspend or otherwise terminate the RNCA and that, if queried by InterNIC, shall confirm that the RNCA is genuine and reflects his intentions. This section shall survive the termination or expiry of this Agreement.

3. PURCHASE PRICE

3.1 The Purchase Price shall be kept in trust and held by the Purchaser's Solicitors in a non-interest bearing account. Upon execution of this Agreement by both parties and, subject to Vendor's compliance with its obligations under Article 2, upon receipt of the confirmation from the Purchaser's Solicitors that the Notice from InterNIC has been received, the Purchaser's Solicitors shall forthwith make available to Vendor for pick-up at *(insert address)*, a cheque payable to "*(insert registrant's or payee's name)*" in an amount in (*insert currency*) funds equivalent to the Purchase Price at the time of conversion.

3.2 Each of Vendor and Purchaser shall be responsible for payment of their own fees, costs and expenses incurred in connection with the sale and purchase of the Domain Name and the payment of any applicable taxes.

4. REPRESENTATIONS, WARRANTIES AND INDEMNITIES BY THE VENDOR

4.1 Vendor represents and warrants to Purchaser as follows and acknowledges that Purchaser is relying on these representations and warranties in connection with the entering into of this Agreement and the purchase of the Domain Name:

(a) "*(Insert registrant's name)*" is a trade name of *(insert company)* and of no other person;

(b) Vendor is the registrant of the Domain Name has sufficient authority and right and full power to enter into this Agreement and perform his obligations hereunder, and in particular, to transfer any and all right, title and interest in and to the Domain Name and *(insert related trade-mark and jurisdiction)* to Purchaser as provided herein free and clear of all encumbrances;

(c) there is no contract, option or any other right of any person binding upon Vendor, or which at any time may become binding upon, Vendor to sell, transfer, assign, license or in any other way dispose of or encumber the Domain Name other than pursuant to the provisions of this Agreement;

(d) Vendor is the sole registrant of the Domain Name and the sole owner of any trade-mark rights in the Domain Name in *(insert jurisdiction)*;

(e) to the best of Vendor's knowledge, the use of the Domain Name prior to and until the execution of this Agreement by Vendor, does not infringe upon or otherwise violate any rights of any other person;

(f) the RNCA is the only filing necessary to transfer to Purchaser all of Vendor's right, title and interest in the Domain Name and upon receipt of the Notice from InterNIC, Purchaser shall be the registrant of and shall possesses all rights in the Domain Name;

(g) Vendor has not knowingly withheld from the Purchaser, knowledge of any circumstance that might cause the registration of the transfer of the Domain Name to be objected to by any person; and

(h) that all registration and renewal fees for the Domain Name have been paid in full.

4.2 Vendor shall defend, indemnify and hold Purchaser and its successors and assigns harmless against all claims (including any damages or compensation paid by the Purchaser to compromise or settle any claim) and all legal costs or other expenses, [in an amount not to exceed the Purchase Price], arising out of any breach of this Agreement by Vendor.

4.3 This Article 4 shall survive the termination or expiry of this Agreement.

5. FORCE MAJEURE

5.1 If either party is prevented from fulfilling its obligations under this Agreement by reason of any supervening event beyond its control including but not by way of limitation, war, national emergency, flood, earthquake, strike or lockout (other than a strike or lockout induced by the party so incapacitated), the party unable to fulfil its obligations shall immediately give notice of this to the other party and shall do everything in its power to resume full performance.

6. ENTIRE AGREEMENT

6.1 This Agreement embodies all the terms and conditions agreed upon between the parties hereto as the subject matter of this Agreement and supersedes and cancels in all respects, all previous representations, warranties, agreements and undertakings, if any, made between the Parties with respect to the subject matter hereof, whether such be written or oral.

7. AMENDMENT, VARIATION, REVOCATION OR MODIFICATION

7.1 No amendment, variation, revocation, modification, cancellation, substitution or waiver of or addition or supplement to any of the provisions of this Agreement shall be binding on the Parties hereto unless the same is duly effected by an instrument in writing signed by all the Parties hereto.

8. SEVERABILITY

8.1 If any of the provisions of this Agreement is found by a court of competent jurisdiction to be void and unenforceable, in whole or in part, under any enactment of law, such provision shall be deemed to be deleted from this Agreement and the remaining provisions of this Agreement shall remain in full force and effect.

9. SUCCESSORS AND ASSIGNS

9.1 This Agreement shall inure to the benefit of and be binding on the respective heirs, personal representatives, successors-in-title or permitted assigns of the Parties hereto.

10. GOVERNING LAW

10.1 This Agreement shall be governed by the laws of *(INSERT PROVINCE)*, Canada, and shall be treated in all respects as a *(INSERT PROVINCE)* contract, without regard to conflicts of laws principles. Any dispute arising out of this Agreement shall be brought to the courts of *(INSERT PROVINCE)*, Canada.

EXECUTED at *(insert jurisdiction)* AS OF THE DATE FIRST WRITTEN ABOVE.

Per ________________________________

Title: ________________________________

EXECUTED at *(insert jurisdiction)* AS OF THE DATE FIRST WRITTEN ABOVE.

Per: ________________________________

Title: ________________________________

CHAPTER 7

WEB SITE HOSTING CONTRACTS

7.1 INTRODUCTION TO WEB SITE HOSTING

As discussed in Chapter 1 (see paragraph 1.5.1), a web site host's function is to run a web site (which is ultimately software), on its server that is connected to the Internet and which Internet users can view and access. A web site host is similar to an ASP in that it runs the web site on its servers, which multiple users can access. Therefore, the issues and terms discussed in Software Hosting Services Agreements (see Chapter 8) are similar in some respects to the issues relating to, and terms of Web Site Hosting Agreements.

However, a critical difference between a Web Site Hosting Agreement and a Software Hosting Agreement, is that in the web site hosting context, usually the software (i.e., the web site) being hosted is owned and supplied by the customer.[1] Therefore, the Web Site Hosting Agreement should include a license from the customer to the web site host. On the other hand, in the software hosting context, the software being hosted by an ASP is usually software that the ASP owns or that the ASP has licensed from a third-party licensor. For a more detailed discussion on software hosting and ASPs, see Chapter 8.

7.2 WHAT RISKS DOES A CUSTOMER FACE IN OBTAINING WEB SITE HOSTING SERVICES AND HOW TO AVOID THEM?

One of the most important issues that a customer has when using another party to host its web site, especially if the web site is critical to the customer's business, is to ensure that access to the web site is quick, reliable and available and that it meets certain service levels. Backup, reporting, disaster recovery and systems management terms, may also be important service requirements. (See Form 8A, Schedule "A")

To allocate some of these risks to other persons, a customer would seek covenants, representations, warranties and indemnities from their web site host, usually an ISP (see Form 7A, Sections 1 and 4), and that the web site hosting services meet required performance levels. ISPs may also be contractually obligated to host the web site on dedicated servers or to have high-speed telecommunications lines or bandwidth, between their servers and the Internet backbone.

---

1 In cases where the web site host was also the developer of the web site, they may have ownership of the web site. See Chapter 5 on web site development, paragraph 5.2.4.

Customers would also be concerned about retaining ownership rights, if any, in the web site, its content and their domain name registrations. Therefore the agreement should deal with ownership and licensing of the web site and any modifications and domain name registrations. (See Paragraph 7.4.4, below) As well, customers would want to have their web site returned to them, and any domain names transitioned back upon termination.

The customer may also want to regularly update the content on the web site or make modifications to the web site. On the other hand, customers generally do not want their web site host to make any modifications to the web site without their prior review or consent. It is common for web site hosts to request having their trade-marks or business name identified on the web site as being the host provider. In such case, the agreement should contain details as to size and placement of the web site host's marks, and care should be taken to ensure that the customer's rights in any of its trade-marks displayed on the web site, are not diluted and that Internet users are not confused as to who the web site belongs to (see also discussion in Chapter 9 regarding web site legal notices).

7.3 WHAT RISKS DOES A WEB SITE HOST FACE IN PROVIDING WEB SITE HOSTING SERVICES AND HOW TO AVOID THEM?

As discussed in Chapter 2, a web site host, often an ISP, might be found liable for its customers' activities, web site and content, including liability for intellectual property infringement (such as copyright and trade-mark infringement), violation of privacy and potential *Criminal Code* offences such as obscenity, child pornography and hate propaganda.

Although an ISP cannot contract out of statutory liability to third parties or criminal liability, the risks faced by the ISP can be reduced with the Web Site Hosting Agreement (see Form 7A). The customer obligations and restrictions in the agreement (see, Form 7A, Section 5) increase customer awareness of potential liabilities. If the customer is in the best position to deal with the risks, there is a good argument that the agreement should be drafted to shift the risks onto the customer and should contain indemnities from the customer for damages that the ISP may suffer.

Another common risk faced by the ISP is the failure of third-party software, hardware, telecommunications backbones or other products or services which were not developed or supplied by the ISP and over which the ISP has little or no control. An ISP can manage this risk by ensuring any limitations on the liability of and disclaimers by their suppliers, are reflected in the Web Site Hosting Agreement. In addition, when acting for an ISP, one should negotiate limitations on the ISP's liability for events outside the control of the ISP, such as disclaimers of any liability for damages or losses resulting from any third-party, including without limitation telecommunications service providers, the ISP's contractors and the Internet backbone. The ISP may also want to provide for system downtime to implement fixes and upgrades.

7.4 PRINCIPAL TERMS OF WEB SITE HOSTING AGREEMENTS

In drafting the Web Site Hosting Agreement, the following principle terms should be included.

7.4.1 Web Site Hosting Services

The Web Site Hosting Agreement must clearly describe the type of web site hosting services being provided. If the services to be provided include more than mere web site hosting (e.g., additional services such as the migration of domain names, customizations or maintenance of the web site), the terms of the Web Site Hosting Agreement should encompass terms required to address those other issues (see Chapter 5 and Form 5A).

The agreement should describe the web site hosting services and performance levels, and any additional activities (e.g., provision of web site or content) in sufficient detail to enable the parties to clearly understand their rights and obligations (see Form 7A, Section 1).

In drafting performance levels, assistance may be required from technical advisers. Common web site hosting performance requirements include:

- availability, accuracy and speed of the hosted web site and related systems;
- regular reporting obligations;
- systems maintenance and response times to customer reported problems;
- back-up and disaster recovery on-site and off-site; and
- compatibility with common web browsers or other interfacing software.

For an example of performance specifications, see Form 8A, Schedule "A".

7.4.2 Customer Restrictions

The purpose of setting out restrictions in the Web Site Hosting Agreement is to draw to the attention of the customer, prohibited and potentially illegal activities. Although an ISP cannot contract out of statutory liability to third parties or criminal liability, the risks faced by the ISP will likely be reduced if the customer is made aware of potential liabilities, and if the customer covenants not to engage in activities that could create liability for the ISP and if the ISP has contractual remedies against the customer for breach of the customer's covenants.

Common restrictions on a customer accessing hosted software services are set out in Checklist 7, below, and Form 7A, Section 5.

7.4.3 Customer Obligations

The agreement should specify the customer's responsibilities for providing the web site and/or any content. The agreement should detail the format and procedure for submitting the web site, content and any future modifications to the web site host. (See Form 7A, Section 5)

7.4.4 Ownership and Licensing

The agreement should clarify who owns the web site and its content (e.g., the customer) and who owns the hardware, servers or other systems where the web site is stored and hosted (e.g., the ISP) or any trade-marks displayed on the web site. To the extent that the web site or content submitted to the web site host is modified, the agreement should specify who owns such modifications. If the customer wishes to retain any and all ownership rights in the web site and content, the customer should require the ISP to assign all ownership rights and obtain waivers (from authors) of any moral rights in the web site and content, in favour of the customer.

As discussed above and in Sections 7.1 and 7.2, if the web site is owned by the customer or its licensors, the Web Site Hosting Agreement should contain a license from the customer to the web site host, to permit the host to run, copy, store, modify or otherwise use the customer's web site to perform the hosting services. The scope of any license granted should be carefully drafted. Consideration should be given as to what specific rights are required to be licensed (e.g., the right to run, copy, store, modify, but not necessarily sublicense or distribute), whether the license is exclusive or non-exclusive and whether there are any territorial, usage or other restrictions or limitations.

7.4.5 Fees and Reporting

There are many different ways to structure fees in Web Site Hosting Agreements. Some of the possibilities upon which fees can be based include each of the following or a combination of the following:

(i) one-time charges, e.g., for implementing hosting service;

(ii) fixed rates, e.g., $x per month or $x per size of web site or bandwidth; or

(iii) variable rates based on the value or amount of Internet traffic to the web site (see Chapter 12, paragraph 12.5.5).

The agreement should also specify whether the fees are inclusive or exclusive of applicable taxes and duties.

It may also be reasonable to impose an obligation on a party to provide regular reports as to the criteria upon which the fees are based and to allow audits of a party's records to verify fees and reports.

7.4.6 Acceptance Testing

Consideration should be given to whether the customer wants to conduct acceptance testing prior to commencement of and payment for the web site hosting services, to ensure that the hosting services will meet the agreed upon performance warranties. For an example of acceptance testing provisions, see Web Site and Content Development Contracts, Chapter 5, paragraph 5.2.6.

7.4.7 Confidentiality and Privacy

In the situation where the customer may be providing confidential information to the web site host, such as technical specifications or proprietary material relevant to the site, it is recommended that the agreement impose a confidentiality obligation on the host.

Where the web site is interactive and may require storage or transmission by the host of personal or private information about individuals, it is recommended that the agreement contain restrictions on the host's use of such information (see Chapter 4). The host should also require a representation and warranty by the customer that it has obtained the requisite privacy consents and an indemnity for any damages that the web site host may suffer if the customer is in breach of this warranty.

As well, in order to comply with any applicable legislation or regulations, to facilitate co-operation with law enforcement agencies, and to ensure that customers are complying with the web site hosting agreement, it is important that the agreement permit (but not obligate) the web site host to monitor, intercept and disclose the content or activity on the customer's web site.

7.4.8 Remedies

The Web Site Hosting Agreement should also set out the remedies that each party has if the other party is in breach of the agreement. Such remedies may include the right for the non-breaching party to terminate the agreement, to receive liquidated damages and to be indemnified for any third-party claims or damages. (See paragraphs 7.4.9 and 7.4.11 and Form 7A, Sections 5 and 9)

7.4.9 Term

See the discussion in respect of the term in Chapter 3, paragraph 3.4.8.

As well, it may be important for the web site host to distinguish suspension of services from termination of the entire agreement, in particular if the host needs to conduct maintenance work on its servers or other systems used in hosting the customer's web site.

7.4.10 Representations and Warranties

In addition to the usual representations and warranties given by parties to a contract, such as that each party has the right to enter into the agreement and that the agreement does not and will not conflict with any other agreement or obligation that a party may have, Web Site Hosting Services Agreements require some additional representations and warranties to minimize the risk of unique liabilities that arise in web site hosting, as discussed in Sections 7.2 and 7.3, above.

When acting for the web site host, it is recommended that the following warranties be obtained from the customer:

- the customer has the right to license the web site, content and/or other materials provided to the host;
- the materials provided to the host do not and will not infringe on any copyright or any trade-mark, patent, trade secret or other intellectual property right of any third-party, in countries where the host will be using the materials or where the host is at risk of being sued for infringement. However, customers will be relatively reluctant to give representations or warranties for any third-party items which were not created by the customer; which the customer does not own; or over which the customer has no control or has not received similar representations or warranties from the customer's developers, suppliers or licensors; and

- where the customer is an individual, that he or she has reached the age of majority,

When acting for the customer, it is recommended that the following warranties be obtained from the web site host:

- the host has the right to provide the web site hosting services;
- performance warranties with respect to the operation of the web site and hosting services (see discussion on performance levels in paragraph 7.4.1, above);
- in the case of dedicated server space for hosting the web site or dedicated bandwidth, the amount and speed of such space or lines, as applicable, and that they are not shared with other customers;
- security or firewall technology is of a certain standard;
- where any web site customizations, content, trade-marks, software, modifications or other materials are being supplied by the web site host, warranties as to title, right to assign or license, non-infringement, performance and no disabling mechanisms;
- where other services such as a development or maintenance are being provided by the web site host, warranties pertaining to such services; and
- the hosting services will be performed in a competent manner by qualified personnel.

7.4.11 Indemnities

In drafting any indemnity, it is important to consider whether the indemnity should apply only to the contracting parties, or whether it should extend to the relevant party's directors, officers, agents, subcontractors and affiliates as well. If the financial ability or viability of a contracting party is of concern, it may be worthwhile to seek a guarantee from a parent or related company.

If it is the customer that is supplying the web site and its content to the web host, then the agreement should provide for an indemnity by the customer to protect the web host from any liability arising out of the customer's web site and its content. The indemnities generally given are indemnities for losses resulting from intellectual property infringement or trade secret misappropriation claims. However, a customer will be relatively reluctant to indemnify the web site host for any items which were not created by the customer (e.g., which were supplied to the customer by third parties or by the web host); which the customer does not own; or over which the customer has no control or corresponding indemnities from the customer's developers, suppliers or licensors.

The web host will generally seek an indemnity from the customer that the web site and its content does not infringe any intellectual property rights of any third-party, in jurisdictions where Internet users may access the web site, where the web host will be hosting the software, or where the web host may otherwise be subject to a claim or judgment. However, it may be reasonable for the parties to impose a limit upon the scope of the indemnity by providing that it applies only in territories where the customer has conducted intellectual property due diligence and registrations, or where it would be reasonable to expect the customer to do so. Furthermore, since patent and trade-mark applications are generally not publicly available until the patent or trade-mark has been issued, one should consider whether the scope of patent and trade-mark indemnities should be limited to only valid patents or trade-marks that have been issued as of the effective date of the agreement. (See additional discussion in Limitations on Liability and disclaimers, below)

An indemnity for a claim of infringement of a third-party's rights may also enable the indemnifying party to, at its option:

(i) modify the infringing material so that it becomes non-infringing;

(ii) replace the infringing material (with consideration given to the criteria to be met by the replacement);

(iii) obtain from the third-party claiming infringement the right to use the infringing material (provided that such rights can be obtained on terms satisfactory to the indemnifying party); or

(iv) request that the web host cease using, remove, return or destroy the infringing material and terminate this agreement.

When acting for the web site host, however, one should carefully review the agreement to ensure that the customer's options referred to above, do not limit any other remedies that the web site host may have against the customer for breach of a non-infringement warranty.

To the extent that the web site host is providing any material to the customer, the customer should obtain an indemnity from the web site host for any damages or claims arising from such material, including an intellectual property infringement indemnity similar to the one discussed above.

7.4.12 Limitations on Liability and Disclaimers

See the discussion in respect of limitations on liability and disclaimers in Chapter 3, paragraph 3.4.11.

7.4.13 General Clauses

As with other commercial agreements, in Internet and e-commerce agreements, one should consider including notice clauses, non-waiver, currency, severability, assignability, survival, entire agreement, force majeure, time of the essence, interpretation, independent contractors, binding on successors, governing law and choice of language clauses.

CHECKLIST 7 – FOR DRAFTING WEB SITE HOSTING AGREEMENTS

- Ensure parties are clearly identified by their full legal names and for on-line agreements, see also checklist in Chapter 9;
- Describe the web site hosting services, e.g., speed, bandwidth, firewall and disaster recovery services;
- Specify how and when the services are available or any exceptions to availability, e.g., suspension of services for maintenance;
- Include web site hosting performance obligations in a schedule;
- Include any additional rights and/or obligations that the web host may have, such as to provide test site, custom developments or modifications to the web site;
- Include ownership (e.g., assignments and waivers of moral rights by authors) and licensing terms with respect to the web site, content, trade-marks, customizations, modifications, domain names or other software or materials being supplied or used under the agreement;
- Include any additional rights and/or obligations that customer may have, such as:
  - compliance with web host's policies,
  - use of the web site hosting services for lawful purposes,
  - adherence to the laws of a particular jurisdiction,
  - compliance with court ordered publication bans;
- Set out restricted customer activities such as:
  - publishing, printing, distributing, possessing, selling, advocating, promoting, or exposing, obscene material, child pornography, or hate propaganda,
  - the use of trade-marks or trade names,
  - the use of copyright works,
  - defamation, libel, harm to reputation, invasion of privacy, misuse or failure to protect personal information, violation of secrecy, unfair competition and other situations that could generate civil liability,
  - export and import restrictions;

- Draft fee and payment terms, specify currency and whether taxes are extra;
- If required, set out reporting requirements and ability to audit reports and records;
- Include confidentiality and privacy provisions and consent by customer to web site host's monitoring and disclosure of web site, content and activities on the web site;
- Set out the remedies that each party has if the other party is in breach of the agreement, e.g., to receive liquidated damages and to be indemnified for any third-party claims or damages;
- Representations, warranties and indemnities given by customer:
    - that it has the right to enter into the agreement,
    - that the agreement does not and will not conflict with any other agreement or obligation,
    - that the customer has the right to license the web site, content or other material provided to the web site host,
    - that materials provided to the web site host do not or will not infringe on any copyright or any trade-mark, patent, trade secret or other intellectual property right of any third-party, in countries where Internet users will be accessing the web site or where the ISP is at risk of being sued for infringement (and consider exceptions for any third-party items which were not created by the customer; which the customer does not own; or over which the customer has no control or has not received similar representations or warranties from the customer's developers, suppliers or licensors),
    - indemnities for losses resulting from intellectual property infringement or trade secret misappropriation claims (and consider exceptions and limitations on indemnities),
    - if the customer is an individual, that this individual has reached the age of majority;
- Representations, warranties and indemnities given by the web site host:
    - that it has the right to enter into the agreement and provide the hosting services,
    - that the agreement does not and will not conflict with any other agreement or obligation,
    - performance warranties with respect to the hosting of the web site,

- in the case of a dedicated server space or bandwidth for hosting the web site, the amount and speed of such space or lines, as applicable, and that they are not shared with other customers,
- that the security or firewall technology is of a certain standard,
- where trade-marks, customizations, modifications, content or other materials, software or browsers are being supplied by the web host, warranties as to title, right to license, non-infringement, performance and no disabling mechanisms (and consider exceptions for any third-party items which were not created by the ISP; which the ISP does not own; or over which the ISP has no control or for which the ISP has not received similar representations or warranties from the ISP's developers, suppliers or licensors),
- where other services such as domain name migration, or development or maintenance of the web site, are being provided by the web site host, warranties pertaining to such services,
- that performance of the services under the agreement will be done in a competent manner by qualified personnel,
- indemnities for losses resulting from intellectual property infringement or trade secret misappropriation claims (and consider exceptions and limitations on indemnities);

• Disclaimers and limitations on liability to consider:
  - as applicable to indemnities,
  - for performance, uninterrupted, confidential, private, secure, dedicated or error free access services,
  - disclaimer of implied warranties,
  - force majeure events,
  - third-party products, acts or omissions,
  - liability by web site host for problems with customer supplied web site or content,
  - indirect damages (which should be described);

• Draft the term, termination and suspension provisions and consider which terms of the agreement survive termination or expiry;

• Consider post-termination or expiry provisions, e.g., return of web site, content or other materials and transitional services;

- Boilerplate provisions, e.g., notice clauses, non-waiver, currency, severability, assignability, entire agreement, further assurances, force majeure, time of the essence, interpretation, independent contractors, binding on successors, survival, governing law and choice of language clauses.

FORM 7A – WEB SITE HOSTING AGREEMENT

This Agreement is made between [*Insert full legal name of ISP*] ("ISP") and [*Insert full legal name of Client*] ("Client"). For good and valuable consideration, the parties agree as follows:

1. WEB SITE HOSTING. Subject to the terms of this Agreement, ISP shall use commercially reasonable efforts to host the Client's Web Site on ISP's web server for access by Internet users (the "Services"). ISP reserves the right to decline to host common gateway Interface script, commonly known as "CGI script". For the purposes of this Agreement, "Web Site" means a series of interconnected web pages intended to be accessible by Internet users with *(insert specifics)* web browsers, including without limitation all software, content, artwork, trade-marks, trade names, logos, text, pictures, sound, graphics, video, data and other materials supplied by Client to ISP. "Internet" means the world-wide network of computers commonly understood as the Internet.

ISP shall: use commercially reasonable efforts to ensure that the Client's Web Site is available to Internet users approximately 24 hours per day; back-up the Client's Web Site at least once every week; and store said back-up materials in a safe and secure environment, fit for the back-up media, and not located at the same location as the ISP's web server.

[At the Client's option and convenience, the Client shall specify Internet index sites, web pages, web sites, search engines and similar Internet resources that maintain information about resources available on the Internet, not to exceed 50, and the ISP shall submit the Client's Web Site to such Internet index sites without additional charge.]

ISP may, but is not obligated to, monitor, intercept and disclose the content or activity on client's Web Site. ISP may suspend the Services [upon prior written notice to Client] during *(insert time frame)* for routine maintenance [which suspension shall not exceed *(insert time limited)*].

2. [Optional - **ALLOCATION OF SERVER SPACE.** ISP agrees to allocate ______server space and _____ transfer bandwidth for the Services].

3. DOMAIN NAME REGISTRATION AND MIGRATION. ISP shall use commercially reasonable efforts to register (Client's proposed domain name), or migrate (Client's existing domain name) (the "Domain Name") from its current Internet service provider, which registration or migration shall form part of the Services. The Client agrees to co-operate with ISP and the domain name registry and to follow ISP's and the domain name registry's instructions in order to effect such registration or migration. Client agrees to comply with all the rules and policies of the *(Name/Country)* domain name registry and shall indemnify and hold ISP harmless of any liability resulting from non-compliance.

The ISP will work co-operatively with the Client to provide project management and migration services necessary for the orderly migration of the Client's Web Site from the web server on which they are currently maintained to the ISP's Web Server. The migration shall be completed within *(Number)* Business Days of receipt of the most recent copy of the Client Web Site.

4. REPRESENTATIONS AND WARRANTIES. The Client represents and warrants that:

(a) it has the right to enter into this Agreement and allow ISP to perform the Services;

(b) the Web Site is owned or licensed by Client and Client has the authority to provide it to the ISP to allow ISP to perform the Services;

(c) it has the right to grant the licenses in this Agreement;

(d) it has unencumbered rights in the Domain Name;

(e) the Domain Name has been registered without committing fraud or misrepresentation;

(f) it has the authority to permit ISP to register and/or transfer the Domain Name;

(g) it has not used the domain name for any illegal purpose;

(h) to the best of the Client's knowledge, the use of the Domain Name does not infringe the trade-mark rights of any third-party in (*insert jurisdiction*); and

(i) it has not received any claim from a third-party that the use of the Domain Name violates the trade-mark rights of any third-party.

5. CLIENT RESPONSIBILITIES AND INDEMNITY. Client agrees to provide ISP with a copy of its Web Site in (HTML) format ready to be placed on ISP's web server without modification or validation, for which extra charges will apply, on (*insert media, e.g., 3.5" diskettes*). Client is responsible for the posting of all Web Site content via file transfer protocol, commonly known as "FTP". Client represents, warrants and covenants that it is and shall at all times be in compliance with all applicable local, provincial, federal and international laws including but not limited to those laws regarding:

(a) court ordered publication bans;

(b) restrictions on publishing, printing, distributing, possessing, selling, advocating, promoting or exposing, obscene or threatening material, child pornography, or hate propaganda and Client understands that these situations could generate criminal liability;

(c) restrictions on the use of trade-marks or trade names, or any work which is protected by copyright, trade secret, patent or other intellectual property laws, including without limitation, software;

(d) restrictions on defamation, libel, harm to reputation, invasion of privacy, misuse or failure to protect personal information, violation of secrecy, confidentiality, unfair competition and other situations which could generate liability; and

(e) export and import restrictions.

Client shall be solely responsible for the design of Client's Web Site and the implications of hosting of Client's Web Site and any and all items, statements or other content transmitted, posted, received or created through Client's Web Site, even if transmitted, posted, received or created by someone else, and Client shall defend, indemnify and hold ISP, its affiliates and their respective directors, officers, employees, agents and contractors harmless from any loss, damage or liability which may result therefrom or for breach of Sections 4 or 5. Client shall comply with all ISP's Internet policies.

Client shall indemnify, defend and hold ISP, its affiliates and their respective officers, directors, contractors and agents harmless from: any and all third-party claims, demands or actions and resulting costs (including without limitation, punitive damages, court costs, arbitration fees, penalties, fines, amounts paid in settlement of claims and reasonable legal fees, disbursements and expenses of investigation) that the Web Site infringes a patent, copyright, trade secret or other intellectual property right enforceable in [Canada].

THIS SECTION SHALL SURVIVE THE TERMINATION OR EXPIRY OF THIS AGREEMENT.

6. OWNERSHIP AND LICENSE. The parties acknowledge that at all times Client is the owner of the Web Site. Client licenses to ISP a non-exclusive, royalty-free, world-wide right to store, copy, reproduce and display the Client's Web Site, as is necessary for ISP to perform the Services.

7. FEES. The Client shall pay to ISP $*(insert amount)* per *(insert time period, e.g., month)* plus all applicable taxes (the "Fees") as follows:

(a) the Client shall pay as a deposit the first and last months' Fees upon execution of this Agreement;

(b) invoices are due and payable within *(insert number)* business days of the invoice date;

(c) interest shall be charged on outstanding balances at a rate of *(insert amount)*% per month or the maximum allowable by law, whichever is less; and

(d) unused Services cannot be transferred or assigned by Client and prepaid fees or deposits are non-refundable.

8. TERM. The term of this Agreement is one (1) year (the "Term") from the commencement of the Services. This Agreement shall automatically renew at the end of the current Term, upon the same terms and conditions except that the Fees in Section 7 shall be at ISP's then current fees. However, this Agreement shall not renew if either party has delivered by fax, courier or regular mail, to the other, a written notice of intent not to renew this Agreement and such notice of intent must be received by ISP not less than *(insert number)* days in advance of the end of the current Term.

9. TERMINATION. Without limiting any other rights or remedies available to ISP under this Agreement, at law or in equity, ISP has the right to terminate this Agreement without notice to the Client if:

(a) Client is in breach of any of its representations, warranties or obligations under Sections 4 or 5 above, and such breach is not cured within *(insert number)* days;

(b) ISP has not received any payment when due under this Agreement; or

(c) bankruptcy or insolvency proceedings are taken by or against the Client or if a receiver, trustee or other similar person is appointed over Client's assets.

In the event of early termination of this Agreement, the Client shall immediately pay to ISP as liquidated damages and not as a penalty and without limiting any other rights or remedies available to ISP under this Agreement, or law or in equity, all amounts due or payable under this Agreement including without limitation amounts which would have been payable by Client over the remainder of the Term.

10. LIMITATIONS ON LIABILITY AND DISCLAIMERS. EXCEPT AS EXPRESSLY PROVIDED IN THIS AGREEMENT, THE SERVICES ARE NOT GUARANTEED AND ARE PROVIDED "AS IS" AND ISP GIVES NO REPRESENTATIONS, WARRANTIES OR CONDITIONS OF ANY KIND, EXPRESS OR IMPLIED, INCLUDING WITHOUT LIMITATION, REPRESENTATIONS, WARRANTIES OR CONDITIONS AS TO UNINTERRUPTED OR ERROR FREE SERVICE, ACCESSIBILITY, PRIVACY OF FILES OR E-MAIL, SECURITY, MERCHANTABILITY, QUALITY OR FITNESS FOR A PARTICULAR PURPOSE AND THOSE ARISING BY STATUTE OR OTHERWISE, OR FROM A COURSE OF DEALING OR USAGE OF TRADE.

IN NO EVENT SHALL ISP, ITS DIRECTORS, OFFICERS, EMPLOYEES, AGENTS, CONTRACTORS OR AFFILIATES, BE LIABLE FOR ANY CLAIM FOR: (A) PUNITIVE, EXEMPLARY, OR AGGRAVATED DAMAGES; (B) DAMAGES FOR LOSS OF PROFITS OR REVENUE, FAILURE TO REALIZE EXPECTED SAVINGS, LOSS OF USE OR LACK OF AVAILABILITY OF CLIENT MATERIALS OR FACILITIES, INCLUDING WITHOUT LIMITATION, ITS COMPUTER RESOURCES, WEB SITE AND ANY STORED DATA; (C) INDIRECT, CONSEQUENTIAL OR SPECIAL DAMAGES; (D) CONTRI-BUTION, INDEMNITY OR SET-OFF IN RESPECT OF ANY CLAIMS AGAINST CLIENT; (E) ANY DAMAGES WHATSOEVER RELATING TO THIRD-PARTY PRODUCTS, CLIENT MATERIALS OR ANY GOODS OR SERVICES NOT DEVELOPED OR PROVIDED BY ISP; OR (F) ANY DAMAGES WHATSOEVER RELATING TO INTERRUPTION, DELAYS, ERRORS OR OMISSIONS.

WITHOUT LIMITING THE FOREGOING, ISP'S, ITS DIRECTORS', OFFICERS', EMPLOYEES', AGENTS', CONTRACTORS' AND AFFILIATES' MAXIMUM TOTAL LIABILITY FOR ANY CLAIM WHATSOEVER, INCLUDING WITHOUT LIMITATION, CLAIMS FOR BREACH OF CONTRACT, TORT (INCLUDING WITHOUT LIMITATION, NEGLIGENCE) OR OTHERWISE, AND CLIENT'S SOLE REMEDY, SHALL BE AN AWARD FOR DIRECT, PROVABLE DAMAGES NOT TO EXCEED THE AMOUNT OF FEES PAID TO ISP UNDER THIS AGREEMENT DURING THE CURRENT TERM. NO ACTION, REGARDLESS OF FORM, ARISING OUT OF THIS AGREEMENT MAY BE BROUGHT BY CLIENT MORE THAN (*INSERT TIME PERIOD, E.G., TWELVE (12) MONTHS*) AFTER THE FACTS GIVING RISE TO THE CAUSE OF ACTION HAVE OCCURRED, REGARDLESS OF WHETHER THOSE FACTS BY THAT TIME ARE KNOWN TO, OR REASONABLY OUGHT TO HAVE BEEN DISCOVERED BY, CLIENT.

THIS SECTION SHALL SURVIVE THE TERMINATION OR EXPIRY OF THIS AGREEMENT.

11. GENERAL.

(a) **Modification and waiver.** This Agreement may not be modified unless agreed to in writing by both the Client and ISP. Any consent by a party to, or waiver of a breach by the other, whether express or implied, shall not constitute a consent to or waiver of or excuse for any other different or subsequent breach unless such waiver or consent is in writing and signed by the party claimed to have waived or consented. Except as otherwise provided herein, no term or provision hereof shall be deemed waived and no breach excused.

(b) **Headings and Gender.** The division of this Agreement into Sections and the insertion of headings, are for convenience of reference only and will not affect the construction or interpretation of this Agreement. Unless the context requires otherwise, words importing the singular include the plural and vice versa and words importing gender include all genders.

(c) **No Assignment.** Neither this Agreement nor any rights or obligations hereunder, may be assigned by the Client in whole or in part, without the prior written consent of ISP.

(d) **Governing Law.** This Agreement is governed by the laws of the Province of *(Insert Province)* and the federal laws of Canada. The parties submit to the non-exclusive jurisdiction of the Courts of *(Insert Province)*. The Parties hereby expressly exclude the application of the United Nations Convention on Contracts for the International Sale of Goods and the *(Insert Name Of Provincial International Sale of Goods Act)*, as amended, replaced or re-enacted from time to time. The Parties have required that this agreement and all documents relating thereto be drawn-up in English. Les parties ont demandé que cette convention ainsi que tous les documents qui s'y rattachent soient rédigés en anglais.

(e) **Execution by Fax.** This Agreement may be validly executed by means of transmission of signed facsimile.

(f) **Severability**. If any part of this Agreement is held to be unenforceable or invalid, it will be severed from the rest of this Agreement, which shall continue in full force and effect.

(g) **Force Majeure.** ISP shall have no obligation to provide Services to the extent and for the period that ISP is prevented from doing so by reason of any cause beyond its reasonable control, including without limitation the inability to use or the failure of any third-party telecommunications carrier or other services.

(h) **Entire Agreement**. This Agreement, and any schedules or other documents referred to herein, constitutes the entire agreement between the parties relating to the Services and supersedes all prior written or oral agreements, representations and other communications between the parties, and shall inure to the benefit of and be binding upon each of the Client and ISP and their respective successors and permitted assigns.

(i) **Survival.** This Section 11 shall survive the termination or expiry of this Agreement.

ACCEPTED AND AGREED TO:	
[*Insert full legal name of client*]	[*Insert full legal name of ISP*]
Per:	Per:
Name:	Name:
Title:	Title:
Date:	Date:

CHAPTER 8

SOFTWARE HOSTING OR APPLICATION SERVICE PROVIDER (ASP) AGREEMENTS

8.1 INTRODUCTION TO SOFTWARE HOSTING OR APPLICATION SERVICE PROVIDER (ASP) SERVICES

As discussed in Chapter 1 (see paragraph 1.5.1), *Application Service Providers*, also known as *ASPs*, *Hosts* or *Outsourcers* (ASPs), play a critical role in the Internet and e-commerce industry. ASPs are parties who will host software on their servers and for a fee, provide a service to others who do not have the software. ASPs will run the software on their own systems and allow others to access their systems and the software to process data; or alternatively the ASPs will simply receive data from others, process the data and return output.

When drafting a Software Hosting Agreement, it is important to consider whether intellectual property licenses from one party to the other are necessary. Whether licenses are required depends on how the hosted software is being accessed and what code or other proprietary material, if any, is being downloaded to the customer. If the situation involves mere data exchange between the parties, (e.g., data is being submitted by the customer to the ASP, processed by the ASP-hosted software and then the output data being transmitted back to the customer), the hosting agreement usually will not contain any licenses from the ASP to the customer. In such context, the ASP, not the customer, is running the software and the customer does not need any rights in or to the software, such as the rights to run, copy, modify or sublicense. The relationship that the customer has with the ASP is that of a service provider or outsourcer and not a software licensor.

On the other hand, if the access to the ASP-hosted software requires the customer to obtain some software from the ASP, such as interfacing software or a browser, or if the access to the hosted software results in the downloading of any code (e.g., HTML, jva applets, JavaScript, ActiveX controls), content or files that are proprietary to the ASP or its licensors, then the hosting agreement will need to include terms governing the customer's use such items.

In addition, if the ASP obtains any proprietary material from the customer, such as data that the ASP needs to copy, store, modify or otherwise use in order to perform the hosting services, the agreement should contain a license from the customer to the ASP.

The agreement should clearly set out who owns the data input, data output and who owns the software, hardware or other systems where the data is being processed and stored (e.g., the ASP). To the extent that the customer will retain any ownership rights in the data output, the ASP should assign all ownership rights and obtain waivers of any moral rights in the data, in favour of the customer.

The ASP's software hosting services are similar to a web site host's services, in that both are performing a service of running software for the benefit of a customer. Therefore, many of the issues and terms applicable to web site hosting apply equally to software hosting. (See Chapter 7) However, one critical difference between an ASP and web site hosting arrangements is that generally, an ASP does not host software that is owned or supplied by the customer. The software being hosted by an ASP is usually software that the ASP owns or that the ASP has licensed from a third-party licensor (which license permits the ASP to use the software for hosting purposes).

8.2 WHAT RISKS DOES A CUSTOMER FACE IN OBTAINING SOFTWARE HOSTING SERVICES AND HOW TO AVOID THEM?

One of the most important issues that a customer has when using an ASP, especially if the software being hosted is critical to the customer's business, is to ensure that access to the software is available and that the processing of any data by the software being hosted, meets certain service levels. Backup, reporting, disaster recovery and systems management terms, may also be incorporated into service level requirements. (See Form 8A, Schedule "A")

Another concern that a customer has is security and access to their data. Given that the role of an ASP is to host software for the benefit of its customers, the ASP's servers where the software is running and where customer data is being processed or stored, will often be shared by many customers. In addition, if customers access the hosted software and transmit or receive data processed by the software over open networks, such as the Internet, the customers face the risk that their access may not be secure and that someone could intercept their data transmissions or misuse their password or other identification.

To allocate these risks, a customer would seek covenants, representations, warranties and indemnities from their ASP (see Form 8A, Section 2 and Schedule "A") and also their ISP (see Chapter 3) that the software hosting services meet required performance levels and that the customer's activities and data are secure and are kept confidential. The ASP may also be contractually obligated to host the software and/or store the data being processed by the software, on dedicated servers, or to have dedicated telecommunications lines between themselves and their customers. Correspondingly, this would require the ASP to establish performance, security and content control mechanisms to ensure compliance with their contractual obligations to the customer.

Customers who transfer data or other materials to an ASP, would also be concerned about retaining ownership rights, if any, in the same. Similarly, customers who receive any software code, documentation, data files or other materials from the ASP, would want to be sure that they are granted sufficient rights to use such materials from the ASP. Therefore, the agreement should contain ownership and license terms, related warranties, as well as intellectual property infringement indemnities. (See paragraphs 8.4.4, 8.4.10 and 8.4.11 below).

Customers may also require customizations to the hosted software application (such as unique branding or custom interface screens), in which case consideration should be given to intellectual property, ownership and licensing terms. The customer may also want to restrict the ASP from allowing other customers of the ASP to access the customized software.

8.3 WHAT RISKS DOES AN ASP FACE IN PROVIDING SOFTWARE HOSTING SERVICES AND HOW TO AVOID THEM?

As discussed in Chapter 2, an ASP might be found liable for its customers' activities, particularly if the customers can upload data or other content to the ASP's servers. The risks of potential liability increase with the amount of control or knowledge[1] that an ASP has of its customers' activities, and include, without limitation, liability for intellectual property infringement (such as copyright and trade-mark infringement), violation of privacy and potential *Criminal Code* offences such as obscenity, child pornography and hate propaganda.

Although an ASP cannot contract out of statutory liability to third parties or criminal liability, the risks faced by the ASP can be reduced with the Software Hosting Agreement (see Form 8A). The customer obligations and restrictions in the agreement (see Form 8A, Section 2) increase customer awareness of potential liabilities. If the customer is in the best position to deal with the risks, there is a good argument that the agreement should be drafted to shift the risks onto the customer and should contain indemnities from the customer for damages that the ASP may suffer.

Another common risk faced by the ASP is the failure of third-party software, hardware, telecommunications backbones or other products or services which were not developed or supplied by the ASP and over which the

---

[1] Note that certain offences, such as strict liability offences, do not require any knowledge by the offender to be found liable.

ASP has little or no control. ASPs can manage this risk by ensuring any limitations on the liability of and disclaimers by their suppliers, are reflected in the hosting agreement. In addition, when acting for an ASP, one should negotiate limitations on the ASP's liability for events outside the control of the ASP, such as disclaimers of any liability for damages or losses resulting from any third-party, including, without limitation, telecommunications service providers, the ASP's contractors and the Internet backbone. The ASP may also want to provide for system down-time to implement fixes and upgrades.

8.4 PRINCIPAL TERMS OF SOFTWARE HOSTING AGREEMENTS

In drafting the Software Hosting Agreement, or any other Internet and e-commerce agreements, it is helpful to have representatives from different areas of the business, such as marketing and technical personnel, give input into what the terms of the agreements should be. Technology, such as encryption techniques and passwords, should also be implemented to support the agreements and their enforcement. In any event, the Software Hosting Agreement between the ASP and the customer should contain the following principle terms.

8.4.1 Software Hosting Services

The Software Hosting Agreement must clearly describe the type of software hosting services being provided. If the services to be provided include more than mere software hosting (such as the license of interfacing or browser software, or the maintenance of a telephone support help desk), the terms of the Software Hosting Agreement should also include the terms of other agreements (such as software license terms or support terms) (see C. Ian Kyer and Mark J. Fecenko, *Kyer and Fecenko on Computer-Related Agreements*, 2nd ed. (Toronto: Butterworths, 1997), Chapters 5 and 6).

The agreement should adequately describe: how the access services are being provided (e.g., by access over the Internet, a dedicated line or through a private network); how many users have access; when the services are available (e.g., twenty-four (24) hours per day, seven (7) days per week, except during scheduled maintenance periods, or by a certain number of users or from a particular location); and what additional obligations each party has (e.g., to provide certain hardware, software or security technology). (See Form 8A, Sections 1 and 2)

The parties may want to negotiate performance covenants and warranties by the ASP, that may be attached as a Schedule (see Form 8A, Schedule "A"). In drafting performance terms, assistance may be needed from technical advisers. Common software hosting performance requirements include:

- Availability, accuracy and speed of the hosted software and related systems;
- Regular reporting obligations;
- Systems maintenance and response times to customer reported problems;
- back-up and disaster recovery on-site and off-site; and
- compatibility with common web browsers or other interfacing software.
- For an example of performance specifications, see Form 8A, Schedule "A".

8.4.2 Customer Restrictions

The purpose of setting out restrictions in the Software Hosting Agreement is to draw to the attention of the customer, prohibited and potentially illegal activities. Although an ASP cannot contract out of statutory liability to third parties or criminal liability, the risks faced by the ASP will likely be reduced if the customer is made aware of potential liabilities, if the customer covenants not to engage in the activities that could create liability for the ASP and if the ASP has contractual remedies against the customer for breach of the customer's covenants.

Common restrictions on a customer accessing hosted software services are set out in Checklist 8, below, and Form 8A, Section 2.

When acting for the ASP, it is important that the customer be responsible for any activity that occurs through the customer's account. (See Form 8A, Section 2.4) This is of particular concern where customers may allow third parties to use their passwords to access the ASP-hosted software. Where security controls, such as encryption technology, are used, the customer may be in a better position to manage the risks of someone else accessing the software in their name.

As well, an ASP may want to include restrictions on the customer subleasing or reselling the software hosting services or allowing simultaneous access by more users than are specified in the agreement.

However, when acting for the customer, particularly where the software hosting services being provided by the ASP are via a dedicated connection, it is important that the ASP be obligated to prevent unauthorized access to the dedicated line by other customers and implement appropriate security controls. (See Form 8A, Sections 1.1, 1.3 and Schedule "A".)

8.4.3 Customer Obligations

The agreement should specify the customer's responsibilities for providing the data, telecommunications access, software (such as web browsers and connectivity software), computer hardware (such as routers, workstations and servers), and peripherals (such as modems and other communications equipment), which are needed to be able to access the hosted software and ensure that the ASP can provide any data processing services.

To the extent that the customer is in a better position than the ASP to maintain control over its access passwords, it is arguable that the customer should be responsible for maintaining the confidentiality of its passwords and should be responsible for all activities and charges resulting from the use of the customer's account or passwords, including unauthorized use. However, if the ASP's obligations include the requirement to maintain adequate security measures to prevent unauthorized access to the services, the customer may not want to agree to such obligation.

The customer should also be obligated to access the software being hosted for lawful purposes. Restrictions on customer's access are discussed in Section 8.4.2, above.

8.4.4 Ownership and Licensing

As discussed above in Section 8.1, whether intellectual property licenses are required depends on how the hosted software is being accessed. Usually, a Software Hosting Agreement contains a license from the customer to the ASP, to permit the ASP to copy, store, modify or otherwise use the customer's data to perform the hosting services. In addition, the customer may need a license from the ASP for any code, content or files that are downloaded from the ASP to the customer (e.g., HTML, java applets, JavaScript, ActiveX controls).

The scope of any licenses granted should be carefully drafted. Consideration should be given as to what specific rights are required to be licensed (e.g., the right to run, copy, store, modify, but not necessarily sublicense or distribute), whether the license is exclusive, sole or non-exclusive[2] and whether there are any territorial, usage or other restrictions or limitations.

---

2 An "exclusive" license means only the licensee can exercise the rights granted, even to the exclusion of the licensor. Exclusivity can be limited in scope. A "sole" license means no one other than the licensee and licensor can exercise the rights granted.

The agreement should also clarify who owns the intellectual property being licensed, and any data and software, hardware or other systems related to the access services. To the extent that any data is submitted by a customer to an ASP, the agreement should clarify that the customer retains any and all ownership rights in the data, and the ASP should assign all ownership rights and obtain waivers of any moral rights (from authors) in any modifications to the data, in favour of the customer.

8.4.5 Fees and Reporting

There are many different ways to structure fees in Software Hosting agreements. Some of the criteria upon which fees can be based include each of the following or a combination of the following:

(i) one-time charges, e.g., for implementing access;

(ii) fixed rates, e.g., $x per month or $x per size of access line; or

(iii) variable rates based on:

(a) value or amount of data being processed;

(b) total on-line access time in a given time period;

(c) ASPs variable fee schedules as provided to its customers from time to time; or

(d) number of users receiving access to the hosted software.

The agreement should also specify whether the fees are inclusive or exclusive of applicable taxes and duties.

It may also be reasonable to impose an obligation on a party to provide regular reports as to the criteria upon which the fees are based and to allow audits of a party's records to verify fees and reports.

8.4.6 Acceptance Testing

Consideration should be given to whether the customer wants to conduct acceptance testing prior to commencement of and payment for the software hosting services, to ensure that the hosting services will meet the agreed upon performance warranties. For an example of acceptance testing provisions, see the web site and content development agreement, Chapter 5, paragraph 5.2.6.

8.4.7 Confidentiality and Privacy

In the situation where the customer may be providing confidential information, such as proprietary data, to the ASP, it is recommended that the agreement impose a confidentiality obligation on the ASP. Similarly, the ASP may want the customer to keep any information it learns about the ASP's software or systems confidential, especially if the ASP has pre-existing confidentiality obligations with its systems' suppliers, such as software licensors.

Where the customer data may contain personal or private information about individuals, it is recommended that the agreement contain restrictions on the ASP's use of such information (see Chapter 4). The ASP should also require a representation and warranty by the customer that it has obtained the requisite privacy consents and an indemnity for any damages that the ASP may suffer if the customer is in breach of this warranty.

As well, in order to comply with any applicable legislation or regulations, to facilitate co-operation with law enforcement agencies, and to ensure that customers are complying with the Software Hosting Agreement, it is important that the agreement permit (but not obligate) the ASP to monitor, intercept and disclose the customer's access to the software.

8.4.8 Remedies

The Software Hosting Agreement should also set out the remedies that each party has if the other party is in breach of the agreement. Such remedies may include the right for the non-breaching party to terminate the agreement, to receive liquidated damages and to be indemnified for any third-party claims or damages.

8.4.9 Term

See the discussion in respect of the term in Chapter 3, paragraph 3.4.8.

As well, it may be important to the ASP to distinguish suspension of services from termination of the entire agreement, in particular if the ASP needs to conduct maintenance work on its servers or the hosted software.

8.4.10 Representations and Warranties

In addition to the usual representations and warranties given by parties to a contract, such as that each party has the right to enter into the agreement and that the agreement does not and will not conflict with any other agreement or obligation that a party may have, Software Hosting Services Agreements require some additional representations and warranties to minimize the risk of unique liabilities that arise in software hosting, as discussed in Sections 8.2 and 8.3, above.

When acting for the ASP, it is recommended that the following warranties be obtained from the customer:

- if applicable, that the customer has the right to license any data, or other materials provided to the ASP;
- the materials provided to the ASP do not and will not infringe on any copyright or any trade-mark, patent, trade secret or other intellectual property right of any third-party, in countries where the ASP will be using or accessing the materials or where the ASP is at risk of being sued for infringement. However, customers will be relatively reluctant to give representations or warranties for any third-party items which were not created by the customer; which the customer does not own; or over which the customer has no control or has not received similar representations or warranties from the customer's developers, suppliers or licensors;
- if the customer is an individual, that he or she is the end user of the software hosting account and has reached the age of majority.

When acting for the customer, it is recommended that the following warranties be obtained from the ASP:

- the ASP has the right to provide access to the hosted software, networks, databases or other systems accessible by the customer under the hosting agreement;
- performance warranties with respect to the speed and error free operation of the hosted software and related data processing;
- in the case of a dedicated server space for hosting the software, storing customer data or dedicated access lines, the amount and speed of such space or lines, as applicable, and that they are not shared with other customers;
- the security or firewall technology is of a certain standard;
- where interfacing software or browsers are being supplied by the ASP to permit the customer to access the hosted software, software licenses and warranties as to title, right to license, non-infringement, performance and no disabling mechanisms;
- where other services such as a help desk are being provided by the ASP, warranties pertaining to such services; and

- performance of the services under the agreement will be done in a competent manner by qualified personnel.

8.4.11 Indemnities

In drafting any indemnity, it is important to consider whether the indemnity should apply only to the contracting parties, or whether it should extend to the relevant party's directors, officers, agents, subcontractors and affiliates as well. If the financial ability or viability of a contracting party is of concern, it may be worthwhile to seek a guarantee from a parent or related company.

Given that the ASP is allowing access by the customer to the hosted software and the ASP's systems, then the agreement should provide for an indemnity by the ASP to protect the customer from any liability arising out of the customer's access. The indemnities generally given are indemnities for losses resulting from intellectual property infringement or trade secret misappropriation claims. However, an ASP will be relatively reluctant to indemnify the customer for any items which were not created by the ASP (e.g., which were supplied to the ASP by third parties or by the customer); which the ASP does not own; or over which the ASP has no control or corresponding indemnities from the ASP's developers, suppliers or licensors.

The customer will generally seek an indemnity from the ASP that the software being accessed does not infringe any intellectual property rights of any third-party, in jurisdictions where the customer will be accessing the software, where the ASP is hosting the software, or where the customer may otherwise be subject to a claim or judgment. However, it may be reasonable for the parties to limit the scope of the indemnity by providing that it applies only in territories where the ASP has conducted intellectual property due diligence and registrations, or where it would be reasonable to expect the ASP to do so. Furthermore, since patent and trade-mark applications are generally not publicly available until the patent or trade-mark has been issued, one should consider whether patent and trade-mark indemnities should be limited to only valid patents or trade-marks that have been issued as of the effective date of the agreement. (See additional discussion in Limitations on Liability and disclaimers, below)

An indemnity for a claim of infringement of a third-party's rights may also enable the indemnifying party to, at its option:

(i) modify the infringing material so that it becomes non-infringing;

(ii) replace the infringing material (with consideration given to the criteria to be met by the replacement);

(iii) obtain from the third-party claiming infringement the right to use the infringing material (provided that such rights can be obtained on terms satisfactory to the indemnifying party); or

(iv) request that the customer cease using, remove, return or destroy the infringing material and terminate this agreement.

When acting for the customer, however, one should carefully review the agreement to ensure that the ASP's options referred to above, do not limit any other remedies that the customer may have against the ASP for breach of a non-infringement warranty. The parties should also consider whether the agreement should provide for a refund of amounts paid under the agreement (especially if amounts were paid for unaccrued services), in the event of early termination as a result of an infringement claim.

To the extent that the customer is providing data to the ASP to be processed by the hosted software, the ASP should obtain an indemnity from the customer for any damages or claims arising from data, including an intellectual property infringement indemnity similar to the one discussed above.

8.4.12 Limitations on Liability and Disclaimers

See the discussion in respect of limitations on liability and disclaimers in Chapter 3, paragraph 3.4.11.

8.4.13 General Clauses

As with other commercial agreements, in Internet and e-commerce agreements, one should consider including notice clauses, non-waiver, currency, severability, assignability, entire agreement, force majeure, time of the essence, interpretation, independent contractors, binding on successors, survival, governing law and choice of language clauses.

CHECKLIST 8 – FOR DRAFTING SOFTWARE HOSTING SERVICES AGREEMENTS

- Ensure parties are clearly identified by their full legal names and for on-line agreements, see also checklist in Chapter 9;
- Describe the Software Hosting Services, e.g., speed, number of users, connection point, remote login, firewall and disaster recovery services;
- Specify how and when the services are available or any exceptions to availability, e.g., suspension of services for maintenance;
- Include software hosting performance obligations in a schedule;
- Include any additional rights and/or obligations that ASP may have, such as to provide a help desk or ancillary software, required for the customer to have access to the hosted software;
- Where interfacing software, browsers, code, documentation or other materials are being supplied by the ASP to permit the customer to access the hosted software, include ownership and licensing terms;
- Include any additional rights and/or obligations that customer may have, such as:
    - compliance with ASP's policies,
    - use of the software hosting services for lawful purposes,
    - adherence to the laws of a particular jurisdiction,
    - compliance with court ordered publication bans,
    - responsibility for telecommunications access, software (such as web browsers and connectivity software), computer hardware (such as routers, workstations and servers), and peripherals (such as modems and other communications equipment);
- Set out restricted customer activities such as:
    - publishing, printing, distributing, possessing, selling, advocating, promoting, or exposing, obscene material, child pornography, or hate propaganda,
    - the use of trade-marks or trade names,
    - the use of copyright works,
    - defamation, libel, harm to reputation, misuse or failure to protect personal information, violation of privacy or secrecy, unfair competition and other situations that could generate civil liability,

- export and import restrictions,
- subleasing or reselling the software hosting services or allowing simultaneous access by more users than are specified in the agreement;

- Allocate responsibility for activities through customer's account or using the customer's password;
- Draft fee and payment terms and specify currency and whether taxes are extra;
- Include any obligations to provide regular reports as to the criteria upon which the fees are based and to allow audits;
- Include confidentiality and privacy provisions and consent by customer to ASP's monitoring, collection, use, storage and disclosure of customer's information and activities;
- Set out the remedies that each party has if the other party is in breach of the agreement, e.g., to receive liquidated damages and to be indemnified for any third-party claims or damages;
- Representations, warranties and indemnities given by customer:

  that it has the right to enter into the agreement,

  - that the agreement does not and will not conflict with any other agreement or obligation,
  - if applicable, that the customer has the right to license any data, or other materials provided to the ASP,
  - that such materials provided to the ASP do not or will not infringe on any copyright or any trade-mark, patent, trade secret or other intellectual property right of any third-party, in countries where the ASP will be using or accessing the materials or where the ASP is at risk of being sued for infringement (and consider exceptions for any third-party items which were not created by the customer; which the customer does not own; or over which the customer has no control or has not received similar representations or warranties from the customer's developers, suppliers or licensors),
  - indemnities for losses resulting from intellectual property infringement or trade secret misappropriation claims (and consider exceptions and limitations on indemnities),
  - if the customer is an individual, that he or she is the end user of the software hosting account and has reached the age of majority;

- Representations, warranties and indemnities given by ASP:
  - that it has the right to enter into the agreement,
  - that the agreement does not and will not conflict with any other agreement or obligation,
  - that the ASP has the right to provide access to the hosted software, networks, databases or other systems accessible by the customer under the hosting agreement,
  - performance warranties with respect to the speed and error free operation of the hosted software and related data processing,
  - in the case of a dedicated server space for hosting the software, storing customer data or dedicated access lines, the amount and speed of such space or lines, as applicable, and that they are not shared with other customers,
  - that the security or firewall technology is of a certain standard,
  - where interfacing software, browsers or other code are being supplied by the ASP to permit the customer to access the hosted software, warranties as to title, right to license, non-infringement, performance and no disabling mechanisms (and consider exceptions for any third-party items which were not created by the ASP; which the ASP does not own; or over which the ASP has no control or for which the ASP has not received similar representations or warranties from the ASP's developers, suppliers or licensors),
  - where other services such as a help desk are being provided by the ASP, warranties pertaining to such services,
  - that performance of the services under the agreement will be done in a competent manner by qualified personnel,
  - indemnities for losses resulting from intellectual property infringement or trade secret misappropriation claims (and consider exceptions and limitations on indemnities);
- Disclaimers and limitations on liability to be considered:
  - as applicable to indemnities,
  - for performance, uninterrupted, confidential, private, secure, dedicated or error free access services,
  - disclaimer of implied warranties,
  - force majeure events,
  - third-party products, acts or omissions,

  - liability by ASP for problems with customer's products,
  - indirect damages (should be described);
- Draft the term, termination and suspension provisions, and consider which terms of the agreement survive termination or expiry;
- Consider post-termination or expiry provisions, e.g., return of software or materials and transitional services;
- Boilerplate provisions, e.g., notice clauses, non-waiver, severability, assignability, survival, entire agreement, force majeure, time of the essence, interpretation, independent contractors, binding on successors, survival, governing law and choice of language clauses.

FORM 8A – SOFTWARE HOSTING AGREEMENT

This Agreement is made between [*Insert full legal name of Application Service Provider*] ("Provider") and [*Insert full legal name of Client*] ("Client"). For good and valuable consideration, the parties agree as follows:

1. SOFTWARE HOSTING.

1.1 Application Services. Subject to the terms of this Agreement, Provider shall use commercially reasonable efforts to host the [*Insert Description Of Software*] (the "Software") on Provider's server for access by [*Insert Description Of Users*] (the "Services"). The Services shall include without limitation [*Insert Details Of Related Services, e.g., Security, Disaster Recovery, Project Management, Training, Development Of Customized Interfaces, Etc.*].

1.2 Provider Warranty. Provider represents, warrants and covenants that the Services are and shall at all times be performed by Provider in accordance with the specific service levels referred to in Schedule A.

1.3 [Optional] **Allocation of Service Space.** Provider agrees to allocate [*Insert amount, e.g., percentage, memory capacity, number of servers*] server space and [*Insert size*] transfer bandwidth for the Services.

2. CLIENT RESPONSIBILITIES.

2.1 Client Responsibilities. Client agrees to provide [*Insert Details Of Client Required Software, Connectivity, Hardware, Data, Etc.*]. Client is responsible for the data input to the Software via file transfer protocol, commonly known as "FTP". Client agrees to comply with all Provider's policies.

2.2 Compliance With Laws. Client represents, warrants and covenants that it is and shall at all times be in compliance with all applicable local, provincial, federal and international laws including but not limited to those laws regarding:

(a) court ordered publication bans;

(b) restrictions on publishing, printing, distributing, possessing, selling, advocating, promoting or exposing, obscene or threatening material, child pornography, or hate propaganda and Client understands that these situations could generate criminal liability;

(c) restrictions on the use of trade-marks or trade names, or any work which is protected by copyright, trade secret, patent or other intellectual property laws, including without limitation, software;

(d) restrictions on defamation, libel, harm to reputation, invasion of privacy, misuse or failure to protect personal information, violation of secrecy, confidentiality, unfair competition and other situations which could generate liability; and

(e) export and import restrictions.

2.3 Client Representations And Warranties. Client represents and warrants that it has the right to enter into this Agreement and allow Provider to perform the Services. THIS SECTION SHALL SURVIVE THE TERMINATION OR EXPIRY OF THIS AGREEMENT.

2.4 Client Indemnity. Client shall be solely responsible for the inputs, selection and use of the Services and all items, statements or other content transmitted, posted, received or created through Client's account, even if transmitted, posted, received or created by someone else, and Client agrees to defend, indemnify and hold Provider, its directors, officers, employees, agents, contractors and affiliates, harmless from any loss, damage or liability which may result therefrom or from breach by Client of this Agreement.

3. FEES.

3.1 Fees. The Client shall pay to Provider $(*insert amount*) per *(insert time period, e.g., month)* plus all applicable taxes (the "Fees") as follows:

(a) the Client shall pay as a deposit the first and last months' Fees upon execution of this Agreement;

(b) invoices are due and payable within *(insert number)* business days of the invoice date;

(c) interest shall be charged on outstanding balances at a rate of *(insert amount)*% per month or the maximum allowable by law, whichever is less; and

(d) unused Services cannot be transferred or assigned by Client and prepaid fees or deposits are non-refundable.

4. OWNERSHIP AND LICENSES.

4.1 Title. The parties acknowledge that at all times Provider or its licensors are the owner of the Software and any hardware, servers, equipment, networks or other software Provider uses in the performance of the Services.

4.2 [Licenses. The Provider licenses to Client the (non-exclusive) (non-assignable, non-transferable, royalty free, non-sublicenseable, irrevocable) right to download and store one (1) copy of *(insert description)* solely for the purpose of receiving the Services. *(insert restrictions on licenses)*.]

5. TERM AND TERMINATION.

5.1 Term. The term of this Agreement is one (1) year (the "Term") from the commencement of the Services. This Agreement shall automatically renew at the end of the current Term, upon the same terms and conditions except that the Fees in Section 3 shall be at Provider's then current fees. However, this Agreement shall not renew if either party has delivered by fax, courier or regular mail, to the other, a written notice of intent not to renew this Agreement and such notice of intent must be received by Provider not less than *(insert number)* days in advance of the end of the current Term.

5.2 Termination. Without limiting any other rights or remedies available to Provider under this Agreement at law or in equity, Provider has the right to terminate this Agreement without notice to the Client if:

(a) Client is in breach of any of its obligations, representations or warranties under Section 2, above and such breach is not cured within (*insert number*) days;

(b) Provider has not received any payment when due under this Agreement; or

(c) bankruptcy or insolvency proceedings are taken by or against the Client or if a receiver, trustee or other similar person is appointed over Client's assets.

In the event of early termination of this Agreement, and without limiting any other rights or remedies available to Provider under this Agreement, at law or in equity, the Client shall immediately pay to Provider as liquidated damages and not as a penalty, all amounts due or payable under this Agreement including without limitation amounts which would have been payable by Client over the remainder of the Term.

6. LIMITATIONS ON LIABILITY AND DISCLAIMERS.

6.1 DISCLAIMER. EXCEPT AS EXPRESSLY PROVIDED IN THIS AGREEMENT, THE SERVICES ARE NOT GUARANTEED AND ARE PROVIDED "AS IS" AND PROVIDER GIVES NO REPRESENTATIONS, WARRANTIES OR CONDITIONS OF ANY KIND, EXPRESS OR IMPLIED, INCLUDING WITHOUT LIMITATION REPRESENTATIONS, WARRANTIES OR CONDITIONS AS TO UNINTERRUPTED OR ERROR FREE SERVICE, ACCESSIBILITY, PRIVACY OF FILES, SECURITY, MERCHANTABILITY, QUALITY OR FITNESS FOR A PARTICULAR PURPOSE AND THOSE ARISING BY STATUTE OR OTHERWISE, OR FROM A COURSE OF DEALING OR USAGE OF TRADE.

6.2 LIMITATION ON LIABILITY. IN NO EVENT SHALL PROVIDER, ITS DIRECTORS, OFFICERS, EMPLOYEES, AGENTS, CONTRACTORS OR AFFILIATES, BE LIABLE FOR ANY CLAIM FOR: (A) PUNITIVE, EXEMPLARY, OR AGGRAVATED DAMAGES; (B) DAMAGES FOR LOSS OF PROFITS OR REVENUE, FAILURE TO REALIZE EXPECTED SAVINGS, LOSS OF USE OR LACK OF AVAILABILITY OF CLIENT MATERIALS OR FACILITIES, INCLUDING ITS COMPUTER RESOURCES, SOFTWARE AND ANY STORED DATA; (C) INDIRECT, CONSEQUENTIAL OR SPECIAL DAMAGES; (D) CONTRIBUTION, INDEMNITY OR SET-OFF IN RESPECT OF ANY CLAIMS AGAINST CLIENT; (E) ANY DAMAGES WHATSOEVER RELATING TO THIRD-PARTY PRODUCTS, CLIENT MATERIALS OR ANY GOODS OR SERVICES NOT DEVELOPED OR PROVIDED BY PROVIDER; OR (F) ANY DAMAGES WHATSOEVER RELATING TO INTERRUPTION, DELAYS, ERRORS OR OMISSIONS.

WITHOUT LIMITING THE FOREGOING, PROVIDER'S, ITS DIRECTORS', OFFICERS', EMPLOYEES', AGENTS', CONTRACTORS' AND AFFILIATES' MAXIMUM TOTAL LIABILITY FOR ANY CLAIM WHATSOEVER, INCLUDING WITHOUT LIMITATION CLAIMS FOR BREACH OF CONTRACT, TORT (INCLUDING, WITHOUT LIMITATION, NEGLIGENCE) OR OTHERWISE, AND CLIENT'S SOLE REMEDY, SHALL BE AN AWARD FOR DIRECT, PROVABLE DAMAGES NOT TO EXCEED THE AMOUNT OF FEES PAID TO PROVIDER UNDER THIS AGREEMENT DURING THE CURRENT TERM. NO ACTION, REGARDLESS OF FORM, ARISING OUT OF THIS AGREEMENT MAY BE BROUGHT BY CLIENT MORE THAN TWELVE (12) MONTHS AFTER THE FACTS GIVING RISE TO THE CAUSE OF ACTION HAVE OCCURRED, REGARDLESS OF WHETHER THOSE FACTS BY THAT TIME ARE KNOWN TO, OR REASONABLY OUGHT TO HAVE BEEN DISCOVERED BY, CLIENT.

7. GENERAL.

7.1 Modification and waiver. This Agreement may not be modified unless agreed to in writing by both the Client and Provider. Any consent by a party to, or waiver of a breach by the other, whether express or implied, shall not constitute a consent to or waiver of or excuse for any other different or subsequent breach unless such waiver or consent is in writing and signed by the party claimed to have waived or consented. Except as otherwise provided herein, no term or provision hereof shall be deemed waived and no breach excused.

7.2 Headings and Gender. The division of this Agreement into Articles, Sections, the insertion of headings, are for convenience of reference only and will not affect the construction or interpretation of this Agreement. Unless the context requires otherwise, words importing the singular include the plural and vice versa and words importing gender include all genders.

7.3 No Assignment. Neither this Agreement nor any rights or obligations hereunder, in whole or in part, may be assigned by the Client without the prior written consent of Provider.

7.4 Governing Law. This Agreement is governed by the laws of the Province of *(Insert Province)* and the federal laws of Canada. The parties submit to the non-exclusive jurisdiction of the Courts of *(Insert Province)*. The Parties hereby expressly exclude the application of the United Nations Convention on Contracts for the International Sale of Goods and the *(Insert Name Of Provincial International Sale Of Goods Act)*, as amended, replaced or re-enacted from time to time. The Parties have required that this agreement and all documents relating thereto be drawn-up in English. Les parties ont demandé que cette convention ainsi que tous les documents qui s'y rattachent soient rédigés en anglais.

7.5 Execution by Fax. This Agreement may be validly executed by means of transmission of signed facsimile.

7.6 Severability. If any part of this Agreement is held to be unenforceable or invalid, it will be severed from the rest of this Agreement, which shall continue in full force and effect.

7.7 Force Majeure. Provider shall have no obligation to provide Services to the extent and for the period that Provider is prevented from doing so by reason of any cause beyond its reasonable control, including without limitation the inability to use or the failure of any third-party telecommunications carrier or other services.

7.8 Entire Agreement. This Agreement and any schedules or other documents referred to herein, constitutes the entire agreement between the parties relating to the Services and supersedes all prior written or oral agreements, representations and other communications between the parties, and shall enure to the benefit of and be binding upon each of the Client and Provider and their respective successors and permitted assigns.

7.9 Survival. Sections 2.4, 5.2 and Article 6 shall survive the termination or expiry of this Agreement.

ACCEPTED AND AGREED TO:	
[Insert name of Provider] Per:	[Insert full legal name of Client] Per:
Name:	Name:
Title:	Title:
Date:	Date:

SCHEDULE "A"

PERFORMANCE SPECIFICATIONS

This document describes the performance specifications for the Services for hosted Software.

1. DEFINITIONS

In this Schedule, the following terms shall have the meanings set forth below:

"**Network Availability**" shall be the percentage of time that the Provider's Systems are available to carry network traffic between the Software and the Point of Access.

"**Point of Access**" shall mean Provider's border router which is used to establish connectivity from Provider's systems to its Internet service provider and the public Internet.

"**Provider's Systems**" shall be the entire physical operation(s) provided to host the Software. This includes all networks and servers, hardware and software utilized in the provision of Services located behind the Point of Access.

"**Server Availability**" shall be the percentage of time that the servers used to host the Software are operational and are successfully executing the necessary web and database server software.

"**Software Availability**" shall be the percentage of time that the hosted Software is accessible by the Client. Software shall be considered accessible unless (*insert qualification, e.g., if there is a complete loss of access by the Client*).

"**System Availability**" means the availability of the Software combined with the availability of Provider's systems, for access by Client to receive the Services.

"**System Availability Period**" shall be defined as twenty-four (24) hours per day, seven days per week less the agreed system maintenance period.

"**System Maintenance Period**" shall mean the time period from *(insert maintenance time period)* during which Software access and Services are not available because of required system maintenance, upgrades, and other Provider's Systems' hosting requirements.

2. PERFORMANCE STANDARDS

2.1 Provider is responsible for delivery of Software access Services on the Provider's Systems up to and including the Point of Access. Provider shall monitor and manage capacity to endeavor to meet commitments regarding disk space, CPU usage, system alarms, connectivity (routers and firewalls) and bandwidth are within operating parameters. The Services shall meet the following performance standards as measured during *(insert measurement period)*, excluding any System Maintenance Period:

- Server Availability = *(insert number)*% ± *(insert number for variance)*%
- System Availability = *(insert number)*% ± *(insert number for variance)*%
- Software Availability = *(insert number)*% ± *(insert number for variance)*%
- Network Availability = *(insert number)*% ± *(insert number for variance)*%

3. PROBLEM RESOLUTION STANDARDS

3.1 Provider shall respond to incidents that have been reported by the Client within the time parameters described as follows: *(insert Provider's support service response times, depending on level of severity)*

4. NETWORK ARCHITECTURE

4.1 Provider shall contract with its Internet service provider(s) to ensure that network packet loss does not exceed 1 percent from the Point of Access to the termination point of the Internet Service Provider's uplink to the public Internet.

4.2 Provider shall implement redundant networking devices: routers, firewalls, switches and balancing devices.

4.3 The Provider's Systems shall support public Internet access through diverse paths and routing to enable disaster recovery.

4.4 Network packets shall travel the round-trip length of the Provider's Systems in (*insert time in milliseconds*) or less. This shall be measured using a standard ping test from a designated Software database server to the end of the Point of Access.

4.5 Provider shall deploy a firewall to filter out network traffic that is not accessing the Software and load balancing devices. The servers to which the load balancer is directing traffic shall not receive packets directly from the Internet.

The Provider's Systems shall include reasonable attacker defences and security measures. The Provider's Systems shall be configured with reasonable security measures regarding data theft (through SSL encryption) and unauthorized network access from other subnets within Provider.

4.6 Any packet processed by the Internet router and forwarded to the Software servers shall first be examined by an intrusion detection ("ID") system. The ID system shall be configured to monitor for network attacks, Java Server attacks, Web Server attacks, Server system attacks, and take appropriate measures should an incident occur. In the event of an attack, the offensive packets shall either be stopped at the Point of Access, edge router, or firewall, or be redirected to another location for further investigation and prosecution, and prevented from entering the Provider's Systems.

4.7 Unauthorized traffic between Client and other software that is hosted on Provider's Systems, shall be denied.

5. PROVIDER SYSTEMS SERVICES

5.1 Provider shall define the Software network and systems architecture and in turn specify which hardware and/or software is required to perform the Services.

5.2 Provider shall procure, at its cost and expense, hardware and/or software used to meet Provider's obligations under this Agreement. Provider shall maintain and support platform operating systems, including required patches. Provider shall periodically review and apply new patches for operating systems as necessary to perform the Services.

5.3 Provider shall monitor server utilization levels and acquire additional hardware as necessary to perform the Services.

5.4 Provider shall carry spare parts inventory in sufficient quantities to support the Services. Such spares will not include CPU or memory. These shall be provided under Provider's support contract with the relevant hardware vendor.

6. SERVER AND DATABASE ARCHITECTURE

6.1 Web and database servers shall support high availability and fault tolerance through the use of multiple web servers and a clustered database server configuration.

6.2 Configuration shall be highly secured through the utilization of a hardened server architecture which is based upon open standards.

7. REPORTING

7.1 Provider shall provide to Client (*insert how often, e.g., weekly*) summary Software access reports and summary reports of Server Availability, System Availability, Software Availability and Network Availability.

7.2 When emergency maintenance that results from hosting server, network or other Provider Systems' failure is required, Provider will provide a reasonable amount of lead-time and arrange, with the Client, a solution that lessens the impact on the Client.

7.3 Provider will provide e-mail notification to the Client prior to scheduled maintenance windows and as soon as possible in the event of emergency maintenance.

8. DATA BACKUPS AND RECOVERY

8.1 Provider shall perform data backup with rotation to off-site storage occurring as follows:

(a) Hot (partial) backups of the database shall be performed at a minimum of daily intervals.

(b) Full backups of the web servers shall be performed at a minimum of weekly intervals.

(c) Cold (full) backups of the database shall be performed at a minimum of weekly intervals as part of the scheduled maintenance window.

8.2 Recovery requests under (*insert size limit*) shall be completed within (*insert number*) hours using the most recent version of the backup. Backups consist of data, databases, applications, and all configuration pieces required to restore the Client data.

CHAPTER 9

WEB SITE LEGAL NOTICES AND DISCLAIMERS

9.1 INTRODUCTION TO WEB SITE LEGAL NOTICES AND DISCLAIMERS

By providing information on a web site, which Internet users may access and possibly use or rely on, a business is opening itself up to potential liability all around the world. For example, if information is put on a web site, whether directly by the web site business, or indirectly by allowing others to upload content, Internet users anywhere in the world, who see this information, whether for free or for a charge, might rely on the information on the web site to make decisions. If the information contains errors and Internet users relying on such information suffer damages, the web site business might be liable.

A contract between the web site business and the Internet users that specifies the terms and conditions under which the Internet users are accessing the web site will help to minimize the risks and potential liabilities that the web site business might face.[1]

9.2 PRINCIPAL TERMS OF WEB SITE LEGAL NOTICES AND DISCLAIMERS

9.2.1 Describing the Parties

Many of the risks faced by web site businesses can be minimized if a web site agreement is entered into between the web site business and users of the web site. However, as with other on-line agreements, the issues of identity and authority of the contracting party becomes important. Technical security measures, such as passwords, cryptography and digital signatures, as discussed in Chapter 2, may need to be implemented to reduce the risks surrounding the identity and authority of the contracting party, particularly if the web site is interactive or contains content that may have liability risks. If the Internet user is a corporation, it is also important to ensure that the individual has the requisite corporate authority to enter into a binding agreement on behalf of the corporation.

---

[1] See Chapter 2 for a more in-depth discussion of web site liability issues.

9.2.2 Access Rights and Restrictions

It is also important to have a good understanding of the applicable intellectual property statutes, such as the Canadian *Copyright Act*.[2] The rights which are granted in the web site terms must be consistent with the rights that the owners of the intellectual property in the web site have. Furthermore, if the business is not the owner of the web site or its content, but rather a licensee, the rights granted to Internet users cannot be broader than the rights that the business has.

The web site terms should also contain proprietary notices, such as copyright and trade-mark notices, which identify the owners of the various rights in the web site and its content.

If the web site is interactive such that Internet users can place content on the web site or participate in discussion groups (such as chat rooms), one needs to consider whether corresponding licenses or assignments of ownership rights and waivers of moral rights in favour of the web site business, should be included in the web site legal terms. It is also recommended that warranties and indemnities in favour of the web site business, be obtained from the Internet users, to protect the web site business from liability for the content delivered by the Internet users, as well as failure by the Internet users to comply with the web site legal terms. One should also consider including additional restrictions on Internet users, similar to the ones discussed in Chapter 3 dealing with Internet access, such as restrictions on posting defamatory, illegal or infringing content.

The web site terms may cross-reference other policies that the web site business expects Internet users to comply with, and that the legal terms and policies may be amended by the business from time to time. However, it is important to recognize that any terms which are not brought to the attention of the Internet user prior to acceptance may not be enforceable.

9.2.3 Distinguish Advertisements from Binding Offers

If the business does not want to be legally bound by Internet users' submissions, e.g., purchase requests, then the web site legal terms should specify that any terms on the web site are not to be construed as "offers" but are merely invitations to treat, or advertising. It should also be clearly stated that any submission by an Internet user will be deemed an offer to purchase and not an acceptance of any terms on the site.

---

2 R.S.C. 1985, c. C-42.

9.2.4 Disclaimers and Limitations on Liability

In Chapter 2, the areas where having a web site could result in liability were discussed, such as if the content on the web site is not the most current, contains errors or is incomplete. Also, interactive web sites where users can upload their own content might contain material that infringes someone else's intellectual property rights, contains viruses or is defamatory or illegal. Hyper-linked third-party web sites may also contain such problems. Furthermore, the operation of the web site might not be consistent, as there may be server outages or down-times. Therefore, the web site legal terms should contain disclaimers and limit the liability of the web site owner for the risks that are peculiar to Internet web sites, as well as disclaimers of potential implied representations, warranties and conditions.

For example, the web site terms and conditions should disclaim any endorsement of or liability for content and hyper-links; implied representations, warranties and conditions, such as quality, merchantability and fitness for a particular purpose; indirect damages or loss of profits; inaccuracy, incompleteness or timeliness of the web site; viruses or data corruption; and damages arising as a result of the transmission, use or inability to use the web site.

9.2.5 Hyper-Linking Terms

Hyper-linking is becoming very common on the Internet to provide Internet users with quick access to other content or web sites. When advising a web site owner, it is important to consider whether there should be any concerns about others hyper-linking directly to the web site. One of the problems with hyper-linking is that third parties may provide "deep links", i.e., links into specific web pages of the site, which divert the home page and potentially any legal terms displayed on such home page. If, after the risk analysis, discussed in Section 9.1, above, one determines that it is important to have all users entering the web site agree to legal terms prior to accessing or using the site, it would also be of concern if hyper-links from other sites could avoid such a process. Therefore, unless technical controls are implemented to prevent deep-linking, it is recommended that the web site legal terms set out clear instructions as to anyone intending to hyper-link to the site as to which page of the web site they should be linking to. Additional hyper-linking terms, such as those dealing with trade-mark rights, are discussed in Chapter 12, and should also be considered.

9.2.6 Jurisdiction

As discussed in Chapter 2, given that a web site may be viewed and content downloaded by Internet users around the world, there is a risk that the web site business may become subject to the laws and regulations of foreign jurisdictions. In order to minimize this risk, the web site legal notice should specify which laws will govern, which courts will the parties bring a dispute in and expressly exclude any conflicts of law and international treaties. In addition, the web site legal notice should contain statements as to where the web site agreement is formed, where the web site is physically located (i.e., the server hosting the web site) and in which jurisdiction the web site is intended to be accessed, e.g., by Canadian residents only. If there are specific jurisdictions that the web site business does not want to be subjected to, the business should implement technical controls, such as requiring Internet users to input postal or area codes, as a screening mechanism.

Note, however, that this does not guarantee that the web site or the business will not be subject to the laws and regulations of foreign jurisdictions. Foreign states or jurisdictions may still claim that their laws apply, or that their courts should hear any disputes, especially if the business has a physical presence in their jurisdiction (such as a warehouse or the server that hosts the web site), or if it actively markets to people in their jurisdiction or allows people from their jurisdiction to access the business' web site.[3]

It is also important to realize and advise web-based clients that many of the same issues that apply to a brick and mortar business selling products internationally or exporting will also apply to a web-based business selling internationally. If a foreign jurisdiction's laws require a business to have a license or permit, to pay local duties or taxes, to not import or sell a product that infringes upon a local intellectual property right (such as a patent), or to comply with other local laws or regulations in order to sell to customers in their state, the business might have to comply with them or else it could be subject to penalties or legal action. It is recommended that businesses seek legal advice from counsel in each of the jurisdictions where there is an expectation of doing business, as any prudent exporter should do.

As with all contracts that are generally prepared for use in Canada, consideration should be given to ensuring compliance with the Quebec Language Charter.[4] Given the likelihood that a web site may be accessed by persons in Quebec, the legal terms should also contain an English language clause.

---

3 This has been the position of some U.S. courts in various U.S. states.

4 *Charter of the French Language*, R.S.Q. 1977, c. 5.

9.2.7 Consents to Use Personal Information

Many web sites permit Internet users to communicate with the web site business or other users. It is also common for web sites to collect information about those accessing the site through the use of *Cookies, Passports, Sniffers* or logs. In Canada, personal data collected, stored, disclosed or otherwise used is subject to the Federal *Personal Information Protection and Electronic Documents Act* (Bill C-6).[5] Therefore, privacy consents should be included in the web site terms if personal information is to be collected. Note that the Federal legislation requires an individual's consent, and it is not clear if merely posting a consent on a web site which deems access to the site as equivalent to consent, is enforceable. It is recommended that where a web site may have privacy issues, consents be expressly obtained from Internet users by means of a more active acceptance procedure, such as clicking on a button or typing in "I consent". To be in compliance with the Act, the web site legal terms should also refer to a method for Internet users to access, correct and delete their personal information.

As with Internet access agreements discussed in Chapter 3 the web site business should specify in the web site legal terms whether they have the right to monitor and disclose the Internet user's activity on the web site. This is particularly important where disclosure to regulatory or law enforcement officials may be required.

9.2.8 Acceptance Procedure

Since web site legal terms are usually agreed to by Internet users on-line, and not by the traditional method of signing paper documents, the issue of whether acceptance has occurred must be addressed.[6] This can be accomplished by specifying in the legal terms the acceptance procedures and when the legal terms are deemed accepted.

For example, the web site legal notice should state that it is binding when the Internet user performs a specific action, such as proceeding to access the web site, clicking on a button, or typing certain words in a box, such as "I agree". By specifying that the action required by the Internet user constitutes their acceptance of the legal terms and their intention to be legally bound, the greater the enforceability. In addition, requiring the Internet user to type in a phrase supports the fact that they have an understanding of the applicable language in which the legal terms are displayed.

---

5 Now S.C. 2000, c. 5. In Quebec, *An Act Respecting the Protection of Personal Information in the Private Sector*, c. P-39.1, would also apply.

6 This issue is discussed in greater detail in Chapter 2.

Given that, in Canada, the mailbox rule (as discussed in Chapter 2) will likely apply to on-line contracts, the acceptance of any offer must be communicated to the offeror. By sending a clear statement that a web site agreement has been successfully completed to the Internet user and by giving the Internet user the opportunity to print out a copy of the web site agreement, it will likely be held to be binding. If writing requirements apply, such as those required under provincial consumer protection legislation, then it is essential that a downloadable, printable, original copy of the completed agreement be provided to the Internet user.

Onerous or unusual terms should be brought to the Internet user's attention, such as by highlighting them in separate sections or requiring individual acceptance, e.g., by click-box, in order to demonstrate the Internet user's intention to be bound by those specific terms. As discussed above, to ensure the enforceability of web site legal terms, it is particularly important that all of the terms are readable before or at the time of acceptance. It is therefore recommended that the web site legal notices and disclaimers not be buried deep in the web site or cross-referenced to other web pages or documents that the Internet user has not seen before entering the web site or agreeing to the web site terms and conditions.

CHECKLIST 9 – FOR DRAFTING WEB SITE LEGAL NOTICES AND DISCLAIMERS

- Draft the web site legal terms in a user-friendly format, by defining the Internet user as "You", the on-line business as the "Company", and both parties as "We" or "Us".
- Adopt technical security measures to verify identity and authority of contracting party.
- Ensure that all of the web site legal terms are readable (e.g., not referenced in other documents or web pages) and highlight the onerous terms. Internet users should be forced to scroll through the web site legal terms and accept them to maximize enforceability. Give Internet users the option to exit the web site if they do not agree with the terms.
- Set out hyper-linking terms such as which page others may hyper-link to (e.g., the home page where the web site terms are displayed), trade-mark rights, restrictions, controls and indemnities.
- Describe what action a party must take to show acceptance and understanding of the web site legal terms and their intent to be legally bound. The requirement to type in a phrase, such as "I accept", is better than to click on a button.
- Carefully draft jurisdiction, governing law and attornment clauses, specifying where the web site agreement is formed, where the server is located, to whom (which jurisdiction) the web site is directed or not intended to be accessed and the agreed upon language.
- Obtain consent for using electronic documents and signatures and specify use of encryption technology.
- Disclaim and limit liabilities for the risks which are peculiar to web sites, in particular liability for content and hyper-links to other web sites.
- Provide access to and retention of electronic documents and a method of correcting errors.

FORM 9A – WEB SITE LEGAL TERMS AND DISCLAIMER

IMPORTANT! YOUR ACCESS TO THIS WEBSITE IS SUBJECT TO LEGALLY BINDING TERMS AND CONDITIONS. CAREFULLY READ ALL OF THE FOLLOWING TERMS AND CONDITIONS BEFORE PROCEEDING. ACCESSING THIS WEBSITE [BY HYPER-LINKING] [BY CLICKING THE "I ACCEPT" BUTTON, BELOW,] IS THE EQUIVALENT OF YOUR SIGNATURE AND INDICATES YOUR ACCEPTANCE OF THESE TERMS AND CONDITIONS AND THAT YOU INTEND TO BE LEGALLY BOUND BY THEM. IF YOU DO NOT AGREE WITH THESE TERMS AND CONDITIONS, PLEASE CLICK ON THE "EXIT" BUTTON BELOW.

This is an agreement between you ("You") and [*insert web site owner's full legal name*] (the "Company"). "We" and "Us" means both You and the Company. The effective date of this Agreement is when You accept this Agreement in accordance with the procedure set out above.

You hereby consent to the exchange of information and documents between Us electronically over the Internet or by e-mail, if to You to [*insert address of Internet user*] or if to Company [*insert address of Company*] and that this electronic Agreement shall be the equivalent of a written paper agreement between Us.

1. Ownership And Copyright. You acknowledge that any and all information, content, reports, data, databases, graphics, interfaces, web pages, text, files, software, product names, company names, trade-marks, logos and trade names contained on this web site (collectively the "Content") including the manner in which the Content is presented or appears and all information relating thereto, are the property of their respective owners as indicated, the Company or its licensors, as the case may be.

2. Permitted Use. The Company hereby grants to You a personal, non-transferable and non-exclusive license to access, read and download one copy of the Content.

3. Restrictions On Use. You agree that You will not:

(i) distribute the Content for any purpose including without limitation compiling an internal database, redistributing or reproduction of the Content by the press or media or through any commercial network, cable or satellite system; or

(ii) create derivative works of, reverse engineer, decompile, disassemble, adapt, translate, transmit, arrange, modify, copy, bundle, sell, sub-license, export, merge, transfer, adapt, loan, rent, lease, assign, share, outsource, host, publish, make available to any person or otherwise use, either directly or indirectly, the Content in whole or in part, in any form or by any means whatsoever, be they physical, electronic or otherwise. You shall not permit, allow or do anything that would infringe or otherwise prejudice the proprietary rights of the Company or its licensors or allow any third-party to access the Content. The restrictions set out in this Agreement shall not apply to the limited extent the restrictions are prohibited by applicable law.

4. License To Use Your Information. With the exception of personal information, You hereby grant to the Company the perpetual, unlimited, royalty-free, world wide, non-exclusive, irrevocable, transferable license to run, display, copy, reproduce, publish, bundle, distribute, market, create derivative works of, adapt, translate, transmit, arrange, modify, sub-license, export, merge, transfer, loan, rent, lease, assign, share, outsource, host, make available to any person or otherwise use, any information or other content You provide on or through this web site or which is sent to the Company by e-mail or other correspondence, including without limitation, any ideas, concepts, inventions, know-how, techniques or any intellectual property contained therein, for any purpose whatsoever. The Company shall not be subject to any obligations of confidentiality regarding any such information unless specifically agreed by the Company in writing or required by law. You represent and warrant that you have the right to grant the license set out above.

5. Personal Information. The Company may from time to time, but is not obligated to, monitor your use of the web site and collect, store, use and disclose to *(insert third parties to whom personal information may be disclosed)* personal information about You for *(insert specific purposes for collection, storage, use and disclosure)* and You hereby consent to such collection, storage, use and disclosure and waive any right of privacy You may have.

YOU MAY ACCESS, CORRECT AND DELETE YOUR OWN PERSONAL INFORMATION STORED BY COMPANY [AND THIRD PARTIES] BY *(INSERT METHOD OR CONTACT INFORMATION).*

6. Limitations on Liability and Disclaimers.

[ALTHOUGH THIS WEB SITE USES ENCRYPTION SECURITY,] THERE IS NO GUARANTEE THAT PERSONAL INFORMATION AND TRANSACTIONS ON THIS WEB SITE OR ON THE INTERNET WILL BE MAINTAINED CONFIDENTIAL AND SECURE. THE USE OF THIS WEB SITE AND THE CONTENT IS AT YOUR OWN RISK AND THE COMPANY ASSUMES NO LIABILITY OR RESPONSIBILITY PERTAINING TO THE

CONTENT, YOUR USE OF THE WEB SITE OR THE RECEIPT, STORAGE, TRANSMISSION OR OTHER USE OF YOUR PERSONAL INFORMATION.

This web site and its Content are not to be construed as a form of promotion [or an offer to sell any product or service]. This web site may contain links to other sites. The Company does not assume responsibility for the accuracy or appropriateness of the information, data, opinions, advice, or statements contained at such sites, and when You access such sites, You are doing so at Your own risk. In providing links to the other sites, the Company is in no way acting as a publisher or disseminator of the material contained on those other sites and does not seek to monitor or control such sites. A link to another site should not be construed to mean that the Company is affiliated or associated with same. THE COMPANY DOES NOT RECOMMEND OR ENDORSE ANY OF THE CONTENT, INCLUDING WITHOUT LIMITATION ANY HYPER-LINKS TO OR CONTENT FOUND, ON OTHER WEB SITES. The mention of another party or its product or service on this web site should not be construed as an endorsement of that party or its product or service.

The Company will not be responsible for any damages You or any third-party may suffer as a result of the transmission, storage or receipt of confidential or proprietary information that You make or that You expressly or implicitly authorize the Company to make, or for any errors or any changes made to any transmitted, stored or received information.

You are solely responsible for the retrieval and use of the Content. You should apply Your own judgment in making any use of any Content, including, without limitation, the use of the information as the basis for any conclusions.

THE CONTENT MAY NOT BE ACCURATE, UP TO DATE, COMPLETE OR UNTAMPERED, AND IS NOT TO BE RELIED UPON.

THE CONTENT IS PROVIDED FOR EDUCATIONAL AND INFORMATIONAL PURPOSES ONLY AND SHOULD NOT BE INTERPRETED AS A RECOMMENDATION FOR ANY SPECIFIC PRODUCT OR SERVICE, USE OR COURSE OF ACTION. THE CONTENT ON THIS WEB SITE IS NOT INTENDED TO BE USED AS A SUBSTITUTE OF ANY KIND FOR PROFESSIONAL ADVICE. IT IS YOUR DUTY TO OBTAIN PROFESSIONAL ADVICE FROM A QUALIFIED *(INSERT INDUSTRY)* PROFESSIONAL TO MEET YOUR *(INSERT DETAILS)* NEEDS. YOU SHOULD NOT ACT OR RELY ON ANY OF THE CONTENT WITHOUT SEEKING ADVICE OF A QUALIFIED PROFESSIONAL.

EXCEPT AS EXPRESSLY PROVIDED IN THIS AGREEMENT, THIS WEB SITE AND ALL CONTENT, PRODUCTS, SERVICES AND SOFTWARE ON THIS WEB SITE OR MADE AVAILABLE THROUGH THIS WEB SITE ARE

PROVIDED "AS IS" WITHOUT ANY REPRESENTATIONS, WARRANTIES, GUARANTEES OR CONDITIONS, OF ANY KIND, WHETHER EXPRESS OR IMPLIED, STATUTORY OR OTHERWISE, INCLUDING BUT NOT LIMITED TO, WARRANTIES AS TO UNINTERRUPTED OR ERROR FREE OPERATION, AVAILABILITY, ACCURACY, COMPLETENESS, CURRENTNESS, RELIABILITY, TIMELINESS, LEGALITY, SUITABILITY, PRIVACY, SECURITY, MERCHANTABILITY, QUALITY, TITLE, NON-INFRINGEMENT OR FITNESS FOR A PARTICULAR PURPOSE, OR THOSE ARISING OUT OF A COURSE OF DEALING OR USAGE OF TRADE.

IN NO EVENT WILL THE COMPANY, ITS AFFILIATES, AGENTS, LICENSORS, SUPPLIERS, OR THEIR RESPECTIVE DIRECTORS OR EMPLOYEES BE LIABLE FOR ANY SPECIAL, INDIRECT, INCIDENTAL, PUNITIVE, EXEMPLARY, AGGRAVATED, ECONOMIC OR CONSEQUENTIAL DAMAGES, HOWSOEVER CAUSED, INCLUDING BUT NOT LIMITED TO: DAMAGES FOR LOSS OF USE, LOST PROFITS OR LOST SAVINGS, EVEN IF THE COMPANY OR ANY OF ITS LAWFUL AGENTS OR EMPLOYEES HAVE BEEN ADVISED OF THE POSSIBILITY OF SUCH DAMAGES OR CLAIM.

IN NO EVENT WILL COMPANY, ITS AFFILIATES, AGENTS, LICENSORS, SUPPLIERS, OR THEIR RESPECTIVE DIRECTORS OR EMPLOYEES, BE LIABLE FOR DAMAGES OR LOSSES RESULTING FROM: VIRUSES, DATA CORRUPTION, FAILED MESSAGES, TRANSMISSION ERRORS OR PROBLEMS; TELECOMMUNICATIONS SERVICE PROVIDERS; LINKS TO THIRD-PARTY WEB SITES; THE INTERNET BACKBONE; PERSONAL INJURY; THIRD-PARTY CONTENT, PRODUCTS OR SERVICES; DAMAGES OR LOSSES CAUSED BY YOU, OR YOUR RESPECTIVE EMPLOYEES, AGENTS OR SUBCONTRACTORS; LOSS OF USE OR LACK OF AVAILABILITY OF FACILITIES INCLUDING COMPUTER RESOURCES, ROUTERS AND STORED DATA; THE USE OR INABILITY TO USE THIS WEB SITE OR THE CONTENT; ANY OTHER WEB SITE ACCESSED TO OR FROM THIS WEB SITE; OR EVENTS BEYOND THE REASONABLE CONTROL OF THE COMPANY, EVEN IF THE COMPANY OR ANY OF ITS LAWFUL AGENTS, OR EMPLOYEES HAVE BEEN ADVISED OF THE POSSIBILITY OF SUCH DAMAGES OR CLAIM.

IN NO CASE WILL THE COMPANY'S, ITS AFFILIATES', AGENTS', LICENSORS', SUPPLIERS', AND THEIR RESPECTIVE DIRECTORS' AND EMPLOYEES' CUMULATIVE TOTAL LIABILITY ARISING UNDER ANY CAUSE WHATSOEVER (INCLUDING WITHOUT LIMITATION BREACH OF CONTRACT, TORT, NEGLIGENCE, GROSS NEGLIGENCE, OR OTHERWISE) BE FOR MORE THAN THE AMOUNT, IF ANY, PAID BY YOU UNDER THIS AGREEMENT TO ACCESS THIS WEB SITE, IN THE YEAR IN WHICH THE CLAIM AROSE.

THE COMPANY ASSUMES NO OBLIGATION TO UPDATE THE CONTENT ON THIS SITE. THE CONTENT ON THIS SITE MAY BE CHANGED WITHOUT NOTICE TO YOU. THE COMPANY IS NOT RESPONSIBLE FOR ANY CONTENT OR INFORMATION THAT YOU MAY FIND UNDESIRABLE OR OBJECTIONABLE. THE COMPANY DISCLAIMS ANY LIABILITY FOR UNAUTHORIZED USE OR REPRODUCTION OF ANY PORTION OF THE WEB SITE. ACCESSING THE CONTENT FROM TERRITORIES WHERE IT MAY BE ILLEGAL IS PROHIBITED.

7. Termination. This Agreement is effective until terminated by the Company, with or without cause, in the Company's sole and unfettered discretion. The Company may terminate this Agreement without notice to You if You fail to comply with any of its terms. Any such termination by the Company shall be in addition to and without prejudice to such rights and remedies as may be available to the Company, including injunction and other equitable remedies.

The disclaimers, limitations on liability, ownership, termination, interpretation, Your license to the Company, Your warranty and the indemnity provisions of this Agreement shall survive the termination or expiry of this Agreement.

8. Indemnity. You agree at all times to indemnify, defend and hold harmless the Company, its agents, suppliers, affiliates and their respective directors and employees against all actions, proceedings, costs, claims, damages, demands, liabilities and expenses whatsoever (including legal and other fees and disbursements) sustained, incurred or paid by the Company directly or indirectly in respect of:

(i) any information or other content You provide on or through this web site or which is sent to the Company by e-mail or other correspondence; or

(ii) Your use or misuse of the Content or this web site, including without limitation infringement claims

9. Governing Law. The Company, this web site and the Content (excluding linked web sites or content) are physically located within the Province of Ontario, Canada. [This web site and its Content are intended to be read by Canadian residents only.] This Agreement will be governed by the laws of the Province of (*insert province*) and the federal laws of Canada and shall be treated in all respects as a (*insert province*) contract, without reference to the principles of conflicts of law. In the event of a dispute, We agree to submit to the non-exclusive jurisdiction of the (*insert province*) courts. We expressly exclude the UN Convention on Contracts for the International Sale of Goods, and the *International Sale of Goods Act (Ontario)* as amended, replaced or re-enacted from time to time. We have required that this Agreement and all documents relating thereto be drawn-up in English. Nous avons demandé que cette convention ainsi que tous les documents qui s'y rattachent soient rédigés en anglais.

10. Interpretation. The division of this Agreement into sections and the insertion of headings are for convenience of reference only and shall not affect the construction or interpretation of this Agreement. In this Agreement, words importing the singular number include the plural and vice versa, words importing gender include all genders; and words importing persons include individuals, sole proprietors, partnerships, corporations, trusts and unincorporated associations. [All references to money amounts in this Agreement, unless otherwise specified, are in Canadian dollars.]

11. Entire Agreement. These terms and conditions and any and all legal notices on this web site constitute the entire agreement between You and the Company with respect to the use of this web site and the Content. No supplement, modification or amendment to this Agreement and no waiver of any provision of this Agreement shall be binding on the Company unless executed by the Company in writing. No waiver of any of the provisions of this Agreement shall be deemed or shall constitute a waiver of any other provision (whether or not similar) nor shall such waiver constitute a continuing waiver unless otherwise expressly provided.

12. Severability. Any provision of this Agreement which is prohibited or unenforceable in any jurisdiction shall, as to that jurisdiction, be ineffective to the extent of such prohibition or unenforceability and shall otherwise be enforced to the maximum extent permitted by law, all without affecting the remaining provisions of this Agreement or affecting the validity or enforceability of such provision in any other jurisdiction.

13. Enurement. This Agreement shall inure to the benefit of and be binding upon each of Us and our respective successors and permitted assigns. You acknowledge having read this Agreement before accepting it, having the authority to accept this Agreement and having received a copy of this Agreement.

© *(insert web site owner's full legal name)*, *(insert year)*, *(insert location)*. *(insert trade-marks on web site)* [is/are] the trade-mark(s) of *(insert name(s) of trade-mark owners/licensors)*.

* * *

The following message may be sent or displayed to the Internet user after acceptance of the web site terms:

"The Agreement between You and the Company for accessing the web site has been successfully completed. Please print a copy of the terms of the Agreement for Your reference. The Agreement has been assigned the following number: *(insert contract identifier)*. A copy of the Agreement will be kept *(insert where, e.g., on-line at a secure web site address, or at the Company's head office)* and to view it, please *(insert instructions)* and refer to the Agreement number above."

CHAPTER 10

ON-LINE EXCHANGES AND PORTALS

10.1 INTRODUCTION TO ON-LINE EXCHANGES AND PORTALS

On-Line *Exchanges* or *Portals* are *Web Sites* that bring together buyers and sellers of products or services. *Portals* can be connecting businesses and consumers (commonly referred to as "*B2C*") or businesses and other businesses (commonly referred to as "*B2B*"). Examples of *Portals* include on-line market places, shopping malls and auctions. *Portals* are also often used for Electronic Data Interchange (*EDI)* between business or trading partners to manage many commercial transactions in a supply chain, such as production, warehousing, inventory control, logistics, retailing and customer relations management (*CRM*).

The main difference between a traditional web site, which offers products or services for sale, and an *Exchange* or *Portal* is that the *Portal* permits multiple parties to share data and enter into transactions among each other. Usually, the owner of the *Portal* is a service provider, who is not one of the buyers or sellers participating on the *Portal* and is not a party to the transactions. On the other hand, a traditional web site that offers products or services for sale is usually owned by one business who is the seller of the products or services being offered and enters into transactions directly with buyers who visit the site.

The operation of a *Portal* is made possible through the use of *Web Pages*, databases, *Browsers* and *Cookies* (see Chapter 1). A Seller that wants to put items for sale on a *Portal* enters a web site. Registration forms, *Passports*, *Cookies* or log-in passwords are used to identify the seller. The seller usually completes a form, detailing the product or service to be put up for sale. This creates a record in a database and a program automatically updates the web page on the *Portal's* web site with the information stored in the database.

When a buyer enters the *Portal*, they access the web site and search with a *Browser* for information on products or services stored in a database. *Cookies* are used to track the buyer's activities and requests. When the buyer is ready to make a purchase, they usually enter a secure web page where the data from the *Cookies* is uploaded to a server that updates the database and where the buyer enters his or her credit card information. The data is encrypted before being sent over the Internet. The server also communicates with the credit card company, confirms the order with the buyer, and requests that the warehouse or seller complete the order.

10.2 WHAT RISKS DO USERS OF PORTALS FACE AND HOW TO AVOID THEM?

One of the important issues that a user has when accessing a portal, especially if the portal is critical to the user's business, is to ensure that access to the portal is available and that the processing of any transactions conducted over the portal meets certain service levels. Backup, reporting, disaster recovery and systems management terms may also be incorporated into service level requirements. (See Form 8A, Schedule "A")

Another concern that a user has is security and privacy, especially since the portal is generally shared by many customers and suppliers and since the portal operator will be collecting information about the user's activities, products or services offered or purchased and transactions completed on the portal. In addition, if users access the portal and transmit or receive data to or from the portal over open networks, such as the Internet, the users face the risk that their access may not be secure and that someone could intercept their data transmissions or misuse their password, credit card information or other important data. Also, the sharing of information among users could give rise to competition concerns.

To allocate these risks, a user of a portal might seek covenants, representations, warranties and indemnities from the portal operator that the portal and transactions conducted on it meet required performance levels and that the user's activities and data are secure and are kept confidential. The portal operator might also be contractually obligated to allocate a certain amount of database space if the user is a seller of products or services, to store the data relating to the user's transactions on dedicated servers, or to have dedicated telecommunications lines between the web server and various users of the portal. Correspondingly, this would require the portal operator to establish performance, security and content control mechanisms to ensure compliance with their contractual obligations to the user.

Sellers who use the portal and upload data or other content to the portal's web site, would also be concerned about retaining ownership rights, if any, in the uploaded content. Similarly, users of the portal who receive any software code, documentation, data files or other materials from the portal, would want to be sure that they are granted sufficient rights to use such materials from the portal operator or its licensors. Therefore, the agreement should contain ownership and license terms, related warranties, as well as intellectual property infringement indemnities. (See Sections 10.4.4, 10.4.8, 10.4.11 and 10.4.12, below)

Sellers using the portal may also require customizations to portal web pages (such as unique branding for a particular marketplace or custom web pages), in which case consideration should be given to intellectual property, ownership and licensing terms. (See also Chapter 5 on Web Site Development).

Sellers may also want to restrict the portal operator from allowing other portal users (e.g., their competitors) to access the portal or certain web pages on the portal.

10.3 WHAT RISKS DOES A PORTAL OPERATOR FACE IN PROVIDING A PORTAL AND HOW TO AVOID THEM?

One of the primary concerns of a portal operator would be assuming responsibility for the risks associated with the transactions occurring between users of the portal and the subject matter of such transactions. Unless the portal operator is also a supplier or purchaser of products or services on the portal, the portal operator should not be a party to any transactions between suppliers and purchasers.

As discussed in Chapter 2, a portal operator might also be liable to third parties for portal users' activities, particularly if the users can upload their own data or content to the portal. The risks of potential liability increase with the amount of control or knowledge[1] that the portal operator has of its users' activities, and include without limitation liability for intellectual property infringement (such as copyright and trade-mark infringement) and violation of privacy.

Although a portal operator cannot contract out of statutory liability to third parties or criminal liability, the risks faced by the portal operator can be reduced with a Portal Services Agreement (see Form 10A). The user's obligations and restrictions in the agreement (see Form 10A, Section 9) increase the user's awareness of potential liabilities. If the user is in the best position to deal with the risks, there is a good argument that the agreement should be drafted to shift the risks onto the customer and should contain indemnities from the user for damages that the portal operator may suffer.

Another common risk faced by the portal operator is the failure of third-party software, hardware, telecommunications backbones or other products or services that were not developed or supplied by the portal operator and over which the portal operator has little or no control. Portal operators can

---

1 Note that certain strict liability offences do not require any knowledge by the offender to be found liable.

manage this risk by ensuring any limitations on the liability of and disclaimers by their suppliers, are reflected in the portal operator's contracts with its users. In addition, when acting for a portal operator, one should negotiate limitations on the portal operator's liability for events outside the control of the portal operator, such as disclaimers of any liability for damages or losses resulting from any third-party, including, without limitation, telecommunications service providers, the portal operator's contractors and the Internet backbone.

Many of the risks faced by portal operators can be minimized if a portal agreement is entered into between the portal operator and users of the portal. However, as with other on-line agreements, the issues of identity and authority of the contracting party becomes important. The portal operator may need to implement a system of verification (e.g., through the use of cryptographic keys) to ensure that the person accepting the on-line agreement terms is the intended party with whom the portal operator desires to form a contract and, if they are a corporation, that the individual has the requisite corporate authority to enter into a binding agreement on behalf of the business.

10.4 PRINCIPAL TERMS OF PORTAL AGREEMENTS

A portal operator might want to have separate agreements with suppliers and customers using the portal, as well as third parties such as credit card companies and finance providers, especially if the portal operator wants to avoid disclosing confidential fee arrangements to other users. In either case, the portal agreement should contain the following principle terms.

10.4.1 Portal Services

The Portal Agreement must clearly describe the portal operator's obligations. More specifically, unless the portal operator is also a supplier or purchaser of products or services on the portal, there is a good argument that the portal operator's obligations should be limited to providing access to the portal. In order to minimize the risk of being responsible for the subject matter or completion of transactions carried out on the portal, the portal operator should try to avoid being a party to any transactions between suppliers and purchasers. Hence, the Portal Services Agreement should clearly set out who the parties are to any transactions occurring on the portal, how such transactions will be entered into and who will bear the risk of any problems relating to the transactions. Consideration should also be given as to whether the portal operator is acting as an agent for any of the users, e.g., in collecting and remitting purchase payments.

If the services to be provided include more than mere portal access (such as the development of content or customized web pages, or the provision of a telephone support help desk), the terms of the Portal Services Agreement should also include the terms of other agreements (such as web site development terms or support terms) **(see Chapter 5 and Form 5A)**.

The agreement should adequately describe: how the portal is to be accessed (e.g., access over the Internet, a dedicated line or through a private network); how many users have access; when the portal is available (e.g., twenty-four (24) hours a day, seven (7) days a week, except during scheduled maintenance periods, or by a certain number of users or from a particular location); and what additional obligations each party has (e.g., to provide certain hardware, software or security technology).

The parties may want to negotiate performance covenants and warranties by the portal operator, which may be attached as a Schedule. In drafting performance terms, assistance may be needed from technical advisers. Common portal performance requirements include:

- availability, accuracy and speed of the portal and related transactions processing;
- regular reporting obligations to sellers;
- commercially reasonable efforts to protect the portal from any virus, worm, or disabling mechanism;
- correction of errors in the portal;
- systems maintenance and response times to reported problems;
- back-up and disaster recovery on-site and off-site; and
- compatibility with common web browsers or other interfacing software.

For an example of performance specifications, see Form 8A, Schedule "A".

10.4.2 Restrictions on Access

The portal agreement should clearly specify what restrictions are imposed upon Internet users who access the portal. When drafting access rights, one must be careful to choose unambiguous words. Simply saying that the Internet user is granted the right or a license to "use" the *Portal* is very broad, not sufficiently clear and could be misinterpreted to include licenses to run, modify, distribute or receive copies of the underlying software or systems. If what is intended is mere access to the portal and reading of web pages with a browser, then that is what the portal agreement should say. If, on the other hand, broader rights are intended to be granted, such as the right to copy, download or upload content, then the portal agreement should specify the precise rights and any restrictions, such as number of copies, territorial limitations and format. For a further discussion on drafting restrictions, see paragraphs 8.4.2 and 9.2.2.

If the portal is interactive such that Internet users can place content on the portal, one needs to consider whether corresponding licenses or assignments of ownership rights and waivers of moral rights in favour of the portal operator, should be included in the portal agreement. It is also recommended that warranties and indemnities in favour of the portal operator, be obtained from the Internet users, to protect the portal operator from liability for the content delivered by the Internet users, as well as failure by the Internet users to comply with the portal agreement. One should also consider including additional restrictions on Internet users, similar to the ones discussed in paragraph 3.4.2 dealing with Internet access, such as restrictions on posting defamatory, illegal or infringing content. Other restrictions may include restrictions on resale of access to the portal or use of any trade-marks on the portal.

10.4.3 Buyer and Seller Obligations

The portal agreement should specify the Internet user's responsibilities for:

- posting of terms relating to the transactions to be entered into with other Internet users, which terms should disclaim any liability or responsibility by the portal operator in respect of the transaction and related goods or services;
- telecommunications access;
- software (such as web browsers and connectivity software); and
- computer hardware and peripherals (such as modems and other communications equipment) which are needed to be able to obtain access to the portal.

To the extent that the Internet user accessing the portal is in a better position than the portal operator to maintain control over its access passwords, one may reasonably argue that the Internet user should be responsible for maintaining the confidentiality of its passwords and should be responsible for all activities and charges resulting from the use of the Internet user's account or passwords, including unauthorized use. However, if the portal operator's obligations include the requirement to maintain adequate security measures to prevent unauthorized access to the portal, the Internet user may not want to agree to such obligation. See also restrictions on access in paragraph 10.4.2, above.

10.4.4 Ownership and Licensing

As with software hosting agreements (see Chapter 8) when drafting a portal agreement, it is important to consider whether intellectual property licenses from one party to the other are necessary. Whether licenses are required depends on how the portal is being accessed and used. If the situation involves mere data exchange between the parties, (e.g., content or data is being submitted by buyers and sellers to the portal operator for processing by the portal's back-end software and database), the portal agreement usually will only require content or data licensing provisions from the buyers and sellers in favour of the portal operator. The agreement should clearly set out who owns any content or data input, data output and who owns the software, hardware or other systems relating to the portal. To the extent that a buyer or seller will retain any ownership rights in the data output, the portal operator should assign all ownership rights and obtain waivers of any moral rights (from authors) in the data, in favour of the buyer or seller.

The portal itself, and the underlying software, are not licensed from the portal operator to the portal users. In such context, the portal operator is running the software, not the buyers or sellers, and the Internet users who access the portal do not need any rights in or to the underlying software or systems. The relationship that the Internet users have with the portal operator is that of a service provider and not a software licensor. On the other hand, if the access to the portal requires the customer to obtain some software from the portal operator, such as interfacing software or a browser, or if the access to the portal results in the downloading of any code (e.g., HTML, java applets, JavaScript, ActiveX controls), content or files that are proprietary to the portal operator or its licensors, then the portal agreement will need to include terms governing the Internet user's use of such items.

With respect to any licensing terms, the scope of any license granted should be carefully drafted. Consideration should be given as to what specific rights are required to be licensed (e.g., the right to run, copy, modify, sublicense, distribute, etc.), whether the license is exclusive, sole or non-exclusive[2] and whether there are any territorial, usage or other restrictions or limitations.

---

2 An "exclusive" license means only the licensee can exercise the rights granted, even to the exclusion of the licensor. Exclusivity can be limited in scope. A "sole" license means no one other than the licensee and licensor can exercise the rights granted.

10.4.5 Fees and Reporting

There are many different ways to structure fees in portal agreements. Different payment mechanisms may apply for different parties, i.e., a buyer or a seller.

Usually, the portal operator charges a fee based on a percentage of the transaction value or number of transactions processed through the portal. Sometimes, fees are also paid to register as a portal user. The portal operator and sellers on the portal, often desire to have the portal operator collect the transaction fees directly from the buyers on the portal and then deduct their percentage when remitting the balance to the sellers. This mechanism reduces the risk on sellers that they have to pay the portal operator regardless of whether they collect any fees from the buyers and the portal operator is ensured of receiving revenues immediately, as opposed to waiting for a seller to pay. However, this type of structure increases the portal operator's risks with respect to involvement in the underlying transaction and the portal agreement would have to be drafted such that the portal operator is acting as an agent for the seller when collecting fees from the buyer. To minimize such risks, the portal agreement should be carefully drafted such that the portal operator is not party to the transactions made through the portal, but rather collects fees from sellers or buyers directly for the service of providing portal access. For a discussion on other criteria upon which fees can be based, see paragraphs 3.4.5 and 8.4.5.

The agreement should also specify whether the fees are inclusive or exclusive of applicable taxes and duties. It may also be reasonable to impose an obligation on a party to provide regular reports as to the criteria upon which the fees are based and to allow audits of a party's records to verify reports and fees.

10.4.6 Acceptance Procedure

If the portal agreement is being entered into electronically or on-line, refer to paragraph 9.2.8.

10.4.7 Confidentiality and Privacy

Given that portal operators often collect information about the users of and activities on the portal (such as pricing of transactions), it is recommended that the portal agreement contain a confidentiality obligation on the portal operator. Similarly, the portal operator may want the Internet users to keep any information they learn about the portal or other Internet users accessing the portal, confidential.

Where data or content is being submitted by or collected from Internet users accessing the portal (which data or content may contain personal or private information), it is recommended that the portal agreement contain restrictions on the portal operator's use of such information. The portal operator should also obtain the requisite privacy consents and indemnities from Internet users (see Chapter 4) with respect to the collection, use, storage and disclosure of data or content and in particular, personal information.

As well, in order to comply with any applicable legislation or regulations, to facilitate co-operation with law enforcement agencies, and to ensure that Internet users are complying with the portal agreement, it is important that the agreement permit (but not obligate) the portal operator to monitor, intercept and disclose the Internet users' access to and activities on the portal.

See also Chapter 4 and paragraph 9.2.7.

10.4.8 Jurisdiction

See paragraph 9.2.6.

10.4.9 Remedies

The portal agreement should also set out the remedies that each party has if the other party is in breach of the agreement. Such remedies may include the right for the non-breaching party to terminate the agreement, to receive liquidated damages and to be indemnified for any third-party claims or damages. See also paragraph 3.4.10.

10.4.10 Term

If applicable, a distinction should be made between the date the agreement becomes effective and the date the portal access services commence. As well, it is important to distinguish suspension of access to the portal from termination of the entire agreement. For example, if the portal operator needs to conduct maintenance work on its servers, it would need the right to suspend access as opposed to terminate it.

For portals where the buyers or sellers have agreed to exclusive relationships or best pricing, it will be important to such parties that the term of the agreement is not too long, and that there is a mechanism in place for terminating the exclusivity if they are not satisfied with the results of the portal access services. It may also be worthwhile considering whether to include an option for early termination in the agreement.

On the other hand, the portal operator may have incurred significant costs in setting up the portal and making arrangements with participants on the portal. Therefore, the portal operator would likely want to negotiate a longer agreement term.

Careful consideration should also be given to the survival of representations, warranties, indemnities and other terms in the portal agreement. Obligations of confidentiality, privacy, and representations, warranties and indemnities relating to title or non-infringement are some of the provisions that one might argue should be made to survive.

Consideration should also be given to the effects of termination, e.g., whether any content will be returned or destroyed and whether any transitional services need to be provided.

10.4.11 Representations and Warranties

In addition to the usual representations and warranties given by parties to a contract, such as that each party has the right to enter into the agreement and that the agreement does not and will not conflict with any other agreement or obligation that a party may have, portal agreements require some additional representations and warranties to minimize the risk of unique liabilities that arise in the provision of portal access services.

When acting for the portal operator, it is recommended that the following warranties be obtained:

- if applicable, that the sellers have the right to license or provide any content onto the portal;
- the content does not and will not infringe on any copyright or any trade-mark, patent, trade secret or other intellectual property right of any third-party, especially in countries where the portal will be operated or where users will be accessing the portal. However, sellers will be relatively reluctant to give representations or warranties for any third-party items which were not created by the seller; which the seller does not own; or over which the seller has no control or has not received similar representations or warranties from the seller's developers, suppliers or licensors;
- if the Internet users are individuals, that they have reached the age of majority.

When acting for the seller or buyer, it is recommended that the following warranties be obtained from the portal operator:

- performance warranties with respect to the speed and error free operation of the portal and related transactions carried out through the portal;
- in the case of an exclusive portal, that it is not used by other buyers or sellers, as the case may be;
- the security or firewall technology is of a certain standard;
- where software is also being licensed as part of the portal access services, software warranties as to title, right to license, non-infringement, performance and no disabling mechanisms;
- where other services such as content development or customized web pages, are being provided by the portal operator, warranties pertaining to such services (see Chapter 5 on Web Site and Content Development Contracts);
- performance of the services under the agreement will be done in a competent manner by qualified personnel; and
- the portal operator has the right to license or provide access to (as the case may be) the portal and any content, software, hardware, or other materials provided on or through the portal.

10.4.12 Indemnities

When acting for a portal operator, one should seek the following indemnities from the Internet users accessing the portal in respect of any claims, demands or other liabilities:

- any negligent or intentional act or omission by Internet users or any breach by Internet users of any provision of the portal agreement, including injury to persons or property and non-compliance with applicable laws;
- any claim relating to an erroneous, failed or aborted transaction caused by Internet-user content;
- any Internet-user content, including any infringements of the intellectual property rights of any person or entity;
- any transaction or the subject matter of any transaction, including infringements of the Intellectual Property rights of any person or entity;
- any claim, expense, action, cause of action, damage and the like arising in any way to and from those accessing Internet-user content except for acts or omissions of the portal provider; and

- any use or misuse of Internet user's ID or password and access to or use of portal by anyone using Internet user's user ID or password except for acts or omissions of the portal provider.

For additional discussion on indemnities, see also paragraphs 3.4.10 and 8.4.11.

10.4.13 Limitations on Liabilities and Disclaimers

See paragraphs 3.4.11 and 9.2.4.

10.4.14 General Clauses

As with other commercial agreements, in Internet and e-commerce agreements one should consider including notice clauses, non-waiver, currency, severability, assignability, entire agreement, force majeure, time of the essence, interpretation, independent contractors, binding on successors, survival, governing law and choice of language clauses.

CHECKLIST 10 – FOR DRAFTING PORTAL AGREEMENTS

- Ensure parties are clearly identified by their full legal names and for on-line agreements, adopt technical security measures to verify identity and authority of contracting party;
- Describe the portal access services, e.g., speed, number of users, connection point, remote login, firewall and disaster recovery services;
- Specify how and when the portal is available or any exceptions to availability, e.g., suspension of services for maintenance;
- Include portal performance obligations in a schedule;
- Include any additional obligations that portal operator may have, such as:
    - to provide ancillary services (e.g., content or customized web page development), software or other materials required for portal access,
    - regular reporting obligations to sellers,
    - taking commercially reasonable efforts to protect the portal from any virus, worm, or disabling mechanism,
    - correction of errors in the portal,
    - systems maintenance and response times to reported problems,
    - backup and disaster recovery on-site and off-site;
- Where interfacing software, browsers, code, content, documentation or other proprietary materials are being supplied by the portal operator or Internet users, include ownership and licensing terms;
- Include any additional obligations that the Internet users may have, such as:
    - compliance with portal operator's policies,
    - use of the portal for lawful purposes,
    - adherence to the laws of a particular jurisdiction,
    - compliance with court ordered publication bans,
    - responsibility for telecommunications access, software (such as web browsers and connectivity software), computer hardware and peripherals (such as modems and other communications equipment),

  - posting of terms relating to the transactions to be entered into with other Internet users, which terms should disclaim any liability or responsibility by the portal operator in respect of the transaction and related goods or services;

- Set out restricted Internet user activities such as:
  - publishing, printing, distributing, possessing, selling, advocating, promoting, or exposing, obscene material, child pornography, or hate propaganda,
  - the use of trade-marks or trade names,
  - the use of copyright works,
  - defamation, libel, harm to reputation, violation of privacy, misuse or failure to protect personal information, violation of secrecy, unfair competition and other situations which could generate civil liability,
  - export and import restrictions, and
  - subleasing or reselling portal access or allowing simultaneous access by more users than are specified in the agreement;
- Allocate responsibility for activities through buyers' and sellers' accounts or using their respective passwords;
- Draft fee and payment terms and specify currency and whether taxes are extra;
- Include any obligations to provide regular reports as to the criteria upon which the fees are based and to allow audits;
- Include confidentiality and privacy provisions and consent by Internet users to portal operator's monitoring, collection, storage, use and disclosure of Internet users' information and activities on the portal;
- Set out the remedies that each party has if the other party is in breach of the agreement, e.g., to receive liquidated damages and to be indemnified for any third-party claims or damages;
- Representations, warranties and indemnities given by Internet users (i.e. buyers and sellers on the portal):
  - that they have the right to enter into the agreement,
  - if the buyer/seller is an individual, that he or she has reached the age of majority,
  - that the agreement does not and will not conflict with any other agreement or obligation,

- that they have the right to license or provide access to (as the case may be) any software, hardware, data, content or other materials provided to the portal operator or on the portal,
- that such materials provided to or on the portal do not or will not infringe on any copyright or any trade-mark, patent, trade secret or other intellectual property right of any third-party, in countries where the portal is operated or accessed or where the portal operator is at risk of being sued for infringement (and consider exceptions for any third-party items which were not created by the buyer/seller; which the buyer/seller does not own; or over which the buyer/seller has no control or has not received similar representations or warranties from the buyer's/seller's developers, suppliers or licensors),
- indemnities for losses resulting from,
  - any negligent or intentional act or omission by Internet user or any breach by Internet user of any provision of the portal agreement including injury to persons or property and non-compliance with applicable laws,
  - any claim relating to an erroneous, failed or aborted transaction, caused by Internet user content,
  - any Internet-user content, including any infringements of the intellectual property rights of any person or entity,
  - any transaction or the subject matter of any transaction, including infringements of the intellectual property rights of any person or entity,
  - any claim, expense, action, cause of action, damage and the like arising in any way to and from those accessing Internet-user content except for acts or omissions of the portal provider,
  - any use or misuse of Internet user's ID or password and access to or use of portal by anyone using Internet user's ID or password except for acts or omissions of the portal provider, and
  - consider exceptions and limitations on indemnities;

- Representations, warranties and indemnities given by the portal operator:
  - performance warranties with respect to availability, accuracy and speed of the portal and related transactions processing,
  - compatibility of the portal with common web browsers or other interfacing software,
  - that it has the right to enter into the agreement,

- that the agreement does not and will not conflict with any other agreement or obligation,
- that the portal operator has the right to provide access to the portal, networks, databases or other systems accessible by the buyers and sellers under the portal agreement,
- in the case of a seller, database storage capacity,
- in the case of an exclusive seller or buyer, that the portal is not shared with other sellers or buyers, as applicable,
- that the security or firewall technology is of a certain standard,
- where interfacing software, browsers or other code are being supplied by the portal operator to permit the customer to access the portal, warranties as to title, right to license, non-infringement, performance and no disabling mechanisms (and consider exceptions for any third-party items which were not created by the portal operator; which the portal operator does not own; or over which the portal operator has no control or has not received similar representations or warranties from the portal operator's developers, suppliers or licensors),
- where other services such as content development or customized web pages are being provided by the portal operator, warranties pertaining to such services (see Chapter 5),
- that performance of the services under the agreement will be done in a competent manner by qualified personnel,
- indemnities for losses resulting from intellectual property infringement or trade secret misappropriation claims (and consider exceptions and limitations on indemnities);

• Disclaimers and limitations on liability to consider:
  - as applicable to indemnities,
  - for performance, uninterrupted, confidential, private, secure, dedicated or error free portal access or related transactions processing,
  - disclaimer of implied warranties,
  - force majeure events,
  - third-party products, acts or omissions,
  - liability by portal operator for problems with seller's products or services or anything relating to the transactions carried out on or through the portal,

- with respect to the terms of any transaction entered on the portal, which terms should be posted and agreed to as between the sellers and buyers, and
- indirect damages (should be described);

- Draft the term, termination and suspension provisions and consider which terms of the agreement survive termination or expiry;
- Consider post-termination or expiry provisions, e.g., return or destruction of software or content and transitional services;
- Boilerplate provisions, e.g., notice clauses, non-waiver, currency, severability, assignability, entire agreement, force majeure, time of the essence, interpretation, independent contractors, binding on successors, survival, governing law and choice of language clauses.

For electronic portal agreements, and agreements pertaining to the transactions that are entered into on the portal, the following additional items should also be considered:

- Draft the on-line portal agreement in a user-friendly format, by defining the Internet user as "You", the on-line business as the "Company" and both parties as "We" or "Us";
- Adopt technical security measures to verify identity and authority of contracting party;
- Ensure that all of the electronic agreement terms are readable (e.g., not referenced in other documents or web pages) and highlight the onerous terms. Internet users should be forced to scroll through the electronic agreement and accept the terms, to maximize enforceability. Give Internet users the option to exit the portal if they do not agree with the terms;
- Describe what action a party must take to show acceptance and understanding of the electronic agreement and his or her intent to be legally bound. The requirement to type in a phrase, such as "I accept", is better than to click on a button;
- Carefully draft jurisdiction, governing law and attornment clauses, specifying where the electronic agreement is formed, where the server is located, to whom (which jurisdiction) the electronic agreement and/or portal is directed or not intended to be accessed and the agreed upon language;
- Obtain consent for using electronic documents and signatures and specify use of encryption technology;

- Disclaim and limit liabilities for the risks that are peculiar to portals and processing of transactions, in particular liability for content and electronic communications problems;
- Provide access to and retention of electronic documents and a method of correcting errors.

FORM 10A – PORTAL SERVICES AGREEMENT

BETWEEN:

[*Insert Name of portal Provider*]

("[*insert name of portal provider*]")

- and -

[*Insert Name of Client*]

(the "Client")

The Client and (*insert name of portal provider)* agree that the terms and conditions contained in this Agreement and any Schedules attached hereto shall govern the provision of portal Services pursuant to this Agreement.

Notwithstanding the date of the signature hereof, the effective date of this Agreement shall be the __ day of _____, or if left blank, the later of the dates set out above (the "Effective Date"). Each Party hereby acknowledges having read this Agreement before signing it, having the authority to sign this Agreement and having received a copy of this Agreement.

1. DEFINITIONS

1.1 In this Agreement the terms below are defined as follows:

"**Agreement**" means this portal Services Agreement and all attached Schedules, as they may be amended from time to time by both of the Parties in writing;

"**Business Day**" means any day other than a Saturday, a Sunday or any day on which banks are generally not open in the city of Toronto, Ontario;

"**Client content**" means Confidential Information, data, text, materials, graphics, information, media or other content provided directly or indirectly by the Client through the use of Portal Services;

"**Confidential Information**" means any and all data, information, software or materials relating to the business and management of either Party, its clients, its affiliates or its licensors, that is designated as confidential or ought reasonably to be considered confidential, including but not limited to: business operations, processes, products, designs, business plans, business opportunities, finances, research, development, know-how, trade-secrets, personnel, clients, methodologies, and Intellectual

Property. Confidential Information shall not include any data, information or materials which:

(i) are or become publicly available through no fault of the receiving Party;

(ii) are already legitimately in the possession of a Party prior to its receipt from the disclosing Party;

(iii) can be shown by the receiving Party to have been independently developed by that Party;

(iv) are rightfully obtained by the receiving Party from a third Party having the right to disseminate the information without restriction on disclosure;

(v) are disclosed by the receiving Party with the written consent of the disclosing Party; or

(vi) are disclosed pursuant to a court order or other legal compulsion.

"**Documentation**" means the documentation provided by (*nsert name of portal provider)* to Client to be able to use the portal Services;

"**Effective Date**" has the meaning set forth on the first page of this Agreement;

"**Fees**" means all amounts due under this Agreement as specified in Schedule "C" plus any and all applicable sales, value added, use, service and border taxes, as well as excise or customs duties presently or hereafter imposed upon any and all such amounts;

"**including**" means including without limitation and "includes" means includes without limitation;

"**Intellectual Property**" means all design and utility patents, application for such patents, industrial design, product get-up, distinguishing guises, trade-marks, trade names, service marks, copyright, trade secrets, know-how and other intellectual property rights as recognized by any jurisdiction and whether registered or not;

"**Portal Services**" means the services specified in Schedule "A";

"**Party**" or "**Parties**" means either *(insert name of portal provider)* or the Client if used in the singular and both *(insert name of portal provider)* and the Client if used in the plural;

"**Term**" has the meaning set forth in Section 10.1; and

"**Transaction**" means an actual or potential transaction as between Client and any third-party.

2. SERVICES

2.1 *(insert name of portal provider)* shall provide to Client the Portal Services.

2.2 Client acknowledges and agrees that the role of *[insert name of portal provider]* in providing Portal Services is limited to providing an interface through which the Client may supply Client content for the purpose of entering into a Transaction, and that *(insert name of portal provider)* is not a party to any such Transaction entered into through the use of Portal Services.

2.3 Without limiting the effect of any provision in this Agreement, Client acknowledges and agrees that in providing Portal Services, *(insert name of portal provider)* does not assume any responsibility, liability, risk, oversight, control, monitoring or any other direct or indirect involvement with respect to any Transaction Client may enter into.

2.4 Notwithstanding the foregoing, *(insert name of portal provider)* may, in its sole discretion, monitor the client's use of Portal Services and disclose such use to law enforcement agencies or pursuant to court order or other legal compulsion.

3. CLIENT RESPONSIBILITIES

3.1 Client's use of the Portal Services is personal, and may only be exercised by Client. Client agrees not to resell or in any way allow access to the Portal Services by any other person or entity without the prior written consent of *(insert name of portal provider)*.

3.2 Client shall not disclose any user ID or password it receives or uses in accessing Portal Services to any third parties. Client may disclose any user ID or password only as required internally within Client's organization, however Client is entirely responsible for any and all activities that occur under their user ID or password. Client agrees to immediately notify *(insert name of portal provider)* of any unauthorized use of Client's user ID, password or any other breach of security that is known or becomes known to Client. Client shall be liable for any unauthorized use or misuse of its user ID or password and access to or unauthorized use of Portal Services by anyone using Client's user ID or password.

3.3 Client shall comply with the laws of the applicable jurisdiction(s) including any laws regarding:

(i) court ordered publication bans;

(ii) restrictions on publishing, printing, distributing, possessing, selling, advocating;

(iii) promoting or exposing, obscene material, child pornography, or hate propaganda, and Client understands that these situations could generate criminal liability;

(iv) restrictions on the use of trade-marks or trade names, or any work which is protected by copyright, trade secret, patent or other intellectual property laws, including without limitation, software; and

(v) restrictions on defamation, libel, harm to reputation, invasion of privacy, misuse or failure to protect personal information, violation of secrecy, unfair competition and other situations which could generate liability.

3.4 Client shall be solely responsible for:

(i) any and all Transactions;

(ii) the drafting and posting of legal terms relating to Transactions which shall exclude *(insert name of portal provider)* from any liability in respect of the Transactions;

(iii) any product or service which is the subject of a Transaction; and

(iv) Client content transmitted, posted, printed, stored, received, routed or created through Client's use of Portal Services on *(insert name of portal provider)*'s system or any other system, including both its content and accuracy.

4. INDEMNIFICATION

4.1 Client shall indemnify and hold *(insert name of portal provider)* and its directors, officers and employees harmless from all claims, demands and other liabilities asserted against such indemnified parties which arise from:

(i) any negligent or intentional act or omission by Client or any breach by Client of any provision of this Agreement including injury to persons or property and non-compliance with applicable laws;

(ii) any claim relating to an erroneous, failed or aborted Transaction, caused by Client Content;

(iii) any Client Content, including any infringements of the Intellectual Property rights of any person or entity;

(iv) any Transaction or the subject matter of any Transaction, including infringements of the Intellectual Property rights of any person or entity;

(v) any claim, expense, action, cause of action, damage and the like arising in any way to and from those accessing Client Content except for acts or omissions of *(insert name of portal provider)*; and

(vi) any use or misuse of its user ID or password and access to or use of Portal Services by anyone using Client's user ID or password except for acts or omissions of (*insert name of portal provider*).

5. COMPENSATION

5.1 Client shall pay to (*insert name of portal provider*) all Fees specified in this Agreement, as follows:

(i) Client shall pay the Registration Fee as set out in Schedule "C", upon execution of this Agreement and any renewal of the Term;

(ii) Client shall pay the Fees set out in Schedule "C" for usage of the Portal Services, which Fees shall be invoiced monthly and are due and payable within thirty (30) days of invoice date;

(iii) interest shall be charged on outstanding balances at the lesser of: two percent (2%) per month or the maximum allowable by law; and unused Portal Services cannot be transferred or assigned by Client and prepaid Fees or deposits are non-refundable.

5.2 Upon renewal and at least sixty (60) days in advance of the end of the then current Term, *(insert name of portal provider)* shall give the Client written notice of any changes to Schedule "C".

6. PROPRIETARY RIGHTS

6.1 The Documentation, Portal Services and *(insert name of portal provider)*'s Confidential Information are proprietary to *(insert name of portal provider)* and its licensors and are protected by Intellectual Property laws, whether under statute or common law. Client shall not directly or indirectly use (other than as expressly provided in this Agreement), modify, copy, network, merge, transfer, hyper-link to, any part of the Documentation, Portal Services or *(insert name of portal provider)*'s Confidential Information, nor may Client use, reproduce or display any trade-marks associated with the Documentation, Portal Services or *(insert name of portal provider)*'s Confidential Information. Except as expressly provided in Section 6.3 below, *(insert name of portal provider)* does not convey to Client any express or implied grant or license with respect to the Documentation, Portal Services or its content, *(insert name of portal provider)*'s Confidential Information or any Intellectual Property.

6.2 The Client's Confidential Information is proprietary to Client and its licensors and are protected by Intellectual Property laws, whether under statute or common law. *(Insert name of portal provider)* shall not directly or indirectly use (other than as required to perform its obligations under this Agreement), modify, copy, network, merge, transfer, hyper-link to, any part of Client's Confidential Information, nor may *(insert name of portal provider)* use, reproduce or display any trade-marks associated with Client's Confidential Information. Except as required to perform its obligations under this Agreement, Client does not convey to *(insert name of portal provider)* any express or implied grant or license with respect to Client's Confidential Information or any Client's Intellectual Property.

6.3 *(Insert name of portal provider)* grants to Client the right to use the Documentation as is reasonably necessary to access and receive the Portal Services, for the Term and in accordance with the terms of this Agreement.

7. CONFIDENTIALITY

7.1 Each Party acknowledges that the Confidential Information of the other Party constitutes valuable, confidential, proprietary information, and agrees that both during the Term and thereafter it shall not, without the express written consent of the other Party, use or disclose to any other person any such Confidential Information of the other Party, except as specifically authorized under this Agreement.

8. WARRANTIES

8.1 *(Insert name of portal provider)* and Client represent and warrant to each other that neither the execution of this Agreement, nor the performance of its obligations hereunder, will breach or result in any default under its articles, by-laws, or other organizational documents, or under any agreement (oral or written), licence or permit to which it is a Party or by which it may be bound.

8.2 *(Insert name of portal provider)* represents, warrants and covenants to Client that:

(i) it will perform Portal Services under this Agreement in a good and workmanlike manner;

(ii) it has used commercially reasonable efforts to protect the Portal Services from any virus, worm, Trojan Horse or any undocumented software locks or drop dead devices which would render inaccessible or impair in any way the operation or availability of the Portal Services;

(iii) *(insert name of portal provider)* will, at its expense, attempt to correct errors in the Portal Services, provided that the errors are attributable to:

(a) *(insert name of portal provider)*'s personnel; or

(b) programs and equipment provided by *(insert name of portal provider)* as part of the Portal Services; and

(c) it owns or has the right to utilize and provide in the manner contemplated by this Agreement all Intellectual Property that it will use in providing the Portal Services to Client in the manner contemplated by this Agreement.

9. LIMITATIONS ON LIABILITY AND DISCLAIMERS

9.1 THE EXPRESS WARRANTIES CONTAINED IN THIS AGREEMENT ARE IN LIEU OF, AND EACH PARTY EXPRESSLY DISCLAIMS, ANY AND ALL OTHER REPRESENTATIONS, WARRANTIES OR CONDITIONS WITH RESPECT TO THE SUBJECT MATTER HEREOF, WHETHER EXPRESS OR IMPLIED, PAST OR PRESENT, STATUTORY OR OTHERWISE IN LAW OR FROM A COURSE OF DEALING OR USEAGE OF TRADE, INCLUDING ANY LEGAL WARRANTIES, IMPLIED WARRANTIES OR CONDITIONS OF MERCHANTABILITY, FITNESS FOR A PARTICULAR PURPOSE, OR OF QUALITY, PRODUCTIVENESS, ACCURACY, PRIVACY, ANONYMITY, COMPATIBILITY, ACCESSABILITY, AVAILABILITY OR PERFORMANCE.

9.2 In no event shall *(insert name of portal provider)* or any of its directors or officers be liable for any claim, even if *(insert name of portal provider)* has been advised of the possibility thereof:

(i) for damages for loss of profits or revenue, loss of data, failure to realize expected savings, interruption, delays errors or omissions or loss of use of Client Content, Transactions or Portal Services;

(ii) for special, indirect, incidental, consequential, or punitive damages;

(iii) for damages arising from Client's failure to perform its obligations in connection with this Agreement, including, without limitation its misuse of the Portal Services or Documentation, or any damages relating to Client Content or the Transactions;

(iv) relating to Client's connectivity to the Internet or access to Portal Services; or

(v) relating to software, hardware or peripherals, including printers, used by Client including obsolescence and incompatibility.

9.3 This Article applies irrespective of the cause of action underlying the claim including breach of contract (even if in the nature of a breach of a condition or a fundamental term or a fundamental breach), tort (including negligence, gross negligence or misrepresentation) or otherwise.

9.4 Without limiting the foregoing, *(insert name of portal provider)*'s and its affiliates' or any of their respective directors', officers', employees', agents' or contractors' maximum total liability for any and all claims whatsoever shall be an award for direct provable damages not to exceed the Fees paid to *(insert name of portal provider)* under this Agreement during the current Term.

9.5 No action, regardless of form, arising out of this Agreement may be brought by Client more than twelve (12) months after the acts giving rise to the cause of action have been discovered.

10. Term and Termination

10.1 Subject to Sections 10.2 and 10.3, the term of this Agreement is for one (1) year from the Effective Date or if renewed, one (1) year from the anniversary date (the "Term").

10.2 This Agreement shall automatically renew at the end of the current Term, upon the same terms and conditions except that Schedule "C" may be amended by *(insert name of portal provider)* in its sole discretion to reflect *(insert name of portal provider)*'s then current fees. However, this Agreement shall not renew if either Party has delivered to the other Party, a written notice of intent not to renew this Agreement and such notice of intent is to be received in accordance with Section 11.1 not less than thirty (30) days in advance of the end of the current Term.

10.3 Either Party shall have the right, on written notice to the other Party and without prejudice to any other remedies which the Parties may have, under this Agreement, in law or in equity, to terminate this Agreement when:

(i) the Party provides thirty (30) days prior written notice to the other Party;

(ii) the other Party shall file a voluntary petition in bankruptcy or insolvency or shall petition for reorganization under any bankruptcy law and such is not dismissed within ten (10) days;

(iii) the other Party shall consent to involuntary petition in bankruptcy or if a receiving order is given against it under the *Bankruptcy and Insolvency Act* or the comparable law of any other jurisdiction and such is not dismissed within ten (10) days;

(iv) there shall be entered an order, judgment or decree by a court of competent jurisdiction, upon the application of a creditor, approving a petition seeking reorganization or appointing a receiver, trustee or liquidator of all or a substantial part of the other Party's assets and such order, judgment or decree continues in effect for a period of thirty (30) consecutive days; provided, however, that such order, judgment or decree may remain in effect for longer than such thirty (30) days, if the other Party is diligently appealing such order, judgment or decree; or

(v) the other Party shall fail to perform any material obligations set forth in this Agreement or is in breach of any representation or warranty under this Agreement and such default or breach in the case of a default or breach which is remediable continues for a period of thirty (30) days after written notice of such failure has been given by the non-defaulting Party.

10.4 In the event of termination of this Agreement prior to the end of the then current Term and without prejudice to any other remedies which the Parties may have in law, equity or under this Agreement, Client shall:

(i) immediately pay to *(insert name of portal provider)* as liquidated damages, and not as a penalty, all amounts due under this Agreement; and

(ii) return all Documentation, Confidential Information and other Intellectual Property provided directly or indirectly by *(insert name of portal provider)* under this Agreement.

11. GENERAL

11.1 Notices. All notices, documents or other communications required or permitted to be given under this Agreement shall be in writing and shall be effectively given if sent by prepaid courier service of registered mail, delivered personally, or sent by facsimile transmission or e-mail to the other Party as set forth in Schedule "B".

Any such notice, document or other communication so given or made shall be deemed to have been given or made and to have been received on the day of delivery if delivered personally, or on the day of facsimile transmission or sending by e-mail, provided that such day is a Business Day and the communication is so delivered, transmitted by facsimile or sent prior to 4:30 p.m. (Toronto, Ontario, Canada time) on such day. Otherwise, such communication will be deemed to have been given and made and to have been received on the next Business Day if sent by courier, personal delivery, e-mail and fax, or on the third Business Day following the mailing thereof; provided that no such communication shall be mailed during any actual or apprehended disruption of postal services.

Each of the Parties hereto shall be entitled to specify a different address for purposes of this Section only by giving notice in accordance with the terms hereof.

11.2 Entire Agreement. This Agreement and the Schedules attached hereto as may be amended by both Parties in writing from time to time, constitute the entire agreement between the Parties pertaining to the subject matter hereof and supersede all prior agreements, understandings, negotiations and discussions, whether oral or written.

11.3 Governing Law. This Agreement shall be governed by, interpreted, and enforced in accordance with the laws of the Province of Ontario and the federal laws of Canada, without reference to principles of conflict of laws. The

Parties submit and consent to the non-exclusive jurisdiction of the courts of the Province of Ontario in any action or proceeding instituted under this Agreement. The Parties hereby expressly exclude the application of the *United Nations Convention on Contracts for the International Sale of Goods* and the *Ontario International Sale of Goods Act*, as amended, replaced or re-enacted from time to time.

11.4 Amendment. Except as otherwise provided in this Agreement, this Agreement may be amended, modified or supplemented only by a written agreement signed by both Parties.

11.5 Severability. Should any provision of this Agreement be found to be invalid or unenforceable by a court of competent jurisdiction, such invalidity shall not affect other provisions of this Agreement which can be given effect without the invalid provision, and such invalid provision shall be deemed severed and the remainder of this Agreement shall remain in full force and effect.

11.6 Survival. Sections *(insert Section and Article numbers)* shall survive the termination or expiry of this Agreement.

11.7 Enurement. This Agreement shall enure to the benefit of and be binding upon each of *(insert name of portal provider)* and the Client and their respective successors and permitted assigns.

11.8 Assignment. Neither Party can assign this Agreement or any rights or obligations hereunder, in whole or in part, except with the prior written consent of the other Party, which consent shall not be unreasonably withheld.

11.9 Waiver. Any waiver of, breach, non-compliance, or consent to depart from, the requirements of any provision of this Agreement shall be effective only if it is in writing and signed by the Party giving it, and only in the specific instance and for the specific purpose for which it has been given. No failure on the part of any Party to exercise, and no delay in exercising, any right under this Agreement shall operate as a waiver of such right. No single or partial exercise of any such right shall preclude any other or further exercise of such right or the exercise of any other right.

11.10 Force Majeure. In the event that the performance of the terms of this Agreement by a Party is delayed, hindered or prevented by a Force Majeure (as defined below) the Party may at its option suspend this Agreement, in whole or in part, without liability or account thereof; provided however that the other Party may terminate this Agreement without liability or waiver of breaches by the first Party unrelated to the Force Majeure event, if such a situation of Force Majeure continues for ninety (90) days.

For the purposes of this Agreement, "Force Majeure" means any cause beyond the reasonable control of the Party seeking to take advantage of such Force Majeure, including, without limitation, any strike, lock-out, labour dispute, act of God, inability to obtain labour, utilities or services, acts of any government authority, enemy or hostile actions, sabotage, war, blockades, insurrections, riots, epidemics, washouts, nuclear and radiation activity or fallout, civil disturbances, explosions, fire or other casualty, unanticipated loads or transactions in portal System, breaches of security, computer viruses, faults in third-party software or equipment, or degradation or failure of telecommunications services. Nothing contained in this Section shall relieve the Client of its obligation to pay for Portal Services provided.

11.12 Further Assurances. Each Party shall do such acts and shall execute such further documents, conveyances, deeds, assignments, transfers and the like, and will cause the doing of such acts and will cause the execution of such further documents as are within its power as any other Party may in writing at any time and from time to time reasonably request be done or executed, in order to give full effect to the provisions of this Agreement.

11.13 Independent Contractors. *(Insert name of portal provider)* and Client acknowledge that *(insert name of portal provider)* is an independent contractor and that Client and *(insert name of portal provider)* shall not be considered to be in an employee-employer, partnership or principal-agent relationship.

11.14 Currency. Unless specified otherwise, all statements of or references to dollar amounts in this Agreement are to Canadian Dollars.

11.15 Headings. The division of this Agreement into Articles and Sections and the insertion of headings are for convenience or reference only and shall not affect the construction or interpretation of this Agreement.

11.16 Number and Gender. In this Agreement, unless there is something in the subject matter or context inconsistent therewith: words in the singular number include the plural and such words shall be construed as if the plural had been used and vice versa; and words importing the use of any gender shall include all genders.

11.17 Counterparts. This Agreement may be executed in any number of counterparts, each of which shall be deemed to be an original and all executed counterparts taken together shall constitute one and the same Agreement. Counterparts may be executed in either original or faxed form and the Parties adopt any signatures received by a receiving fax machine as original signatures of the Parties and any faxed document will be deemed to be an original written document.

11.18 Language. The Parties to this Agreement have required that this Agreement and all deeds, documents and notices relating to this Agreement, be drawn up in the English language. Les Parties aux présentes ont exigé que le présent contrat et tous autres contrats, documents ou avis afférents aux présentes soient rédigés en langue anglaise.

AGREED TO BY:	
CLIENT:	*(INSERT NAME OF PORTAL PROVIDER)*
ADDRESS:	ADDRESS:
SIGNATURE:	SIGNATURE:
I HAVE AUTHORITY TO BIND THE CORPORATION.	I HAVE AUTHORITY TO BIND THE CORPORATION.
NAME:	NAME:
TITLE:	TITLE:
DATE:	DATE:

SCHEDULE "A"
SERVICES

Services

Commencement Date: ______________________________

Portal Services consist of *(insert description of portal functionality).*

Support

Portal support is available *(insert times and time zone).*

In case of an operations problem after hours, your call to the Support centre *(insert phone number)* will offer two options:

(i) If the problem is an emergency (cannot wait), you are directed to an extension that will be routed to a phone on stand-by and you will be contacted within *(insert number)* minutes.

(ii) If the problem is not an emergency, can wait until business hours, you are asked to leave a message that will be followed up with you in the morning of the next business day.

The Support Centre – Help Desk Service, is available to our customers Monday through Friday, *(insert times and time zone)*, for assistance regarding any aspect of the contracted services.

SCHEDULE "B" NOTICES

Notices to *(insert name of portal provider)* shall be sent to:

Notices to Client shall be sent to:

SCHEDULE "C"
FEES

- Annual Registration Fee Per Trading Partner: $x
- Plus monthly fees, for documents and messages exchanged through Portal, based on the following rate:
  - Document Fee: (covers volume based on document exchange)
  - $x per transaction document*
  - Kilo-Character Fee: (covers volume based on document content)
  - $x*
  - (*Plus all applicable taxes)
- All payments are due within thirty (30) days of the invoice date.
- The base rates indicated above will be discounted as per the following section.

Discount Benefits.

- Customers processing in excess of x per month will have document charges waived.
- The Base Kilo-Character rate of $x/KC will be discounted as follows:
  - A discount of x% will be applied to accounts processing over x per month;
  - A discount of x% will be applied to accounts processing over x per month;
  - A discount of x% will be applied to accounts processing over x per month;
  - A discount of x% will be applied to accounts processing over x per month;
  - A discount of x% will be applied to accounts processing over x per month;
- For customers that can commit to volumes over x per month for one year, further discounts can be negotiated.

- The Base Document rate of $x/Document will be discounted as follows:
    - A discount of x% will be applied to accounts processing over x Documents per month;
    - A discount of x% will be applied to accounts processing over x Documents per month;
    - A discount of x% will be applied to accounts processing over x Documents per month;
    - A discount of x% will be applied to accounts processing over x Documents per month;
    - A discount of x% will be applied to accounts processing over x Documents per month.

FORM 10 B – PORTAL LEGAL TERMS AND DISCLAIMERS

IMPORTANT! YOUR ACCESS TO THE INFORMATION ON THIS PORTAL IS SUBJECT TO TERMS AND CONDITIONS. CAREFULLY READ ALL OF THE FOLLOWING TERMS AND CONDITIONS BEFORE PROCEEDING. TYPING IN "I ACCEPT" IN THE BOX BELOW INDICATES YOUR ACCEPTANCE OF THESE LEGAL TERMS AND DISCLAIMERS. IF YOU DO NOT AGREE WITH THESE TERMS AND DISCLAIMERS, PLEASE CLICK ON THE "EXIT" BUTTON BELOW.

Any and all information, product names, company names, domain names, trade-marks or trade names, patents, copyrights, or other proprietary rights (whether or not registered), reports, web pages, graphics, data, databases, files, multimedia, software or content *(NOTE TO DRAFT: DESCRIBE CONTENT OF PORTAL AND CONSIDER ALL POSSIBLE INTELLECTUAL PROPERTY RIGHTS)* as used in or accessed through this portal, including the manner in which the information is presented or appears and all information relating thereto (the "Content"), are the property of their respective owners as indicated, *(insert name of portal provider)* or its licensors.

You are solely responsible for the retrieval and use of the Content, transactions, products and/or services available on or through this portal. You should apply your own judgement in making any use of the Content, including, without limitation, the use of the Content as the basis for any conclusions or for the sale or purchase of any products or services or other transactions.

THE CONTENT ON THIS PORTAL, PRODUCTS AND/OR SERVICES AVAILABLE ON OR THROUGH THIS PORTAL, MAY NOT BE ACCURATE, UP TO DATE, COMPLETE, ERROR FREE, OR UNTAMPERED, AND IS NOT TO BE RELIED UPON.

(INSERT NAME OF PORTAL PROVIDER), ITS DIRECTORS, OFFICERS OR AFFILIATES SHALL NOT BE LIABLE, EITHER DIRECTLY OR INDIRECTLY, FOR ANY SPECIAL, INDIRECT, ECONOMIC OR CONSEQUENTIAL DAMAGES; DAMAGES FOR LOSS OF USE, LOST PROFITS, LOST SAVINGS, VIRUSES, OR DATA CORRUPTION; OR DAMAGES ARISING AS A RESULT OF THE TRANSMISSION, USE OR INABILITY TO USE THIS PORTAL OR THE CONTENT, TRANSACTIONS, PRODUCTS OR SERVICES AVAILABLE ON OR THROUGH THIS PORTAL, OR ANY OTHER WEB SITE OR PORTAL ACCESSED TO OR FROM THIS PORTAL.

(INSERT NAME OF PORTAL PROVIDER)'S, ITS DIRECTORS', OFFICERS' OR AFFILIATES' MAXIMUM COLLECTIVE TOTAL LIABILITY FOR ANY CLAIMS WHATSOEVER, INCLUDING CLAIMS FOR BREACH OF

CONTRACT, TORT (INCLUDING NEGLIGENCE OR GROSS NEGLIGENCE) OR OTHERWISE, EVEN IF ADVISED OF THE POSSIBLITY OF SUCH DAMAGES, AND YOUR SOLE REMEDY, SHALL BE AN AWARD FOR DIRECT, PROVABLE DAMAGES NOT TO EXCEED THE AMOUNT OF *(INSERT LIMITATION ON LIABILITY FOR DIRECT DAMAGES, E.G., VALUE OF THIS AGREEMENT/ACCESS, FEES RECEIVED BY PORTAL PROVIDER).*

(INSERT NAME OF PORTAL PROVIDER), AND ITS DIRECTORS, OFFICERS AND AFFILIATES GIVE NO REPRESENTATIONS, WARRANTIES, GUARANTEES OR CONDITIONS OF ANY KIND, EXPRESS OR IMPLIED, WHETHER ARISING BY STATUTE OR FROM A COURSE OF DEALING OR USAGE OF TRADE, AS TO THE USE OF THIS PORTAL OR THE CONTENT, TRANSACTIONS, PRODUCTS OR SERVICES ON OR THROUGH THIS PORTAL, INCLUDING WITHOUT LIMITATION, ANY REPRESENTATIONS, WARRANTIES, GUARANTEES OR CONDITIONS AS TO UNINTERRUPTED OR ERROR FREE OPERATION, QUALITY, ACCURACY, RELIABILITY, COMPLETENESS, TIMELINESS, LEGALITY, SUITABILITY, NON-INFRINGEMENT, TITLE, CONFIDENTIALITY, PRIVACY, MERCHANTABILITY, OR FITNESS FOR PURPOSE.

Unless prior written permission is obtained from *(insert name of portal provider)* and its licensors, the Content may not be reproduced, published, copied, linked to, framed, tagged, embedded, merged, modified, recompiled, licensed, distributed, sold, stored in an electronic retrieval system, downloaded (except by your browser as a single user) or transmitted, in whole or in part, in any form or by any means whatsoever, be they physical, electronic or otherwise.

This portal is physically located on a server in Ontario, Canada and the laws of the province of Ontario and the federal laws of Canada shall apply without regard to the conflict of laws principles. This portal is intended to be read by Canadian residents only. This portal and the Content are not to be construed as any form of recommendation, promotion, endorsement, or an offer to sell any product or service, by or to enter any transaction with *(insert name of portal provider).*

The parties hereby expressly exclude the application of the *United Nations Convention on Contracts for the International Sale of Goods* and the *International Sale of Goods Act (Ontario),* as amended, replaced or re-enacted from time to time. You also agree and hereby irrevocably submit to the exclusive personal jurisdiction and venue of the courts of the Province of Ontario with respect to any disputes. The parties have required that this Agreement and all documents relating thereto be drawn up in English. Les parties ont demandé que cette convention ainsi que tous les documents qui s'y rattachent soient rédigés en anglais.

These legal terms and disclaimers (and any *(insert name of portal provider)* policies on the portal, and any agreements between buyer(s) and *(insert name of portal provider)* or seller(s) and *(insert name of portal provider)*) constitute the entire agreement between you and *(insert name of portal provider)* with respect to the use of this portal and the Content. No supplement, modification or amendment to these legal terms and disclaimers and no waiver of any provision of these legal terms and disclaimers shall be binding on *(insert name of portal provider)* unless executed by *(insert name of portal provider)* in writing. No waiver of any of the provisions of these legal terms and disclaimers shall be deemed or shall constitute a waiver of any other provision (whether or not similar) nor shall such waiver constitute a continuing waiver unless otherwise expressly provided.

Any provision of these legal terms and disclaimers which is prohibited or unenforceable in any jurisdiction shall, as to that jurisdiction, be ineffective to the extent of such prohibition or unenforceability and shall be severed from the balance of these legal terms and disclaimers, all without affecting the remaining provisions of these legal terms and disclaimers or affecting the validity or enforceability of such provision in any other jurisdiction.

(Insert name of portal provider) and *(insert other trade-marks in portal)* are the trade-marks of *(insert names of respective trade-mark owners).*

IF YOU AGREE WITH THESE LEGAL TERMS AND DISCLAIMERS AND INTEND TO BE LEGALLY BOUND BY THEM, TYPE "I ACCEPT" IN THE BOX BELOW. IF YOU DO NOT AGREE WITH THESE TERMS AND DISCLAIMERS, PLEASE CLICK ON THE "EXIT" BUTTON BELOW.

CHAPTER 11

E-CONTRACTS

11.1 INTRODUCTION TO E-CONTRACTS

Like traditional brick and mortar businesses, on-line businesses also sell products and services. However, the method of doing business on-line has some peculiarities that require additional drafting considerations. The following chapter will focus on drafting effective on-line "e-contracts", also commonly referred to as "click-wrap" agreements. Before reading this chapter, one needs to understand the primary legal issues involving e-commerce. These issues are addressed in Chapter 2.

E-contracts do not differ extensively from traditional paper contracts, in that they both set forth the terms and conditions of the transaction, which may include the following clauses: description of the product or service, delivery and payment terms, each party's rights and obligations, ownership or licensing, confidentiality, force majeure, representations, warranties, indemnities, limitations on liability and disclaimers, term and termination, definitions, interpretation, governing law, jurisdiction, dispute resolution, assignment, notice and severability. However, given an e-contract's intangible format, there are certain provisions that require more attention than in traditional paper contracts.

11.2 E-CONTRACT UNIQUE TERMS

11.2.1 Describing the Parties to the e-Contract

Every lawyer knows that in any commercial agreement, it is important to clearly and accurately identify the parties to the contract. However, in e-commerce, one of the key issues (as discussed in Chapter 2) is knowing the identity, legal capacity, competency and authority of the party one is contracting with. This issue can be overcome by adopting certain security procedures.[1] Thereafter, the e-contract can be drafted in a more user-friendly format by defining the customer as "You", the on-line business as the "Company" and both parties as "We" or "Us".

---

1 See Chapter 2 for a description of some of the technical controls that may be adopted to increase assurance of identity.

11.2.2 Acceptance Procedure

Since an e-contract is formed on-line, and not by the traditional method of signing paper documents, the issue of whether acceptance has occurred must be addressed.[2] This can be accomplished by specifying in the e-contract the acceptance procedures and when the contract is deemed accepted.

For example, the e-contract should state that it is binding when the Internet user performs a specific action, such as proceeding to access a web site, clicking on a button, or typing certain words in a box, such as "I agree". By specifying that the action required by the Internet user constitutes their acceptance of the e-contract and their intention to be legally bound, the greater the enforceability of the e-contract. In addition, requiring the Internet user to type in a phrase, supports the fact that they have an understanding of the applicable language in which the legal terms are displayed.

Given that in Canada the mailbox rule (as discussed in Chapter 2) will likely apply to e-contracts, the acceptance of any offer must be communicated to the offeror. By sending a clear statement that an e-contract has been successfully completed to the customer and by giving the customer the opportunity to print out a copy of the e-contract, it will likely be held to be binding. If writing requirements apply, such as those required under provincial consumer protection legislation, then it is essential that a downloadable, printable original copy of the completed contract be provided to the consumer.

If the e-contract is subject to certain conditions such as availability of products or credit acceptance then it is important that such conditions be clearly indicated along with all other important terms. Onerous or unusual terms should be brought to the reader's attention, such as by highlighting them in separate sections or requiring individual acceptance, e.g., by click-box, in order to demonstrate the contracting party's intention to be bound by those specific terms. To ensure the enforceability of an e-contract, it is particularly important that all of the terms are readable before or at the time of acceptance. It is recommended that the e-contract terms not be buried in other documents or linked to other web pages.

Note that in some cases, consumers have the right to repudiate contracts during a cooling-off period. For example, in Ontario consumers have forty-eight (48) hours after signing to get out of an otherwise binding executory contract.

---

2 This issue is discussed in greater detail in Chapter 2.

11.2.3 Establish Jurisdiction

As discussed in Chapter 2, another issue of electronic commerce is when and where the e-contract has been formed, i.e., jurisdiction. As with web site terms, setting out which laws will govern, which courts will the parties bring a dispute in and expressly excluding any conflicts of law and international treaties is important to limit the risk of being subject to the laws of foreign countries where one does not want to do business (see paragraph 9.2.6). In addition, the e-contract should contain statements as to when and where the e-contract is formed, where the web site of the party presenting the e-contract is located (i.e., the server hosting the web site) and which language the parties have agreed that the e-contract be written in.

If there are specific jurisdictions that the business does not want to be subjected to, the business should implement technical controls, such as requiring potential e-contracting parties to input postal or area codes, as a screening mechanism.

As with all contracts that are generally prepared for use in Canada, consideration should be given to ensuring compliance with the Quebec Language Charter.[3] Given the likelihood that an e-contract may be entered into by persons in Quebec, the legal terms should also contain an English language clause.

11.2.4 Disclaimers and Limitations on Liability

As with traditional contracts, it is important to disclaim implied representations, warranties and conditions, such as those arising under sale of goods legislation or other statutes. Given the peculiar risks of the electronic environment in which e-contracts are formed, certain unique disclaimers and limitations on liability should be considered. These include disclaimers or limitations for liability arising from viruses, data corruption, failed messages, damages arising as a result of transmission errors or problems, telecommunications providers and third-party products or services, over which the parties have no control.

11.2.5 Signature and Writing Requirements

To deal with the issues of signature and writing requirements of certain types of contracts, as discussed in Chapter 2, the e-contract should specify what constitutes a "signature" and that an electronic document is equivalent to paper. In particular, the parties should agree to the transmission, signing and use of electronic documents and signatures. Also, technological controls and security

---

3 *Charter of the French Language*, R.S.Q. 1977, c. 5.

procedures should be agreed upon and implemented. Furthermore, access to and retention of electronic documents and a method of correcting errors should be provided to ensure integrity and reliability and to satisfy the writing requirements.

CHECKLIST 11 – FOR DRAFTING E-CONTRACTS

- Draft the e-contract in a user-friendly format, by defining the Internet user as "You", the on-line business as the "Company" and both parties as "We" or "Us";
- Ensure that all of the terms are readable (e.g., not referenced in other documents or web pages) and highlight the onerous terms;
- Describe what action a party must take to show acceptance and understanding of the e-contract;
- Carefully draft jurisdiction, governing law and attornment clauses, specifying where the e-contract is formed, where the server is located and the agreed upon language;
- Obtain consent for using electronic documents and signatures and specify use of encryption technology;
- Disclaim and limit liabilities for the risks that are peculiar to e-commerce;
- Provide access to and retention of electronic documents and a method of correcting errors.

FORM 11A – E-CONTRACT (CLICK-WRAP AGREEMENT) TERMS

1. e-Contract Terms Identifying Contracting Parties and Effective Date. This Agreement is between you, the purchaser of the products or services on this web site ("You") and *(insert company name)* (the "Company"). "We" and "Us" means both You and the Company. The effective date of this Agreement is when You accept this Agreement in accordance with the procedure set out [below].

2. e-Contract Acceptance Procedure, Signature and Error Correction Terms. IMPORTANT! YOUR PURCHASE OF GOODS OR SERVICES ON THIS WEB SITE IS SUBJECT TO LEGALLY BINDING TERMS AND CONDITIONS. CAREFULLY READ ALL OF THE APPLICABLE TERMS AND CONDITIONS AS SET OUT BELOW. IF YOU ACCEPT THESE TERMS AND CONDITIONS, TYPE "I ACCEPT" IN THE BOX BELOW. THAT ACTION IS THE EQUIVALENT OF YOUR SIGNATURE AND INDICATES YOUR ACCEPTANCE OF THE TERMS AND CONDITIONS AND THAT YOU INTEND TO BE LEGALLY BOUND BY THEM. IF THERE IS AN ERROR IN THE TERMS AND CONDITIONS OR IF YOU DO NOT AGREE WITH THEM, PLEASE CLICK ON THE "BACK" BUTTON OF YOUR BROWSER TO MAKE A CORRECTION OR CLICK ON THE "CANCEL" BUTTON BELOW TO EXIT THIS WEB SITE.

3. e-Contract Terms Consenting to Electronic Documents. You hereby consent to the exchange of information and documents between Us electronically over the Internet or by e-mail, if to You to *(insert address of Internet user)* or if to Company *(insert address of Company)* and that this Agreement in electronic form shall be the equivalent of an original written paper agreement between Us.

4. e-Contract Jurisdiction and Language Clause. The Company, this web site and its server is physically located within the Province of *(insert province)*, Canada. This Agreement will be governed by the laws of the Province of (*insert province*) and the federal laws of Canada and shall be treated in all respects as a *(insert province)* contract, without reference to the principles of conflicts of law. In the event of a dispute, We agree to submit to the non-exclusive jurisdiction of the *(insert province)* courts. We expressly exclude the *UN Convention on Contracts for the International Sale of Goods*, and the (*provincial*) *International Sale of Goods Act (Ontario)* as amended, replaced or re-enacted from time to time. We have required that this Agreement and all documents relating thereto be drawn-up in English. Nous avons demandé que cette convention ainsi que tous les documents qui s'y rattachent soient rédigés en anglais.

5. e-Contract Disclaimer and Limitation of Liability. EXCEPT AS EXPRESSLY PROVIDED IN THIS AGREEMENT, COMPANY DOES NOT MAKE OR GIVE ANY REPRESENTATION, WARRANTY OR CONDITION OF ANY KIND, WHETHER EXPRESS OR IMPLIED, STATUTORY OR OTHERWISE, INCLUDING WITHOUT LIMITATION WARRANTIES AS TO UNINTERRUPTED OR ERROR FREE TRANSACTIONS, PRIVACY, SECURITY, MERCHANTABILITY, QUALITY, TITLE, NON-INFRINGEMENT OR FITNESS FOR A PARTICULAR PURPOSE, OR THOSE ARISING OUT OF A COURSE OF DEALING OR USAGE OF TRADE.

IN NO EVENT WILL THE COMPANY BE LIABLE FOR ANY INDIRECT, INCIDENTAL OR CONSEQUENTIAL DAMAGES, HOWSOEVER CAUSED, INCLUDING BUT NOT LIMITED TO, ANY LOST PROFITS, LOST SAVINGS, LOSS OF USE OR LACK OF AVAILABILITY OF FACILITIES INCLUDING COMPUTER RESOURCES, ROUTERS AND STORED DATA, PUNITIVE, EXEMPLARY, AGGRAVATED OR ECONOMIC DAMAGES, ARISING OUT OF THE PRODUCTS OR SERVICES PROVIDED BY COMPANY OR OTHERWISE RELATED TO THIS AGREEMENT, EVEN IF THE COMPANY OR ANY OF THEIR LAWFUL AGENTS, CONTRACTORS, OR EMPLOYEES HAVE BEEN ADVISED OF THE POSSIBILITY OF SUCH DAMAGES OR CLAIM. IN NO CASE WILL THE COMPANY'S TOTAL LIABILITY ARISING UNDER ANY CAUSE WHATSOEVER (INCLUDING WITHOUT LIMITATION BREACH OF CONTRACT, NEGLIGENCE, GROSS NEGLIGENCE, OR OTHERWISE) BE FOR MORE THAN THE AMOUNT PAID BY YOU UNDER THIS AGREEMENT FOR THE SPECIFIC PRODUCT OR SERVICE TO WHICH THE CLAIM RELATES. IN NO EVENT WILL COMPANY BE LIABLE TO YOU FOR DAMAGES OR LOSSES RESULTING FROM VIRUSES, DATA CORRUPTION, FAILED MESSAGES, DAMAGES ARISING AS A RESULT OF: TRANSMISSION ERRORS OR PROBLEMS, TELECOMMUNICATIONS SERVICE PROVIDERS, THE COMPANY'S CONTRACTORS, THE INTERNET BACKBONE, THIRD-PARTY SUPPLIER OF PRODUCTS OR SERVICES, DAMAGES OR LOSSES CAUSED BY YOU, OR YOUR RESPECTIVE EMPLOYEES, AGENTS OR SUBCONTRACTORS, OR OTHER EVENTS BEYOND THE REASONABLE CONTROL OF THE COMPANY.

FOR THE PURPOSES OF THIS SECTION, THE "COMPANY" SHALL INCLUDE THE COMPANY'S AFFILIATES AND THE COMPANY'S AND ITS AFFILIATES' RESPECTIVE DIRECTORS, OFFICERS, EMPLOYEES, AGENTS AND CONTRACTORS.

THIS SECTION SHALL SURVIVE THE TERMINATION OR EXPIRY OF THIS AGREEMENT.

6. e-Contract Confirmation of Contract and Print Request. The Agreement between You and the Company for the purchase of *(insert description of products and services)* has been successfully completed. Please print a copy of the terms of the Agreement for your reference. The Agreement has been assigned the following number: *(insert contract identifier)*. A copy of the Agreement will be kept *(insert where, e.g., on-line at a secure web site address, or at the Company's head office)* and to view it, please *(insert instructions)* and refer to the Agreement number above.

CHAPTER 12

INTERNET ADVERTISING AND LINKING

12.1 INTRODUCTION TO INTERNET ADVERTISING AND LINKING

With the increasing volume of traffic on the Internet, the burgeoning world of electronic commerce and with Internet advertising becoming a source of profit generation and traffic diversion, the contractual issues associated with advertising on the Internet are becoming more important. An Internet advertisement is in effect a computer program, capable of displaying certain information to Internet browsers, usually as text or pictures but can also encompass sound or video. The computer program is written in the same or similar language as web pages (see discussion in Chapter 1 regarding the Internet). As a computer program, the Internet advertisement is only run when certain actions of the user occur. The resulting display is downloaded into the user's computer where it is viewed on-screen. Advertising on the Internet for products and services has some unique characteristics as compared to advertising in other forms of media. Traditionally, advertisements are broadcast or pushed to the public at large, either through print or telecommunications media. On the other hand, Internet advertising is usually pulled down (or downloaded) by the user as they select or use an area on the Internet where such advertising is located.

In this chapter, the word *Advertiser* shall mean the party who has products or services to sell on the Internet and would like to post an advertisement or link with a web host. The term *Web Host* is not to be confused with a general web site host, as discussed above in Chapter 7. In this Chapter, the term *Web Host* is used to describe the host of the advertisement or link of the advertiser on the host's web site. An Internet user who is browsing the web host's web site will, upon choosing to click on the advertiser's advertisement or link or upon the instructions received by the web browser, be *hyper-linked*, as discussed below, to the advertiser's own web site.

The underlying assumption of this chapter is that each party already has their own fully operational web site, which is being hosted by their own respective web site hosts (usually also their Internet service providers). The agreements in Forms 12A and 12B, do not contain web site hosting or Internet access terms, as these would generally be subject to separate agreements, and have been previously discussed in Chapters 3 and 7 and in Forms 3A, 3B and 7A.

Some of the areas where Internet advertisements can be found are:

(i) on web pages (including bulletin boards and search engine pages), either on one particular web site or a collection of web sites, often called cyber malls;

(ii) on frames;

(iii) in software programs, such as web browsers or screen savers; and

(iv) in e-mail, such as automatic mailings either to subscribers or in spam.[1]

Internet advertisements can come in many forms, such as static, rotating or targeted. A *static* advertisement is written to be displayed in one of the above-mentioned areas without rotation, such as a banner ad that appears constantly across the top of a particular web page. A *rotating* advertisement is written to randomly rotate to different locations in one of the above-mentioned areas and may or may not be seen by an *Internet user*. A *targeted* advertisement is written to be seen by an *Internet user* who either enters specific information or who browses to specific advertising areas on the Internet. For example, a user with an interest in history that conducts a search using a web browser on a historical subject may be shown an advertisement by an antique shop on the search results web page. The same web page may show a different advertisement to a user who conducted a search on a different topic. Behind the scenes of a targeted advertisement is the web host's software which is analyzing the information entered by the user and selecting the advertisement targeted to that specific user's interests. An example of an Internet Advertising Agreement that contains the above forms of advertising as options, is attached as Form 12A.

Internet *linking*, as requested by the advertiser, is merely another form of targeted advertising using a *hyper-link*.[2] A hyper-link can either be presented on its own in the content of the web host's web site or within the *Advertiser's* advertisement on the web host's web site. When the Internet user clicks on a hyper-link, they activate a function, such as the transferring of the user to another web page or site or the addition of the user onto an e-mail mailing list.

Another form of hyper-link is an *embedded* or *inline* link. An embedded link may contain code that automatically performs a function as soon as the web page is loaded, such as the display of graphic images or information being stored in files on a server or another data base, without any action on behalf of the Internet user. A hyper-link is often used together with the various forms of advertising discussed above, to provide the user with access to more detailed information if required.

---

1 This is also referred to as junk e-mail. For a discussion of e-mail, see Chapter 1.

2 See discussion in Chapter 1.

Some advertisers prefer to cross-market their products or services with other advertisers. For example, a book company that sells travelogues may display a travel agency's advertisement on the book company's web site with a link to the travel agency's web site, and simultaneously, the travel agency may display the book company's advertisement on the travel agency's web site with a link to the book company's web site. This form of co-operative advertising is also sometimes referred to in the Internet industry as co-branding. Often the co-branding or linking is accomplished using a Linking Agreement in which revenue is shared between the linked companies. For an example of a revenue sharing Linking Agreement, please refer to Form 12B.

12.2 RISKS FACED BY ADVERTISERS IN ADVERTISING AND LINKING ON THE INTERNET

Advertisements only generate business if they are seen by Internet users. Web hosts offering Internet advertising services go to great lengths and expense to get their web sites registered in various Internet search directories and to embed codes into their web sites (known as *metatags*) that will be read by web browsers. A hyper-link that directs an Internet user to a web page other than the page on which an advertisement may be found may be disturbing to the web host or the respective advertiser, who generate revenues from the advertising. Thus, recently, web site owners have become more concerned about unauthorized links to their web sites.[3]

12.2.1 Intellectual Property Laws

It used to be thought that there was no liability for merely linking one's web site to another. However, if the hyper-link itself (especially an embedded link, as discussed above) consists of a graphic image, video, sound or other literary or artistic work, there could be a potential infringement of copyright. Similarly, a hyper-link that consists of a trade-mark, trade name, logo, design or other

---

[3] See for example, *Shetland Times Ltd. v. Wills* (Edinburgh, Scotland, F.S.R. (Ct. Sess. O.H.) October 24, 1996) in which Lord Hamilton J., of the Court of Sessions, issued an injunction to prevent a link by *The Shetland Times* that directly accessed text on the Shetland News web site, but bypassed Shetland News advertising. Also see *Ticketmaster Corp. v. Microsoft Corp.*, Civ. 97-3055 DDP (C.D. Cal. April 28, 1997) in which Ticketmaster obtained an injunction and damages against Microsoft for a link from Microsoft's Seattle Sidewalk web site, which linked to Ticketmaster's web site, bypassing numerous advertising pages. However, in the more recent case of *Ticketmaster Corp. v. Tickets.com, Inc.*, 2000 U.S. Dist. LEXIS 4553, 54 U.S.P.Q.2d (BNA) 1344 (C.D. Cal. 2000); *Ticketmaster Corp. v. Tickets.com, Inc.*, 2000 U.S. Dist. LEXIS 12987 (C.D. Cal. 2000), Tickets.com was not prevented from deep linking to the ticket purchasing web pages of the Ticketmaster web site.

device, could give rise to trade-mark infringement, a passing off action or reverse passing off.[4]

On the other hand, a link may equally be considered as nothing more than a footnote, bibliography or similar reference, simply pointing and transporting users to related information. Since there is no actual reproduction of a copyright work by the referring web page or web site, it would appear that a link would not be a direct infringement of a copyright owner's reproduction right. However, it is arguable that the Internet user who views the work, receives a copy, which is stored in the random access memory (RAM) of his or her computer. A link may also be challenged as an infringement of the copyright owner's distribution right.[5]

In Canada, it may also be possible to argue that a link to a web site that contains infringing content constitutes authorizing infringement under the *Copyright Act*.[6] A similar concept of contributory infringement exists under U.S. copyright laws.

Furthermore, the Internet advertisements or links themselves can give rise to intellectual property concerns. Advertisements and links can be very complex, since they may consist of software and multi-media such as text, graphics, sound, video, lyrics and other literary or artistic works. An advertiser should be careful not to include in its advertisement, both in the software that underlies the advertisement and/or link and in the content, any material that might infringe the intellectual property rights[7] or violate any confidentiality obligations of any third parties.

Also, an infringement or violation by the advertiser could potentially impose liability on the web host, depending upon how much control they may have over the content of the advertisement/link and/or the *Advertiser's* web site and whether the courts have jurisdiction over the web host.[8]

---

4 Passing off or "palming off" occurs when one directs attention to one's goods or services, using the trade-mark, trade name or trade dress of another so as to cause confusion. Reverse passing off occurs when original trade-marks or source identifiers of goods or services are removed and substituted so as to cause confusion as to designation or origin.

5 *Canadian Copyright Issues on the Internet: What Every Corporate Counsel Must Know*, by Sheldon Burshtein (Toronto, 1998).

6 R.S.C. 1985, c. C-42.

7 For a discussion of intellectual property rights, see Chapter 2.

8 For a discussion of Internet Service Provider liability, see Chapters 2 and 7 above.

12.2.2 Criminal Laws

Hyper-links to inappropriate materials, such as child pornography, hate literature or other types of illegal content, may be construed as facilitating the commission of an offence or other criminal activity.

12.2.3 Other Advertising Legal Issues

The fact that the Internet is accessible world wide raises the possibility that the advertisements can be read by users in different jurisdictions and subject to numerous local, national or international statutory or common laws affecting advertising.[9] Whether Internet advertising is subject to the laws of any particular jurisdiction should definitely be given careful consideration. A detailed analysis of applicable laws and regulations that would impact Internet advertising, the advertisers and the web hosts is outside the scope of this book.

12.3 HOW CAN THE RISKS OF INTERNET ADVERTISING AND LINKING BE AVOIDED?

12.3.1 Internet Legal Notices

Web site terms and conditions, such as the ones discussed above in Chapter 9, may be an effective means of reducing the risks associated with Internet advertising and linking.

Terms that prohibit users from downloading the contents of a site unless the user is visiting their site exclusively, or the user displays pages in a frame less than the entire size of display space on a browser program, could give the advertiser a cause of action if it discovers an unauthorized link to its web site.

---

9 Some of the Canadian federal legislation and regulations affecting advertising include: the *Competition Act*, R.S.C. 1985, c. C-34; *Food and Drugs Act*, R.S.C. 1985, c. F-27, s. 5(1); *Trade-marks Act* R.S.C. 1985, c. T-13; *Consumer Packaging and Labelling Act*, R.S.C. 1985, c. C-38; *Hazardous Products Act*, R.S.C. 1985, Chapter H-3; *Textile Labelling Act*, R.S.C. 1985, c. T-10; *Tobacco Products Control Act*, R.S.C. 1985 (4th Supp.), Chapter 14, s. 4; *Telecommunications Act*, S.C. 1993, c. 38; *Broadcasting Act*, S.C. 1991, c. 11. Some of the provincial legislation and regulations include: Ontario *Business Practices Act*, R.S.O. 1990, Chapter B.18; *Liquor Licence Act*, R.S.O. 1990, Chapter L.19; *Motor Vehicle Dealers Act*, R.S.O. 1990, Chapter M.42; Quebec: *Consumer Protection Act*, R.S. 1980, c. P.-40.1. Some of the industry regulations include: the *Canadian Association of Broadcasters* (CAB) *Broadcast Code for Advertising to Children*, 1988; the CAB *Code of Ethics*, 1989; the *Canadian Broadcasting Corporation Advertising Standards*, 1993.

12.4 PRINCIPAL TERMS IN INTERNET ADVERTISING AND LINKING AGREEMENTS

12.4.1 Description of the Advertisement and/or Link and Location of Web Sites

The agreement should contain a brief description of the format of the advertisement and/or link, e.g., whether it is graphics based (i.e., GIF or PCX), file or text-based (i.e., TXT). In the case of an advertisement or graphical link, a hard copy print-out may be attached as a Schedule and if attached, should reference the fact that the print-out may not be in the same scale/size as that advertisement and/or link will appear in the particular location or display.

The agreement should also detail the web host's web site (i.e., URL address) where the advertisement and/or link is to be found and the *Advertiser's* web site address to which Internet users will be connected upon clicking on the advertisement and/or link.

12.5 OBLIGATIONS

12.5.1 Services Provided by the Web Host

The agreement should provide sufficient description as to the nature of the services being provided by the web host. It is important to define clearly:

(i) where the advertisement and/or link will or will not be displayed, such as on particular web pages, frames, software programs or responding e-mail;

(ii) the location and placement of the advertisement and/or link; and

(iii) the size or prominence of the advertisement and/or link, as it appears to users and/or relative to other advertisements and/or links.

Consideration should also be given as to whether the advertisement and/or link will be displayed exclusively or along with other advertisers that could potentially be competitors of the advertiser.

In the case of an advertisement, the format of the advertisement is important. For example, will it be static, rotating or targeted.[10]

---

10 See Section 12.1.

If the advertisement is to be rotating, the agreement should specify randomness and frequency of the rotation. If the advertisement is targeted, the agreement should cover what markets, search results, key words, categories or pages will trigger the display of the advertisement.

The parties may want to negotiate performance guarantees by the web host. Such guarantees could be similar to the obligations and representations found in the Web Site Hosting or ASP Agreements [see Chapters 7 and 8] or more specific to the results generated by the advertisement or link, as discussed in paragraph 12.5.5, Fees and Reporting, below. If guaranteed minimums are given by the web host, the agreement should also address what the advertiser's remedies will be if such minimums are not met. For example, the advertiser may want an extension of the contract term, or a refund of fees paid.

12.5.2 Changes to the Web Host's Web Site or the Advertisement

The agreement should address whether the web host is permitted to modify its web site, the advertisement or the link. A web host may object to controls by the advertiser over the web host's web site. However, an advertiser may have specific concerns such as: the type of content or other advertising displayed on or linked to the web host's web site; or the order or positioning of web pages on the web site, which could affect the impact or visibility of the advertisement or link.

If the agreement permits the web host to make modifications to the advertiser's advertisement or link, either upon the advertiser's request or as required by the web host, the agreement should specify clearly what restrictions the web host would have in performing such modifications. Such restrictions should include the fact that the overall look of the advertisement or link will either stay the same, or be as requested by the advertiser. However, in order to carry out the web host's services efficiently, the web host should at least be given the right to make *minor* editorial or format changes to the advertisement or link without the *Advertiser's* prior consent. In such case, the advertiser would want to ensure that such modifications do not adversely affect the appearance of the advertisement or link to Internet users.

The agreement should also address the procedure for the advertiser to provide or request changes to the advertisement or link. If the changes are minor, the web host might not charge extra fees. However, substantial changes, whether made by the advertiser or the web host, might result in additional service charges to the advertiser. If the advertiser requests the web host to make substantial changes to the advertisement, the same issues as discussed in Chapter 5, Web Site and Content Development Contracts, may arise and reference to the terms of Form 5A is recommended.

If the web host is given permission under the agreement to modify the advertiser's advertisement or link in any way, the ownership section of the agreement should address who owns such modifications. (See also discussion in paragraph 12.5.4, below, regarding ownership)

12.5.3 Obligations of the Advertiser

An Internet advertisement is generally provided by the advertiser to the web host. In such case, the agreement should specify the obligations of the advertiser, such as the format in which the advertisement is to be supplied (i.e., file format and delivery format).

An Internet link, on the other hand, will likely be programed by the web host into its web site. The agreement should specify whether the link will be textual (such as a highlighted or underlined word) or graphical (such as a logo or button).

12.5.4 Ownership and Licensing

With respect to an advertisement, it is important that the agreement distinguish ownership of the advertisement from ownership of the area where the advertisement is displayed. Generally speaking, if the advertiser is supplying its own advertisement, then it usually wants to retain ownership of the advertisement, while the web host wants to remain the owner of the web site, software or other area on which the advertisement is displayed. The agreement should contain a licensing provision that grants to the web host the right to set up, reproduce, use and publicly display the advertisement and/or link in order to perform the web host's services under the agreement.

With respect to a link that does not contain any intellectual property, an express license grant is not necessary. In the case of a web host linking an advertisement to the respective *Advertiser's* web site, the agreement merely needs to state that the web host *shall* link the advertisement to the *Advertiser's* web site. In the case of a request by one party seeking permission to link to another party, the agreement merely needs to provide a grant of such permission.

Caution should be exercised when the advertisement or link contains intellectual property, especially trade-marks (such as word marks or design marks), whether they have been registered or not. If the advertisement or link contains any trade-marks, the agreement should contain sufficient quality controls by the trade-mark owner and an inurement clause, as are commonly found in trade-mark licenses (*see for example Sections 2.3 and 2.4 of Form 12B*) to ensure the trade-mark owner's rights in the trade-marks are not diluted.

The license grant, or permission to link, should specify whether the advertisement or link is to be displayed on the web host's web site (or other location) on an exclusive, sole or non-exclusive basis.[11] A web host may be interested in being the exclusive host for the advertiser. On the other hand, the advertiser likely would not want to restrict its advertising or links to one web host. Conversely, the advertiser may have concerns about the web host's ability to provide advertising or linking space to other advertisers, such as the advertiser's competitors.

The license grant to the web host would normally be a world wide grant, unless the web host is requested by the advertiser to limit access to its web site (where the advertiser's advertisement or link is located). A territorial limitation might be preferred where the products or services being advertised are subject to strict regulation in certain jurisdictions, such as the sale of securities or Internet gambling.

The parties may also want to control links from one another's web sites to other sites which either of them may consider undesirable or risky to be associated with, such as pornographic sites or sites that may contain infringing material.

Terms governing the operation of and access to the web site on which the advertisement or link is displayed are usually contained in separate web site hosting and Internet access agreements, as discussed in Chapters 7 and 3, respectively.

12.5.5 Fees and Reporting

There are many different ways to structure fees in advertising or linking agreements. The following is a list of some of the factors upon which fees can be based:

(i) fixed rates, e.g., $x per month;

(ii) number of impressions, that is the number of times an area containing the advertisement, is downloaded by the Internet

---

[11] An "exclusive" license means only the licensee can exercise the rights granted, even to the exclusion of the licensor. Exclusivity can be limited in scope. A "sole" license means no one other than the licensee and licensor can exercise the rights granted.

user, regardless of whether the user waits long enough to view the whole advertisement;

(iii) number of actual displays (often referred to as page views), that is the number of times the entire advertisement is displayed in whole;

(iv) clicks (often referred to as click-throughs or depressions), that is the number of times an Internet user actually clicks on a hyper-link in the advertisement to directly access the advertiser's web site or additional information on the product or service being sold;

(v) user actions, such as filling out a questionnaire or requesting a brochure; or

(vi) actual sales revenue, in which case the web host would only get paid if the Internet user followed the advertisement and/or link through to purchasing the advertiser's product or service on-line.

A web host would prefer certainty in payment, such as method (i) above, especially if it does not have much control over the content and placement of the advertisement and/or link, or if the advertiser's product or service is not in high demand. Advertisers, on the other hand, prefer a more *results-oriented* approach, such as methods (iv) through (vi) above. If a results-oriented approach is selected, the agreement should include an obligation on the web host not to artificially increase the results obtained.

Using various software tools, it is possible for a web host to monitor and report to the advertiser on the effectiveness of its advertisement and/or link or the tracking of Internet users. However, it should be noted that because of the characteristics of the Internet, such as the ability of web sites to *cache* or store third-party sites, have mirrored sites, or the disablement by an Internet user of *Cookies* or the entering of incorrect information in *Passports*, the information gathered by a web host may not be entirely accurate or complete. Therefore, the party gathering such information may want to disclaim any liability in relation to such information or related reports. Privacy issues, as discussed in previous chapters, should also be considered with respect to the collection of any personal information.

The parties should also address whether additional fees for changing the advertisement will be charged. If one of the parties feels that the proposed fee structure is unfair, it may want to consider a shorter term for the agreement or the ability to adjust the fee structure.

It may also be reasonable to impose an obligation on a party to provide regular reports as to the criteria upon which the fees are based and to allow audits of a party's records to verify fees.

12.6 CONFIDENTIALITY AND PRIVACY

In the situation where the parties to the Internet advertising or linking contract are exchanging confidential or personal information, such as web site user traffic, click-through rates, purchases made by customers or sales revenue figures, it is recommended that the agreement contain a confidentiality clause and privacy representations, warranties and covenants. This is especially important in light of the privacy legislation that may apply to collection of personal information, discussed in Chapter 4.

12.7 TERM

If applicable, a distinction should be made between the date the agreement becomes effective and the date the link or advertisement commences being displayed on the web host's web site.

From the *Advertiser's* point of view, it is important that the term of the agreement is not too long, especially if the advertisement or link fails to generate the anticipated revenue. Hence, one should consider including an option for early termination in the agreement. On the other hand, the web host may have incurred significant costs in setting up the advertisement on its web site. This may be particularly true if the advertisement is complex, with many rotations or programed targets. Therefore, the web host would likely want to negotiate a longer agreement term. In order to free up advertising space, a web host may also want to have the ability to terminate the agreement early if, advertiser fails to pay or becomes bankrupt.

Careful consideration should also be given to the survival of representations, warranties, indemnities and other terms in the Internet advertising and linking agreements.

12.8 REPRESENTATIONS AND WARRANTIES

In addition to the usual representations and warranties given by parties to a contract, such as that each party has the right to enter into the agreement and that the agreement does not and will not conflict with any other agreement or obligation that a party may have, Internet advertising and linking agreements require some additional representations and warranties to minimize the risk of unique liabilities that arise in Internet advertising and linking, as discussed in Section 12.2, above.

The parties should represent and warrant that their web sites, web pages, advertisements, links, frames, content or other material to which either of them may be associated, do not and will not:

(i) violate or infringe the rights of any third parties in any jurisdiction, including without limitation, patent, copyright, trade-mark, trade secret, privacy, publicity, confidentiality or other proprietary rights;

(ii) violate the laws, statutes or regulations of any jurisdiction;

(iii) include any material that is illegal, harmful, pornographic, abusive, hateful, obscene, threatening, racist, discriminatory or defamatory or that encourages illegal activities; and

(iv) contain links to sites displaying the type of material defined in paragraph (iii) above.

In addition, an advertiser would generally want the web host to represent and warrant that:

(i) performance of the services under the Internet Advertising Agreement will be done in a competent manner by qualified personnel;

(ii) the web host is the owner of the web site (or other area) where the advertisement or link is displayed;

(iii) the web host's web site will always be available and running and has been programed efficiently enough to be downloaded quickly by Internet users (*see also Chapter 7 and Form 7A)*; and

(iv) the web host's web site is viewable by the currently common web browsers.

It is of particular concern to advertisers that the web host's web site is easily and quickly viewable by Internet browsers, especially when the fees payable by the advertiser are not results-oriented, as discussed above. Internet users do not have a lot of patience and if the web page loads too slowly, they may exit the web site before the advertisement or link to the advertiser has the opportunity to be displayed. As discussed above, the advertiser may also request that the web host give performance or results guarantees.

In return, a web host will likely ask that the following representation and warranty to be given by the advertiser:

The Advertiser is the owner of the advertisement (or link) or has the right to grant a license to the web host to use the advertisement or link for the performance of the web host's obligations under the agreement.

12.9 INDEMNITIES

In drafting any indemnity, it is important to consider whether the indemnity should apply only to the contracting parties, or whether it should extend to the relevant party's directors, officers, agents, subcontractors and affiliates as well. If the financial ability or viability of a contracting party is of concern, it may be worthwhile to seek a guarantee from a parent or related company.

The indemnities generally given in advertising and linking contracts are indemnities for losses resulting from intellectual property infringement or trade secret misappropriation claims. The advertiser will generally seek an indemnity from the web host that the web host's web site, or services does not infringe any intellectual property right of any third-party world wide. The web host may try to limit a patent or trade-mark indemnity to Canada, or other territories where it is economically feasible for the web host to conduct appropriate intellectual property due diligence and registrations. Given that patent and trade-mark applications might not be publicly available until the patent or trade-mark has been issued, consideration should be given to limiting the scope of indemnities for patent or trade-mark infringement to only valid patents or trade-marks that have been issued as of the effective date of the agreement.

The web host may seek the same intellectual property indemnities from the advertiser in respect of the web host's possession, use, or modification (if permitted in the agreement) of the advertisement or other property provided by advertiser, including, without limitation, any information, software, documentation or data received from the advertiser.

An indemnity for a claim of infringement of a third-party's rights with respect to an advertisement might also include the ability of the advertiser to, at its option:

(i) modify the advertisement so that it becomes non-infringing;

(ii) replace the advertisement (consider the criteria for the replacement);

(iii) obtain from the third-party claiming infringement the right to use the advertisement (provided that such rights can be obtained on terms satisfactory to the advertiser); or

(iv) request that the web host cease using, remove, return or destroy the infringing advertisement and terminate this agreement.

When acting for the web host, however, one should carefully review the agreement to ensure that the advertiser's options, referred to above, do not limit any other remedies the web host may have against the advertiser for breach of a non-infringement warranty.

In addition, indemnity for claims arising from statements or other content transmitted, posted, received or created through the respective party's web site, even if transmitted, posted, received or created by someone else (especially intellectual property infringement claims), are sometimes given. If the contracting party does not have control over what goes through or onto their web site, the parties must negotiate who will bear the risk of any third-party claims.

12.10 LIMITATIONS ON LIABILITY AND DISCLAIMERS

As discussed above in paragraph 12.5.5, a party that is obligated to report to another on Internet user traffic or activities may want to disclaim liability for inaccuracies in such reports, given the inherent complexities of the Internet.

Unforeseen circumstances or events beyond a party's control (also known as Force Majeure) are often included in an excusable delays clause. As with all types of Internet contracts, reliance is placed on third parties, such as telecommunications providers, domain name recognition systems and other Internet service providers. It is up to the contracting parties to carefully define Force Majeure and to allocate between them the risks of such events occurring.

In drafting the Internet advertising and/or linking agreement, one should consider including a provision that exculpates the web host from responsibility for any problem with the advertiser's web site, server, computer hardware or software that was not caused by any of the services performed by a web host under the agreement. Furthermore, the web host may want to attribute responsibility to the advertiser, in the form of payment to the web host at the web host's then standard billing rates, for all costs incurred in the evaluation, correction or performance of services relating to problems with the advertiser's web site, server, computer hardware or software.

Exclusions are often drafted for intellectual property infringement indemnities if such infringement occurs as a result of unauthorized use or modification of the property that is determined to be infringing, or continued use of the infringing property after the party using it has been notified of the infringement or after it has been provided with modifications that would have avoided the infringement.

Unlike most commercial agreements, which tend to limit liability for indirect and consequential damages, it is important for the parties entering into an Internet advertising or linking agreement to realize that most of the advertiser's damages, as a result of a web host's breach of contract, would be in the form of a loss of potential profits. Therefore, excluding indirect and consequential damages entirely may not be sufficient to protect the advertiser, unless the relationship is one of cross-advertising and revenue sharing, similar to the situation in Form 12B.

The following suggestions may address some of these issues.

First, the parties may want to negotiate in advance an amount of liquidated damages, representing the potential profits to be earned by the advertiser as a result of the advertisement or link. This approach may be difficult if the advertiser has not had much e-commerce experience.

Second, the parties may want to exclude indirect and consequential damages for only certain kinds of claims, such as negligence, but not breach of contract or intellectual property infringement claims, where damages could be indirect.

Limitations similar to those found in the Web Site Hosting Agreement (see Form 7A, as discussed in Chapter 7), should also be considered. Unless expressly warranted, a web host will try to obtain a disclaimer for uninterrupted or error free operation, accessibility, privacy and security of its web site.

Often, a maximum limit on liability is imposed, based on a certain amount of advertising fees paid by the advertiser over a certain time period, such as the twelve (12) months preceding the claim. It is important to note, that this limit may not be sufficient to indemnify claims where high damages may be awarded, such as in intellectual property infringement lawsuits.

12.11 GENERAL CLAUSES

As with other commercial agreements, Internet and e-commerce agreements, one should consider including notice clauses, non-waiver, currency, severability, assignability, entire agreement, force majeure, time of the essence, interpretation, independent contractors, binding on successors, survival, governing law and choice of language clauses.

CHECKLIST 12A – TO MINIMIZE LIABILITY FOR ADVERTISING AND LINKING

- Add legal notices to web sites, containing, among other terms, disclaimers of responsibility (especially for other web sites), limitations on liability, prohibitions on linking and notices of ownership rights (see also Chapter 9);
- Require Internet users to click on an "I accept" button, to acknowledge that they have read and agree with the terms;
- Do not use another entity's logo, design, trade name, trade-mark, or content as a link or in the advertisement or underlying software, without permission, and clearly indicate the source of any content or embedded material;
- Seek permission to link to another entity's web site, or alternatively, link only to the home page of such web site;
- Avoid framing other web sites and implied affiliations with other persons or entities;
- Give notice to Internet users when they are leaving the web site via a link;
- Do not copy any collection of links that might be available from other sources.

CHECKLIST 12B – FOR DRAFTING INTERNET ADVERTISING AND LINKING AGREEMENTS

- Ensure parties are clearly identified by their full legal names and for on-line agreements, see also checklist in Chapter 9;
- Describe advertising and linking services. Provide details about the advertisement and/or link, e.g., will it be static, rotating, targeted, where will it be positioned, size, keywords that will trigger it, will it be a graphics-based and/or text-based file, and will it be linked to the *Advertiser's* web site;
- Consider whether the parties will have reporting obligations and allocate risk between the parties for inaccurate or incomplete information due to Internet user tracking difficulties;
- Describe *Advertiser's* obligations, such as delivery of advertisement and/or link and required format;
- Reference web host's web site and the *Advertiser's* web site and ownership of web sites, domain names, advertisement and/or link, trade-marks and any modifications;
- Provide license grant/permission to web host for use of advertisement and/or link, and specify exclusivity, territory and restrictions on rights, e.g., modification, trade-mark controls;
- Provide detailed payment structure. Fees will be based on form of advertisement and/or link, e.g., static, rotating, targeted and any guarantees, e.g., minimum number of impressions, page views, clicks, Internet user actions, or sales revenue. Consider when fees will be paid, whether taxes are included and rate of interest on overdue accounts. If required, set out reporting requirements and ability to audit reports. Be cautious of inaccuracies in Internet traffic reports;
- Include any obligations to provide regular reports as to the criteria upon which the fees are based and to allow audits;
- Set out confidentiality obligations, especially if reports regarding web site traffic or revenues are being exchanged between the parties;
- Specify term of agreement and start date of advertisement and/or link if different from effective date of agreement. Allow time for web host to set it up. Web host should not be obligated to commence services until the advertisement and/or link has been provided in an appropriate form from advertiser;
- Provide for guarantees as to minimum number of impressions, page views, clicks, Internet user actions, or sales revenue. Outline what the remedies to

the advertiser will be if such minimums are not met (e.g., extension of duration of advertisement, termination of contract, refund of fees, etc.);

- Set out a procedure for changing the advertisement and/or link;
- Determine early termination rights;
- Consider excusable delays (*Force Majeure*), such as failures by Internet service or telecommunications providers;
- Consider boilerplate provisions, e.g., notice clauses, non-waiver, currency, severability, assignability, entire agreement, force majeure, time of the essence, interpretation, independent contractors, binding on successors, survival, governing law and choice of language clauses.

FORM 12A – INTERNET ADVERTISING AGREEMENT

THIS ADVERTISING AGREEMENT is made between (*insert full legal name of Company that will be placing the ad on its web site*) a (*jurisdiction*) corporation with its head office located at (*insert address*) (*web host*) and (*insert full legal name of the Company that has the advertisement*) a (*jurisdiction*) corporation with its head office located at (*insert address*) (*Advertiser*) effective as of (*insert date*) Effective Date.

RECITALS:

WHEREAS, web host maintains an Internet web site [relating to (*insert description of contents of Web Host's web site*)] located at http:// (*insert Web Host's web site Internet address*) (*the Web Host's Web Site*);

WHEREAS, Advertiser maintains an Internet web site [relating to (*insert description of contents of Advertiser's web site*)] located at http://(*insert Advertiser's web site Internet address*) (the Advertiser's Web Site);

WHEREAS, Advertiser desires to place an advertisement on the Web Host's Web Site consisting of a graphical [and/or text-based] file supplied by the Advertiser [Note: if the advertisement is to be developed by the Advertiser, terms similar to the Web Site Development Agreement Form 5A, should be inserted – see Chapter 5] a hard copy of which is attached as Schedule A, which contains a hyper-link that, when clicked by a mouse, moves Internet users from the Web Host's Web Site to the Advertiser's Web Site (the Advertisement); and

WHEREAS, web host is willing to place [and maintain] the Advertiser's advertisement on the Web Host's Web Site in accordance with the terms of this Agreement;

NOW THEREFORE, in consideration of ONE CANADIAN DOLLAR ($1.00 Cdn.) and other good and valuable consideration, the receipt and sufficiency of all of which is hereby acknowledged, the Web Host and Advertiser, intending to be legally bound, agree as follows:

1. ADVERTISING SERVICES.

Web Host shall provide to Advertiser space on the Web Host's Web Site for the Advertisement that will be displayed on the Web Host's Web Site (the Services).

The Services shall be provided as follows:

[Static Display. The Advertisement will be displayed without rotation on the Web Host's Web Site [on the following web pages (*insert specifics, e.g., size, positioning, location, address, etc.*)]; or Random Display. The Advertisement will be displayed on the Web Host's Web Site in random rotation (*insert specifics, e.g., size, positioning, randomness and frequency*); or Targeted Result Display. The Advertisement will be displayed on the Web Host's Web Site [on the following web pages (*insert specifics, e.g., content, location, address, etc.*)] in response to searches by Internet users using the (*insert keywords, markets, search results, categories or pages that will trigger the display of the ad*) accessing the web host's Web Site; or Targeted Page Display. The Advertisement will be displayed on the following specific pages of the Web Host's Web Site (*insert specifics, e.g., content, location, address, etc.*) (the Targeted Page). The contents of the Targeted Page shall remain similar to the contents on the Effective Date.]

[Impression means the number of times a [page; or frame; or (*insert specific area*)] of the Web Host's Web Site containing the Advertisement, is downloaded by an Internet user, regardless of whether or not the user waits long enough to view the whole Advertisement.]

[Page Views means the number of times the entire Advertisement is displayed in whole to an Internet user downloading the [page; or frame; or (*insert specific area*)] of the web host's Web Site containing the Advertisement]

[Clicks means the number of times an Internet user actually clicks on a hyper-link in the Advertisement to directly access the [Advertiser s Web Site; or additional information on the Advertiser's products or services being sold; or (*specify Internet address to where link is connected*)]

[The Web Host does not guarantee [the number of Impressions that will be displayed] or [the number of Page Views that will be displayed] or [the number of Clicks that will occur] or [the number of (*insert specific user actions that Advertisement is expected to generate*) that will be completed]; or [that any actual sales revenue to Advertiser will occur]]; or

[During the Term, at least (*insert number or dollar amount, as applicable*) of [Impressions; or Page Views; or Clicks; or (*insert specific user actions that Advertisement is expected to generate*); or actual gross [net] sales revenue to Advertiser from on-line purchases] [, as defined above] will [be displayed; or occur; or be generated directly from the Advertisement as evidenced by an Internet user being transferred to the Advertiser's Web Site through the Advertisement displayed on the Web Host's Web Site and subsequently completing a purchase transaction with the Advertiser] in each calendar month (the Minimum Monthly [Impressions; or Page Views; or Clicks; or User Actions; or Sales Revenue])]

[The following paragraph is optional to be added if the Services are Static Display or Random Display: The Web Host will take commercially reasonable efforts to ensure the Minimum Monthly [Impressions; or Page Views; or Clicks; or User Actions; or Sales Revenue] are met each month. If the Minimum Monthly [Impressions; or Page Views; or Clicks; or User Actions; or Sales Revenue] are not reached in any calendar month, the sole remedy of the Advertiser shall be to have the Web Host extend the term of the Agreement at no additional charge to Advertiser until the Advertisement receives the total number of [Impressions; or Page Views; or Clicks; or User Actions; or Sales Revenue], calculated by multiplying the Minimum Monthly [Impressions; or Page Views; or Clicks; or User Actions; or Sales Revenue] by the number of months in the initial Term of the Agreement.]

Web Host shall not be responsible for any problem with Advertiser's Web Site, server, computer hardware or software that was not caused by any Services performed by Web Host. Advertiser will be responsible to pay Web Host for all costs incurred for all evaluation, correction or similar services performed by Web Host relating to such problem on a time and materials basis at Web Host's then standard billing rates.

Web Host reserves the right to refuse any Advertisement that does not completely conform to every detail, instruction, method, and guideline set forth in the Web Host's written advertising specifications, a copy of which is attached as Schedule "B".

Web Host reserves the right to refuse any Advertisement that:

(i) does not arrive [fifteen] days before the Start Date, as defined in Section 13, below;

(ii) is in breach of the warranties given by Advertiser in Section 9, below;

(iii) is otherwise in Web Host's sole discretion, unacceptable or inappropriate; or

(iv) is advertising for (*insert details of products or services, e.g., gambling, tobacco, firearms, etc.*).

2. REPORTING.

To the extent possible, Web Host shall use reasonable efforts to provide the Advertiser, on a [regular/monthly] basis with usage statistics regarding the number of (*insert details upon which Fees are based, e.g., Impressions, Page Views, Clicks or User Actions*) per [month] (the Reports). The parties recognize and acknowledge, however, that the characteristics of the Internet, including without limitation caching or site mirroring by third parties, may impede Web Host's ability to gather complete usage information. Advertiser acknowledges that all information and the Reports provided by Web Host shall be subject to the confidentiality obligations of Section 8 and Advertiser shall use all such information and Reports solely for its internal business purposes.

[To the extent possible, Advertiser shall use reasonable efforts to provide the Web Host, on a [regular/monthly] basis with reports of its monthly Sales Revenue (the Reports). Web Host shall have the right [once each calendar quarter] upon reasonable prior notice to Advertiser and only during regular business hours, to [have an independent Chartered Accountant] conduct a review of Advertiser's financial records solely for the purpose of verifying the Reports for accuracy and completeness as they may apply to Fees paid or payable to the Web Host under this Agreement. Web Host acknowledges that all information it learns from and the Reports provided by Advertiser shall be subject to the confidentiality obligations of Section 8. (*insert details*)

[The Web Host shall provide Advertiser with Reports only as a courtesy to the Advertiser. Web Host makes no guarantee that Reports will be accurate. Web Host shall not be held liable for any claims as they relate to Reports.]

3. CHANGES.

The Web Host shall [not] be entitled to make changes to the Web Host's Web Site, including but not limited to the content, the format, the web pages, the order or positioning of web pages, [the specific placement or rotation of the Advertisement], [the keywords, markets, search results, categories or pages, that would trigger the Advertisement to a targeted Internet user], the Internet addresses or domain names of web pages, any advertisements or hyper-links on the Web Host's Web Site [without the prior [written] consent of the Advertiser].

The Web Host shall be entitled to make [editorial or format] modifications to the Advertisement, provided that the modifications do not [materially] change the appearance of the Advertisement.

The Advertiser may [request the Web Host to make; or supply the Web Host with][minor] modifications to the Advertisement (*if applicable insert frequency, e.g., once a month*). Any such modifications will [not] be subject to additional fees [payable at the Web Host's standard rates which are then in effect].

(*If modifications to the Advertisement by Web Host are substantial, insert terms from Form 5A*).

Such changes to the Advertisement shall be implemented (*insert timing, e.g., within x days of Web Host receiving the changes from the Advertiser*).

4. ADVERTISER'S RESPONSIBILITIES.

Advertiser will deliver [or transmit] the Advertisement to Web Host in a (*insert format details, e.g., graphics based (i.e., GIF or PCX) file or text-based (i.e. TXT) file, file size*) and stored on a (insert media, e.g., 3.5 diskette, CD, etc.) [or by on-line transmission].

The Advertisement provided by Advertiser must be viewable by standard (*or insert specific, such as Netscape Navigator Version 2.0 and Microsofts Internet Exchange Version 2.0*) web browsers [and shall contain a hyper-link to the Advertiser's Web Site.]

[Or Advertiser will post the Advertisement on Advertiser's Web Site (*or insert other location*) which Web Host can access and download.]

(*If the Advertisement is to be delivered on-line or downloaded from the Advertiser's Web Site to the Web Host, consider adding terms governing the electronic transmission. See, for example, C. Ian Kyer and Mark J. Fecenko,* Kyer and Fecenko on Computer-Related Agreements: A Practical Guide, 2nd ed. (Toronto: Butterworths, 1997), Chapter 11, EDI Trading Agreements.)

5. OWNERSHIP.

The parties acknowledge that at all times the Web Host is the owner [or licensee from Web Host's licensors], of the Web Host's Web Site, including without limitation any content on the Web Host's Web Site and the Web Host's Web Site domain name. The Advertiser is the owner [or licensee from the Advertiser's licensors] of the Advertisement, the Advertiser's Web Site, the Advertiser's Web Site domain name and all graphics, files, code, data or other materials provided by Advertiser to the Web Host under this Agreement.

The use of any trade-marks or trade names in the Advertisement shall inure to the benefit of the Advertiser.

6. LICENSE GRANT.

The Advertiser grants to the Web Host the [non-]exclusive, world-wide, royalty-free license and right to set up, reproduce, use [, modify] and publicly display the Advertisement, solely for the purposes of performing the Services under this Agreement and promoting the Advertiser's Web Site and products [and/or services]. (*If the Advertisement contains a trade-mark, insert appropriate trade-mark license terms and restrictions. See for example trade-mark controls in Section 2.4 of Form 12B. See also license terms, as set out in Section 2.2 of Form 12B).*

7. PAYMENT.

Advertiser shall pay Web Host $ (*insert amount and currency*) per [month] or $ (*insert amount and currency*) per (*insert number*) of Impressions per [month]; or $ (insert amount and currency) per Page Views per [month]; or $ (*insert amount and currency*) per (insert number) of Clicks per [month]; or $ (*insert amount and currency*) per (*insert number*) of User Actions per [month]; or Advertiser shall pay Web Host (insert percentage) % of Advertiser's Sales Revenue per [month] (the Fees).

The Fees shall be due (*insert details, e.g., number of days after the Start Date, first or last day of each month, etc.*). If the Fees are not made when due, Web Host may, in addition to any other rights or remedies available to it under this Agreement, in law or in equity, terminate this Agreement and/or remove the Advertisement from the Web Host's Web Site immediately (upon notice to Advertiser) and all Fees for Services performed up to the date of termination shall immediately become due and payable.

The Fees are exclusive [inclusive] of any and all [reasonable expenses incurred by Web Host and] applicable taxes and duties, including without limitation, PST, GST, HST and withholding taxes, with the exception of Web Host's income taxes. Web Host will have no obligation to perform any Services when any amount required to be paid by Advertiser remains due and unpaid beyond the date such amount is due.

Advertiser will pay the Fees as set forth above, without deduction, set-off, defence or counterclaim for any reason.

All outstanding fees are subject to interest equal to the lesser of (*insert percentage*) % per annum or the highest interest rate permitted by applicable law.

8. CONFIDENTIAL INFORMATION.

(This section is optional, but is recommended in the case where the parties are exchanging confidential information, such as web site user traffic, click-through rates, purchases made by customers or Sales Revenue figures.)

8.1 Confidentiality Obligations. Advertiser and Web Host shall each:

(i) hold the Confidential Information (as defined below) of the other in trust and confidence and avoid the disclosure or release thereof to any other person or entity by using the same degree of care as it uses to avoid unauthorized use, disclosure, or dissemination of its own Confidential Information of a similar nature, but not less than reasonable care; and

(ii) not use the Confidential Information of the other party for any purpose whatsoever except as expressly contemplated under this Agreement or as is necessary to perform the Services.

Each party shall disclose the Confidential Information of the other only to those of its employees or subcontractors having a need to know such Confidential Information for the performance of the Services and shall take all reasonable precautions to ensure that its employees or subcontractors comply with the provisions of this Section 8.1.

8.2 Definition. The term "Confidential Information" shall mean any and all information or proprietary materials (in every form and media) not generally known in the relevant trade or industry and which has been or is disclosed or made available by either party (the "Disclosing Party") to the other (the "Receiving Party") in connection with the efforts contemplated in this Agreement, including without limitation:

(i) all statistics of either party's web site user traffic;

(ii) sales revenues;

(iii) existing or contemplated products, services, designs, technology, processes, technical data, engineering, techniques, methodologies and concepts and any information related thereto; and

(iv) information relating to business plans, sales or marketing methods and customers or customer requirements.

8.3 Exclusion. The obligations of either party under this Section 8 will not apply to information that the Receiving Party can demonstrate:

(i) was in its possession at the time of disclosure and without restriction as to confidentiality;

(ii) at the time of disclosure is generally available to the public or after disclosure becomes generally available to the public through no breach of agreement or other wrongful act by the Receiving Party;

(iii) has been received from a third-party without restriction on disclosure and without breach of agreement by the Receiving Party;

(iv) is independently developed by the Receiving Party without regard to the Confidential Information of the other party; or

(v) is required to be disclosed by law or order of a court of competent jurisdiction or regulatory authority, provided that the Receiving Party shall furnish prompt written notice of such required disclosure and reasonably co-operate with the Disclosing Party, at the Disclosing Party's expense, in any effort made by the Disclosing Party to seek a protective order or other appropriate protection of its Confidential Information.

9. WARRANTIES.

9.1 Each party represents and warrants that their respective web sites, web pages, advertisements, links, frames, content or other material to which either of them may be associated, do not and will not:

(i) violate or infringe the rights of any third parties in any jurisdiction, including without limitation, patent, copyright, trade-mark, trade secret, privacy, publicity, confidentiality or other proprietary rights;

(ii) violate the laws, statutes or regulations of any jurisdiction;

(iii) include any material which is illegal, harmful, pornographic, abusive, hateful, obscene, threatening, racist, discriminatory or defamatory or which encourages illegal activities; and

(iv) contain links to sites displaying the type of material defined in paragraph (iii) above.

In addition, Web Host represents and warrants that:

(i) performance of the Services will be done in a competent manner by qualified personnel;

(ii) the Web Host is the owner of the web site (or other area) where the advertisement or link is displayed;

(iii) (*insert details regarding availability, up-time and speed of downloading of the Web Host's Web Site [see also Chapter 7. Similar representations and warranties can be found in the Web Site Hosting Agreement Form 7A]*);

(iv) the Web Host's web site is viewable by the currently common web browsers (*or insert specific details about browsers*);

In addition, Advertiser represents and warrants that it is the owner of the Advertisement and has the right to grant the license to the Web Host set out in Section 6, above.

10. INDEMNIFICATION.

10.1 Intellectual Property Rights Indemnity. Web Host and Advertiser (in such case, the Indemnifying Party) each agree to indemnify and hold harmless the other (in such case, the Indemnified Party) from and against any costs and damages awarded against the Indemnified Party by a court pursuant to a final judgment as a result of, and defend the Indemnified Party against, any claim of infringement of any copyright, [Canadian] patent, [Canadian] trade-mark or misappropriation of any trade secret related to: in the case of indemnification by Web Host, the Web Host's Web Site or Services; or in the case of indemnification by Advertiser, the Web Host's possession, use [or modification] of the Advertisement or other property provided by Advertiser, including without limitation any information, software, documentation or data.

10.2 Intellectual Property Rights Exclusions. Advertiser shall have no obligation under Section 10.1 or other liability for any infringement or misappropriation claim resulting or alleged to result from:

(i) use of Advertisement or other property provided by Advertiser, other than for the performance of the Services and as specified in this Agreement;

(ii) modification of the Advertisement by any person or entity, other than the Advertiser or pursuant to the Advertiser's instructions; or

(iii) Web Host continuing the allegedly infringing activity after being notified thereof or after being informed or provided with modifications that would have avoided the alleged infringement.

10.3 Infringement Remedies. In the event of an infringement or misappropriation claim as described in Section 10.1, above, arises, or if Advertiser reasonably believes that a claim is likely to be made, Advertiser may, at its option and in lieu of indemnification:

(i) modify the applicable Advertisement or other property provided by Advertiser so that it becomes non-infringing;

(ii) replace the applicable Advertisement or other property provided by Advertiser with material that is non-infringing;

(iii) obtain for the Web Host the right to use the Advertisement, if such rights can be obtained on terms satisfactory to the Advertiser; or

(iv) request that the Web Host cease using, remove [return or destroy] the infringing or violative Advertisement or other property provided by the Advertiser and terminate this Agreement.

[This Section 10 sets forth the exclusive remedy and entire liability and obligation of each party with respect to intellectual property infringement or misappropriation claims, including without limitation trade-mark or copyright infringement claims and trade secret misappropriation.]

11. DISCLAIMER.

EXCEPT AS EXPRESSLY PROVIDED IN SECTION 9, WEB HOST DOES NOT MAKE OR GIVE ANY REPRESENTATION, WARRANTY OR CONDITION OF ANY KIND, WHETHER SUCH REPRESENTATION, WARRANTY OR CONDITION BE EXPRESS OR IMPLIED, INCLUDING WITHOUT LIMITATION [WARRANTIES AS TO UNINTERRUPTED OR ERROR FREE OPERATION OF THE WEB HOST'S WEB SITE, ACCESSIBILITY, PRIVACY, SECURITY,] ANY WARRANTY OF MERCHANTABILITY, QUALITY OR FITNESS FOR A PARTICULAR PURPOSE, WHETHER STATUTORY OR COMMON LAW, OR ANY REPRESENTATION, WARRANTY OR CONDITION ARISING OUT OF A COURSE OF DEALING OR USAGE OF TRADE.

12. LIMITATION OF LIABILITY AND RELEASE.

12.1 Exclusion of Indirect Damages. Except as expressly provided herein, in no event shall either party be liable to the other party or any other person or entity for any special, exemplary, indirect, incidental, consequential or punitive damages of any kind or nature whatsoever (including, without limitation, lost revenues, profits, savings or business or contribution or indemnity in respect of any claim against the party) or loss of records or data, whether in an action based on contract, warranty, strict liability, tort (including, without limitation, negligence) or otherwise, even if such party has been informed in advance of the possibility of such damages or such damages could have been reasonably foreseen by such party.

12.2 Limitation of Liability. In no event shall either party's liability to the other party or any other person or entity arising out of or in connection with this Agreement or the Services exceed, in the aggregate, the total Fees paid by Advertiser to Web Host for the particular Services [in the preceding year] with respect to which such liability relates, whether such liability is based on an action in contract, warranty, strict liability or tort (including, without limitation, negligence) or otherwise. Web Host will not be liable for any damages claimed by Advertiser based upon any third-party claim, except for claims by Web Host's subcontractors against Advertiser relating to work performed at Web Host's request under this Agreement.

[No action arising out of or in connection with this Agreement or any of the Services provided hereunder may be brought by either party more than one (1) year after the cause of action has accrued, except that an action for non-payment of any Fees due to web host hereunder may be brought within two (2) years of the date of the termination of performance under this Agreement.]

13. TERM AND TERMINATION.

13.1 Term. The Services will be provided from (*insert date that Advertisement is scheduled to be available and accessible on the Web Host's Web Site, e.g., within x days from delivery by Advertiser of the Advertisement to Web Host in accordance with Section 4 above*) (the "Start Date") to the earlier of: (i) the termination of this Agreement as provided in this Agreement; or (ii) (*insert expiry date*) (the "Term").

13.2 Termination for Breach. In addition to other rights or remedies, this Agreement may be terminated by either party (the "Non-Breaching Party") in whole or in part upon written notice to the other party if any of the following events occur by or with respect to such other party (the "Breaching Party"):

(i) the Breaching Party commits a material breach of any of its obligations hereunder and fails to cure such breach within thirty (30) days after receipt of notice of such breach or fails to reach an agreement with the Non-Breaching Party regarding the cure thereof; or

(ii) any insolvency of the Breaching Party, any filing of a petition in bankruptcy by or against the Breaching Party, any appointment of a receiver for the Breaching Party, or any assignment for the benefit of the Breaching Party's creditors.

13. Early Termination by Advertiser. Advertiser may terminate this Agreement by giving at least (*insert number*) days prior written notice to the Web Host of the termination effective date. Advertiser shall pay all Fees incurred up to the [end of the month in which the] effective date of Termination [occurs], in accordance with Section 7.

14. SURVIVAL.

In the event of termination or upon expiration of this Agreement, Sections (*insert section numbers*) hereof will survive and continue in full force and effect.

15. FORCE MAJEURE.

Each party will be excused from delays in performing, or from its failure to perform under this Agreement to the extent and for the period that such delays or failures result from causes beyond the party's reasonable control [except payment obligations], including without limitation, acts of God, riot, embargoes, acts of governmental authorities, fire, earthquake, flood, accident, strikes (*may want to insert specific details, such as failure by Internet service provider or telecommunications provider or facilities*). Without limiting the generality of the foregoing, Advertiser acknowledges that Advertiser's failure or delay in furnishing necessary information, or delays or failure by Advertiser in completing tasks required of Advertiser or in otherwise performing Advertiser's obligations in this Agreement, will be considered an excusable delay or excusable failure to perform by Web Host and may impede or delay completion of the Services.

16. INDEPENDENT CONTRACTORS.

The parties are separate and independent legal entities. Nothing contained in this Agreement shall be deemed to constitute either Web Host or Advertiser as agent, representative, partner, joint venturer or employee of the other for any purpose. Neither party has the authority to bind the other or to incur any liability on behalf of the other, nor to direct the employees of the other.

17. GENERAL.

17.1 Governing Law. This Agreement will be governed by the laws of the Province of (*insert province*) and the federal laws of Canada and shall be treated in all respects as a (*insert province*) contract, without reference to the principles of conflicts of law. The parties agree to attorn to the non-exclusive jurisdiction of the (*insert province*) courts. The parties acknowledge and agree that this Agreement relates solely to the performance of services, not the sale of goods and, accordingly, will not be governed by the *UN Convention on Contracts for the International Sale of Goods*, and the *International Sale of Goods Act (insert name of provincial)* as amended, replaced or re-enacted from time to time. The parties have required that this agreement and all documents relating thereto be drawn-up in English. Les parties ont demandé que cette convention ainsi que tous les documents qui s'y rattachent soient rédigés en anglais.

17.2 Assignment. Neither party may assign or otherwise transfer any of its rights, duties or obligations under this Agreement without the prior written consent of the other party, except either party may, upon prior written notice to the other party, but without any obligation to obtain the consent of such other party, assign this Agreement or any of its rights hereunder to any affiliate of such party, or to any entity who succeeds, by purchase, merger, operation of law or otherwise, to all or substantially all of the capital stock, assets or business of such party, if such entity agrees in writing to assume and be bound by all of the obligations of such party under this Agreement.

[Any transfer of control of substantially all of the assets or business of Advertiser to a third-party by any means, including without limitation, stock acquisition or merger, shall be deemed to be an assignment for purposes of this Section 17.2.]

17.3 Notices. All notices required by this Agreement will be given in writing to the other party and delivered by registered mail, international air courier, facsimile, or the equivalent. Notices will be effective when received as indicated on the facsimile, registered mail, or other delivery receipt. All notices will be given by one party to the other at its address stated on the first page of this Agreement unless a change thereof previously has been given to the party giving the notice.

17.4 No Modification. This Agreement may not be modified or waived except by a written amendment executed by duly authorized officers or representatives of both parties.

17.5 Counterparts. This Agreement may be executed in several counterparts, each of which will be deemed an original, and all of which taken together will constitute one single Agreement between the parties with the same effect as if all the signatures were upon the same instrument. (*If this agreement is to be executed electronically, insert provisions in Form 11 dealing with on-line acceptance of a contract and electronic data exchange terms referred to in chapter 11 of C. Ian Kyer and Mark J. Fecenko,* Kyer and Fecenko on Computer-Related Agreements: A Practical Guide, *2nd ed. (Toronto: Butterworths, 1997).*)

17.6 Severability. If any provision in this Agreement is held by a court of competent jurisdiction to be invalid, void or unenforceable, then such provision shall be severed from this Agreement and the remaining provisions will continue in full force.

17.7 Entire Agreement. This Advertising Agreement and all Schedules attached hereto constitute the complete and exclusive statement of the agreement between the parties (the Agreement) and supersede all proposals, oral or written, and all other prior or contemporaneous communications between the parties relating to the Services, the Advertisement and the subject matter of this Agreement. In the event of any inconsistency or conflict between this Advertising Agreement and any Schedules attached hereto, the terms of this Advertising Agreement shall supersede. This Agreement shall be binding upon and enure to the benefit of the parties hereto and their respective successors and permitted assignees.

IN WITNESS WHEREOF, Web Host and Advertiser have caused this Agreement to be signed and delivered by their duly authorized officers, all as of the date first herein above written.

(*insert full legal name of Advertiser*)	(*insert full legal name of Web Host*)
Signature:______________________	Signature:____________________
Name: _______________________	Name:________________________
Title:________________________	Title:_________________________
Date:________________________	Date:_________________________

SCHEDULE "A"
HARD COPY OF ADVERTISEMENT

(not necessarily same as displayed size)

[SCHEDULE "B"
WEB HOST'S ADVERTISING SPECIFICATIONS]

FORM 12B – INTERNET LINKING AGREEMENT

THIS LINKING AGREEMENT is made between (*insert full legal name of Company*) a (*jurisdiction*) corporation with its head office located at (*insert address*) (ABC) and (*insert full legal name of Company*) a (*jurisdiction*) corporation with its head office located at (*insert address*) (XYZ) effective as of (*insert date*) Effective Date.

RECITALS:

WHEREAS, XYZ operates a Web Site, as defined below, relating to (*insert details of XYZ's products or services*) rendered in association with the trade-mark (*insert XYZ's trade-mark*) at the following URL address: http://(*insert Internet address*), which address is subject to change (XYZ's Web Site);

WHEREAS, ABC operates a Web Site identified in Schedule E hereto at the URL address listed in Schedule E, which address is subject to change (*ABC's Web Site*);

WHEREAS, ABC wishes to obtain a [graphic or text] link to XYZ's Web Site which Users of ABC's Web Site can click on or otherwise select to move to XYZ's Web Site;

WHEREAS, XYZ is willing to provide such link to XYZ's Web Site for ABC; and

WHEREAS, the parties desire to share in the advertising revenues associated with such link.

NOW THEREFORE, in consideration of the promises and mutual covenants and agreements set forth herein, the parties agree as follows:

1. DEFINITIONS

"Advertising Revenue" means, in relation to a party, the gross revenue derived from advertising placed on such party's Web Site that is invoiced by such party in a calendar quarter.

"Confidential Information" means all data and information relating to the business and management of either party, including without limitation this Agreement, any proprietary information and trade secrets, technology and accounting records to which access is obtained hereunder by the other party, and any such data and information that is furnished or disclosed by either party to the other party provided, however, that Confidential Information shall not include any data or information which:

(i) is or becomes publicly available through no fault of the party obtaining or receiving same;

(ii) is already in the rightful possession of a party prior to such party obtaining or receiving same;

(iii) is independently developed by the party receiving same;

(iv) is rightfully obtained by the party receiving same from a third-party;

(v) is disclosed with the prior written consent of the party whose information it is; or

(vi) is disclosed pursuant to court order or other legal compulsion,

provided the party making such disclosure provides prior written notice thereof to the other party to enable such other party to seek a protective order or otherwise prevent such disclosure.

"**HTML**" means the computer language commonly known as Hypertext Markup Language used in documents on the World Wide Web to indicate how Web Browsers should display such documents to the User and should respond to User actions.

"**HTTP**" means the client/server protocol commonly known as Hypertext Transfer Protocol used to access information.

"**Internet**" means the world-wide collection of computer networks and gateways that use the TCP/IP suite of protocols to communicate with one another.

"**Link**" means the Internet hyperlink to XYZ's (*insert details of XYZ's web pages*) from ABC's Web Site, as described in Schedule E.

"**Losses**" has the meaning set forth in Section 3.11.

"**ABC's Bridge Page**" means the Web Page of ABC's Web Site located at the URL identified in Schedule E.

"**ABC's Image**" means the graphic image and trade-marks set forth in Schedule B.

"**ABC's Web Site**" has the meaning set forth in the Recitals above.

"**XYZ's Database**" means XYZ's (*insert description of database that Internet users can access on XYZ's Web Site*).

"**XYZ's Image**" means the graphic image and trade-marks set forth in Schedule A, including without limitation the trade-mark (*insert XYZ's trade-mark*).

"**XYZ's Search Pages**" means the Web Pages of XYZ's Web Site located at URL address: http:// (*insert Internet address*) providing the functionality of a search of XYZ's Database.

"**XYZ's Web Site**" has the meaning set forth in the Recitals above.

"**User**" means a person on the Internet using a Web Browser or other facility to view the World Wide Web.

"**Web Browser**" means software that enables a User to view documents on the World Wide Web, to follow hyper-links among them, or to transfer files to and from Web Sites.

"**Web Page**" means a document or file that is formatted using HTML and that is intended to be accessible by Users with a Web Browser.

"**Web Site**" means a series of interconnected Web Pages; and

"**World Wide Web**" means all of the interlinked hypertext documents residing on HTTP compliant servers on the Internet.

2. XYZ'S OBLIGATIONS

2.1 Access. Provided that ABC is in compliance with the terms of this Agreement, XYZ shall permit Users of the Link to access XYZ's Web Site subject to the terms of XYZ's Database and/or software licenses.

2.2 Image License. Subject to the terms of this Agreement, XYZ grants to ABC a non-exclusive, world-wide, royalty-free license to reproduce and publicly display XYZ's Image on ABC's Bridge Page and frames (surrounding XYZ's Search Pages) solely for the purposes of providing the Link and accessing and promoting XYZ's Web Site. [*Note to Draft: Any use/marketing on other pages or off-site?*] This license is also subject to the quality control provisions of Section 3.3. ABC may, with the prior written approval of XYZ, display XYZ's Search Pages within a frame on ABC's Web Site. ABC shall not otherwise use XYZ's Image without XYZ's prior written consent, which consent may be withheld for any reason. XYZ shall provide ABC with a copy of XYZ's Image in (*insert details*) format.

2.3 Ownership. The parties acknowledge that at all times XYZ is the owner of XYZ's Image and the use of any trade-marks or trade names therein shall inure to the benefit of XYZ. Any and all graphics, code, data or other materials provided by XYZ to ABC under this Agreement shall be owned by XYZ.

2.4 Quality Control. XYZ shall place ABC's Image on XYZ's Search Pages to which the Link connects, in the same script colour and typeface specified in Schedule B and shall place ABC's Image at the location specified in Schedule B so that ABC's Image is immediately visible by a User when loaded into the Web Browser on a standard VGA monitor at 640 by 480 resolution when the Web Browser is running in full screen configuration. In such configuration, ABC's Image shall not be less than the size described in Schedule B. ABC's Image shall be visible by the User when the User first loads XYZ's Search Pages through the Link. The placement and size of ABC's Image on XYZ's Search Pages, as well as the content and organization of such XYZ's Search Pages, shall be subject to the prior and continuous review and approval of ABC. This Agreement shall be conditional upon such approval being provided by ABC to XYZ. In the event ABC does not provide its approval as aforesaid, this Agreement shall for all purposes be void and of no effect whatever. The foregoing condition has been stipulated for the sole benefit of ABC, and may be waived by ABC at its entire discretion without the consent or approval of XYZ. ABC shall also have the right, at all times during the term of this Agreement, to review and control the use of ABC's image by XYZ and to request XYZ to implement any changes to ABC's Image and/or XYZ's Search Pages to which such Link is connected and XYZ shall at all times comply with such request(s).

2.5 User Information (Quarterly Reports). To the extent permissible by law, XYZ shall, within thirty (30) days after the end of each calendar quarter during the term of this Agreement, deliver a report to ABC showing the Advertising Revenue collected during such calendar quarter from advertisements on XYZ's Search Pages upon which ABC's Image was placed and a computation of the payment due to ABC, pursuant to Section 4.

2.6 Sale of Advertising. Subject to the revenue sharing provisions of Section 4, XYZ shall have the right to sell banner advertising space on XYZ's Search Pages upon which ABC's Image is placed provided, however that XYZ shall not sell such banner advertising to the competitors of ABC specified on Schedule E. The price at which such advertising space is sold shall be determined solely by XYZ.

2.7 Representations and Warranties. XYZ represents, warrants and covenants that on the Effective Date and at all times during the term of the Agreement:

(a) XYZ has the right to enter into this Agreement, and this Agreement does not conflict with any other agreement or obligation by which XYZ is bound;

(b) [to the best of XYZ's knowledge,] XYZ's Web Site does not violate the rights of any third parties in any jurisdiction, including without limitation, patent, copyright, trade-mark, trade secret, privacy, publicity or other proprietary rights; and

(c) [to the best of XYZ's knowledge,] XYZ's Web Site does not violate the laws, statutes, or regulations of any jurisdiction.

2.8 DISCLAIMER OF OTHER WARRANTIES. EXCEPT AS EXPRESSLY PROVIDED HEREIN, XYZ'S WEB SITE, XYZ'S SEARCH PAGES, XYZ'S DATABASE, XYZ'S IMAGE AND THE LINK ARE PROVIDED AS IS AND WITHOUT WARRANTY OR CONDITION OF ANY KIND. XYZ GIVES NO REPRESENTATIONS, WARRANTIES OR CONDITIONS OF ANY KIND, EXPRESS OR IMPLIED, INCLUDING WITHOUT LIMITATION WARRANTIES AS TO UNINTERRUPTED OR ERROR FREE OPERATION, ACCESSIBILITY, PRIVACY, SECURITY, MERCHANTABILITY, QUALITY OR FITNESS FOR A PARTICULAR PURPOSE, WHETHER ARISING BY STATUTE OR OTHERWISE, OR FROM A COURSE OF DEALING OR USAGE OF TRADE.

2.9 Indemnification. XYZ agrees to defend, indemnify, and hold harmless ABC, its officers, directors, employees and agents, from and against any claims, actions, or demands, including without limitation reasonable legal and accounting fees, alleging or resulting from the breach of the Warranties in Section 2.7. ABC shall provide notice to XYZ promptly of any such claim, suit, or proceeding and shall assist XYZ, at XYZ's expense, in defending any such claim, suit, or proceeding.

2.10 Usage Information. To the extent possible, XYZ shall use reasonable efforts to provide ABC on a regular basis with usage statistics regarding the number of searches performed by Users of XYZ's Search Pages who used the Link from ABC's Web Site. The parties recognize and acknowledge, however, that the characteristics of the Internet (including caching or site mirroring by third parties) may impede XYZ's ability to gather complete usage information. ABC acknowledges that all information provided by XYZ shall be subject to the confidentiality obligations of Section 6 and ABC shall use all such information solely for its internal business purposes.

2.11 Development of Bridge Page. Subject to Sections 2.3 and 2.12 and the terms of Schedule E, at the request of ABC, XYZ shall develop ABC's Bridge Page. (*Insert standard Web Page Design Terms, such as specifications, acceptance testing, modifications, etc. See Web-Site Design Contract, Form 5A*)

2.12 Retention of Rights. Except as expressly licensed in Section 2.2 of this Agreement, XYZ retains all rights in XYZ's Web Site, XYZ's Search Pages, XYZ's Database, XYZ's Image, XYZ's trade-marks, copyrights, and other intellectual property rights.

3. ABC'S OBLIGATIONS

3.1 Establishment of Link. ABC shall establish the Link onto ABC's Bridge Page.

3.2 Image License. Subject to the terms of this Agreement, ABC grants to XYZ a non-exclusive, world-wide, royalty-free license to reproduce and publicly display ABC's Image on XYZ's Search Pages. This license is also subject to the quality control provisions of Section 2.4. XYZ shall not otherwise use ABC's Image without ABC's prior written consent, which consent may be withheld for any reason. ABC shall provide XYZ with a copy of ABC's Image in ____format.

3.3 Quality Control. ABC shall place XYZ's Image on ABC's Bridge Page in the same script colour and typeface specified in Schedule A and shall place XYZ's image at the location specified in Schedule A so that XYZ's Image is immediately visible by a User when loaded into the Web Browser on a standard VGA monitor at 640 by 480 resolution when the Web Browser is running in full screen configuration. In such configuration, XYZ's Image shall not be less than the size described in Schedule A. XYZ's Image shall be visible by the User when the User first loads ABC's Bridge Page. ABC's Bridge Page shall contain a legend in the following terms: (*insert XYZ's trade-mark*) is a registered trade-mark *of (insert name of XYZ*) used under licence by (*insert name of ABC*) The placement and size of XYZ's Image on ABC's Bridge Page, as well as the content and organization of ABC's Web Site and frames, shall be subject to the prior and continuous review and approval of XYZ. This Agreement shall be conditional upon such approval being provided by XYZ to ABC. In the event XYZ does not provide its approval as aforesaid, this Agreement shall for all purposes be void and of no effect whatever. The foregoing condition has been stipulated for the sole benefit of XYZ, and may be waived by XYZ at its entire discretion without the consent or approval of ABC. XYZ shall also have the right, at all times during the term of this Agreement, to review and control the use of XYZ's image by ABC and to request ABC to implement any changes to XYZ's image and/or ABC's Bridge Page, frames, links or other portions of ABC's Web Site and ABC shall at all times comply with such request(s).

3.4 User Information. To the extent permissible by law, ABC shall, within thirty (30) days after the end of each calendar quarter during the term of this Agreement, deliver a report to XYZ showing the Advertising Revenue collected during such calendar quarter from ABC's Bridge Page and frames, upon which the Link and/or XYZ's Image was placed and a computation of the payment due to XYZ, pursuant to Section 4.

3.5 Ownership. The parties acknowledge that at all times ABC is the owner of ABC's Image and the use of any trade-marks or trade names therein shall inure to the benefit of ABC. Any and all graphics, code, data or other materials provided by ABC to XYZ under this Agreement shall be owned by ABC.

3.6 Sale of Advertising. Subject to the revenue sharing provisions of Section 4, ABC shall have the right to sell banner advertising space on ABC's Bridge Pages or on the frame within which XYZ's Search Pages are displayed, provided, however that ABC shall not sell banner advertising to the competitors of XYZ specified in Schedule E. The price at which such advertising space is sold shall be determined solely by ABC.

3.7 ABC's Web Site Content. ABC acknowledges that this Agreement and the license granted in Section 2.2 were made based on the content and organization of ABC's Web Site on the Effective Date. Without limiting any other of XYZ's rights or remedies, XYZ may terminate the Agreement in accordance with Section 7.1 if ABC materially alters the content or structure of ABC's Web Site, Bridge Page, frames or links. ABC shall give notice to XYZ of any material change in the content or structure of ABC's Web Site, Bridge Page, frames or links.

3.8 Representations and Warranties. ABC represents, warrants and covenants that on the Effective Date and at all times during the term of the Agreement:

(a) ABC has the right to enter into this Agreement and this Agreement does not and will not conflict with any other agreement or obligation by which ABC is or shall be bound;

(b) ABC's Web Site, ABC's Bridge Page, links and frames do not and will not violate the rights of any third parties in any jurisdiction, including without limitation, patent, copyright, trade-mark, trade secret, privacy, publicity or other proprietary rights;

(c) ABC's Web Site, ABC's Bridge Page, links and frames do not and will not violate the laws, statutes or regulations of any jurisdiction;

(d) ABC's Web Site, ABC's Bridge Page, links and frames do not and will not include any material which is harmful, pornographic, abusive, hateful, obscene, threatening, or defamatory or which encourages illegal activities or racism or promotes software or services which deliver unsolicited E-mail; and

(e) ABC's Web Site, ABC's Bridge Page, links and frames do not and will not contain links to sites displaying the type of material defined in Section 3.8(d).

3.9 Uptime, Linking and Compatibility Requirements.

(a) ABC acknowledges that the availability of ABC's Web Site to Users is important for maximizing Advertising Revenues. Consequently, ABC agrees to use reasonable commercial efforts to make ABC's Web Site available to Users twenty-four (24) hours each day, seven (7) days per week.

(b) On the Effective Date, ABC's Web Site is linked to the Web Sites listed in Schedule C. ABC agrees to give notice to XYZ of other Web Sites that have a hyper-link to ABC's Web Site within thirty (30) days after the end of the calendar month in which such hyper-link is established.

(c) ABC shall ensure that ABC's Web Site can be viewed without modification by the Web Browsers listed in Schedule D. This obligation may be met by having an alternative version of ABC's Web Site.

3.10 Responsibility of ABC and Indemnity. ABC agrees to adhere to all local, provincial/state, federal and international laws including but not limited to those laws regarding:

(a) court ordered publication bans;

(b) restrictions on publishing, printing, distributing, possessing, selling, advocating, promoting or exposing, obscene or threatening material, child pornography, or hate propaganda and ABC understands that these situations could generate criminal liability;

(c) restrictions on the use of trade-marks, trade names or on the use any work which is protected by copyright, trade secrets, patents or other intellectual property laws, including without limitation, software;

(d) restrictions on defamation, libel, harm to reputation, invasion of privacy, misuse or failure to protect personal information, violation of secrecy, confidentiality, unfair competition and other situations which could generate liability; and

(e) export and import restrictions.

ABC agrees to be solely responsible for the design of ABC's Web Site, ABC's Bridge Page, any frames and the implications of linking to and from the foregoing and any and all items, statements or other content transmitted, posted, received or created through ABC's Web Site, Bridge Page, frames and links even if transmitted, posted, received or created by someone else, and ABC agrees to defend, indemnify and hold XYZ, its directors, officers, employees, agents, contractors and affiliates, harmless from any Losses which may result therefrom.

3.11 Intellectual Property Indemnification. ABC agrees to indemnify XYZ, its directors, officers, agents, subcontractors and affiliates and hold them harmless from any and all damages, losses or expenses (including without limitation, punitive damages, court costs, arbitration fees, penalties, fines, amounts paid in settlement of claims, reasonable legal fees and expenses of investigation) (hereinafter referred to as the Losses) which XYZ, its directors, officers, agents, subcontractors or affiliates, may incur, suffer or become liable for as a result of, or in connection with, any claim asserted against XYZ to the extent such claim is based upon a contention that ABC's Web Site, ABC's Bridge Page, any frames, the link(s), and all items, statements or other content transmitted, posted, received or created through ABC's Web Site, even if transmitted, posted, received or created by someone else, or any portion thereof, infringes any patents, copyrights, trade secrets, trade-marks or other intellectual property rights of any third-party, provided that XYZ has notified ABC in writing of such claim.

3.12 Retention of Rights. Except as otherwise expressly provided under this Agreement, ABC retains all rights in ABC's Web Site, trade-marks, copyrights and other intellectual property rights.

4. REVENUE SHARING

4.1 Revenue Sharing. ABC shall pay XYZ the percentage specified in Schedule E of ABC's Advertising Revenue generated by the sale of banner advertising on ABC's Bridge Page (or in the frame surrounding ABC's Bridge Page or XYZ's Search Pages) upon which the Link was placed on XYZ's Image displayed. XYZ shall pay ABC the percentage specified in Schedule E of XYZ's Advertising Revenue generated by the sale of banner advertising on XYZ's Search Pages, provided, however, that ABC acknowledges that currently the placement of banner advertising on XYZ's Search Pages is technologically limited to a static banner advertisement on the first page of each function. Each party shall be responsible for payment of all taxes and duties applicable to its respective percentage of Advertising Revenue received.

4.2 Payment Schedule. Each party shall make such payments within thirty (30) days of the end of each calendar quarter for the Advertising Revenue invoiced during such calendar quarter.

4.3 Records. Each of the parties agrees to keep accurate books of account and records at its principal place of business covering all Advertising Revenues and associated commissions. Upon reasonable notice of not less than seven (7) business days, but in no event more than once per year (unless the immediately preceding audit showed a material underpayment), either party shall have the right, subject to suitable confidentiality measures, to cause an independent accountant to inspect those portions of the books of account and records which relate to the percentage of Advertising owed to the other party, to confirm that the correct amount owing under Section 4.1 has been paid. Each party shall maintain such books of account and records which support each statement for at least two years after the termination or expiration of this Agreement or after the final payment made by such party to the other, whichever is later.

5. LIMITATIONS ON LIABILITY

5.1 IN NO EVENT SHALL XYZ, ITS DIRECTORS, OFFICERS, EMPLOYEES, AGENTS, CONTRACTORS OR AFFILIATES, BE LIABLE FOR ANY CLAIM FOR: (A) PUNITIVE, EXEMPLARY, OR AGGRAVATED DAMAGES; (B) DAMAGES FOR LOSS OF PROFITS OR REVENUE, FAILURE TO REALIZE EXPECTED SAVINGS, LOSS OF USE OR LACK OF AVAILABILITY OF ABC'S OR THIRD-PARTY MATERIALS OR FACILITIES, INCLUDING WITHOUT LIMITATION, BRIDGE PAGES, LINKS, FRAMES, COMPUTER RESOURCES, WEB SITES, CONTENT AND ANY STORED DATA; (C) INDIRECT, CONSEQUENTIAL OR SPECIAL DAMAGES EVEN IF ADVISED OF THE POSSIBILITY OF SAME; (D) CONTRIBUTION, INDEMNITY OR SET-OFF IN RESPECT OF ANY CLAIMS AGAINST ABC; (E) ANY DAMAGES WHATSOEVER RELATING TO THIRD-PARTY PRODUCTS OR SERVICES, LINKS, SOFTWARE OR WEB SITES; (F) ANY DAMAGES WHATSOEVER RELATING TO ABC'S WEB SITES, FRAMES, LINKS, PRODUCTS, SERVICES OR SOFTWARE; OR (G) ANY DAMAGES WHATSOEVER RELATING TO INTERRUPTION, DELAYS, ERRORS OR OMISSIONS.

5.2 WITHOUT LIMITING THE FOREGOING, THE MAXIMUM TOTAL LIABILITY OF XYZ, ITS DIRECTORS, OFFICERS, EMPLOYEES, AGENTS, CONTRACTORS AND AFFILIATES, FOR ANY CLAIM WHATSOEVER, INCLUDING WITHOUT LIMITATION, CLAIMS FOR BREACH OF CONTRACT, TORT (INCLUDING WITHOUT LIMITATION, NEGLIGENCE) OR OTHERWISE, AND ABC'S SOLE REMEDY SHALL BE AN AWARD FOR DIRECT AND PROVABLE DAMAGES NOT TO EXCEED $10,000 CANADIAN.

5.3 THIS SECTION 5 SHALL SURVIVE THE TERMINATION OR EXPIRY OF THIS AGREEMENT.

6. CONFIDENTIALITY

6.1 Each of XYZ and ABC shall use reasonable efforts (and, in any event, that are no less than the efforts used to protect its own Confidential Information) to protect from disclosure such information that is the Confidential Information of the other. Each of XYZ and ABC shall divulge such Confidential Information only to its employees, agents or lawyers or accountants who require access to it for the purposes of this Agreement or as otherwise provided in this Agreement.

6.2 Each of XYZ and ABC (the "Indemnifying Party") agree to indemnify the other (the "Indemnified Party") for all Losses incurred by the Indemnified Party as a result of a failure of the Indemnifying Party to comply with its obligations under this Section 6.1 provided that the Indemnified Party has given prompt notice of any such claim and, to the extent that a claim may lie against a third-party for the unauthorized disclosure of such Confidential Information, the right to control and direct the investigation, preparation, action and settlement of each such claim and, further, provided that the Indemnified Party reasonably cooperates with the Indemnifying Party in connection with the foregoing and provides the Indemnifying Party with all information in the Indemnified Party's possession related to such claim and such further assistance as reasonably requested by the Indemnifying Party.

6.3 This Article 6 shall survive the termination of this Agreement.

7. TERMINATION

7.1 Term and Termination for Breach. The initial term of this Agreement will be for the period specified in Schedule E from the Effective Date and will automatically renew for 30-day periods thereafter unless terminated by either party. Either party may terminate this Agreement:

(a) after the initial term for any reason on thirty (30) days prior written notice or

(b) at any time in the event of a material breach by the other party that has not been cured within fifteen (15) days written notice thereof.

Upon termination, each party shall promptly return to the other all of the Confidential Information and proprietary materials of the other party in its possession or control.

(a) ABC acknowledges that XYZ may terminate this Agreement if the content or structure of ABC's Web Site changes materially, upon fifteen (15) days prior written notice, unless ABC removes the material to which XYZ objects or revises ABC's Web Site to return to the original format.

(b) This Agreement may be terminated by a party immediately, without notice:

(i) upon the institution by or against the other party of insolvency, receivership, or bankruptcy proceedings or any other proceedings for the settlement of the other party's debts;

(ii) upon the other party making an assignment for the benefit of creditors; or

(iii) upon the other party's dissolution.

8. MISCELLANEOUS PROVISIONS

8.1 Notices. Any notice, demand or other communication (in this section, a "notice") required or permitted to be given or made under this Agreement and shall be sufficiently given or made if:

(a) delivered in writing and in person during normal business hours on a Business Day and left with a receptionist or other responsible employee of the relevant party at the applicable address set forth below;

(b) sent by prepaid first class mail; or

(c) sent by any electronic means of sending messages, including e-mail or facsimile transmission, which produces a hard copy confirmation ("Electronic Transmission") during normal business hours on a Business Day charges prepaid [and confirmed by prepaid first class mail];

in the case of a notice to XYZ, addressed to it at:

[Address]

Attention: ______________________

Fax No.: ______________________

E-mail: ______________________

with a copy to: ______________________

Address: ______________________

and in the case of a notice to ABC, addressed to it at:

[Address]

Attention: ______________________

Fax No.: ______________________

E-mail: ______________________

with a copy to: ______________________

Address: ______________________

Each notice sent in accordance with this section shall be deemed to have been received:

(a) if delivered, on the day it was delivered;

(b) if mailed, on the fifth Business Day after it was mailed (excluding each Business Day during which there existed any general interruption of postal services due to strike, lockout or other cause); or

(c) on the same day that it was sent by Electronic Transmission, or on the first Business Day thereafter if the day on which it was sent by Electronic Transmission was not a Business Day.

Any party may change its address for notice by giving notice to the other parties as provided in this Section.

8.2 Waiver and Amendments. This Agreement may not be modified unless agreed to in writing by both ABC and XYZ. Any consent to or waiver by a party of a breach by the other party, shall not constitute a consent to or waiver of or excuse for any such breach, or for any other or subsequent breach unless such waiver or consent is in writing and signed by the party claimed to have waived or consented. Except as otherwise provided herein, no term or provision hereof shall be deemed waived and no breach excused.

8.3 Assignment. Neither this Agreement nor any rights or obligations hereunder, in whole or in part, may be assigned by ABC without the prior written consent of XYZ. This Agreement shall inure to the benefit of and be binding upon each of ABC and XYZ and their respective successors and permitted assigns.

8.4 Governing Law. This Agreement is governed by and shall be interpreted in accordance with the laws of the Province of Ontario and the federal laws of Canada. The parties submit to the non-exclusive jurisdiction of the Courts of Ontario. The Parties hereby expressly exclude the application of the *United Nations Convention on Contracts for the International Sale of Goods*, and the *International Sale of Goods Act* (Ontario) as amended, replaced or re-enacted from time to time. The parties have required that this agreement and all documents relating thereto be drawn up in English. Les parties ont demandé que cette convention ainsi que tous les documents qui s'y rattachent soient rédigés en anglais.

8.5 Execution. This Agreement may be validly executed by means of transmission of signed facsimile thereof (*if this agreement is to be executed electronically, insert provisions in Form 11 dealing with on-line acceptance of a contract and electronic data exchange terms referred to in Chapter 11 of C. Ian Kyer and Mark J. Fecenko,* Kyer and Fecenko on Computer-Related Agreements: A Practical Guide, *2nd ed. (Toronto: Butterworths, 1997)*.)

8.6 Severability. If any part of this Agreement is held to be unenforceable or invalid, it will be severed from the rest of this Agreement, which shall continue in full force and effect.

8.7 Force Majeure. XYZ shall have no obligation to perform under this agreement to the extent and for the period that XYZ is prevented from doing so by reason of any cause beyond its reasonable control, including without limitation the inability to use or the failure of any third-party telecommunications carrier or other services.

8.8 Independent Contractors. The parties are separate and independent legal entities. Nothing contained in this Agreement shall be deemed to constitute either XYZ or ABC as agent, representative, partner, joint venturer or employee of the other for any purpose. Neither party has the authority to bind the other or to incur any liability on behalf of the other, nor to direct the employees of the other.

8.9 Survival. The obligations, representations, warranties and indemnities in Sections 2.3, 2.8, 2.12, 3.5, 3.8, 3.10, 3.11, 3.12, 5 and 6 shall survive termination or expiry of this Agreement.

8.10 Entire Agreement. This Agreement and any Schedules or other documents referred to herein constitute the entire agreement between the parties relating to the subject matter herein and supersedes all prior written or oral agreements, representations and other communications between the parties.

IN WITNESS WHEREOF, this Agreement is executed as of the Effective Date set forth above.

(insert full legal name of XYZ)		*(insert full legal name of ABC)*	
By:	____________________	By:	____________________
Name:	____________________	Name:	____________________
Title:	____________________	Title:	____________________

SCHEDULE "A"
XYZ'S IMAGE

(Insert XYZ's Image)

(insert XYZ's trade-mark) is a registered trade-mark of, used under license by (*insert full legal name of ABC*).

XYZ'S IMAGE SPECIFICATIONS

Location: *(insert details, e.g., top right corner of ABC's Bridge Page)*

Size: *(insert details, e.g., _____ pixels by _____ pixels)*

SCHEDULE "B"
ABC'S IMAGE

(Insert ABC's Image)

ABC'S IMAGE SPECIFICATIONS

Location: *(insert details, e.g., top right corner of ABC's Bridge Page)*

Size: *(insert details, e.g., _____ pixels by _____ pixels)*

SCHEDULE "C"
LIST OF LINKS TO ABC'S WEB SITE

(Insert list of hyper-links)

SCHEDULE "D"
WEB BROWSERS

(Insert list of web browsers)

SCHEDULE "E"
ADDITIONAL TERMS

1. ABC's Web Site:

   URL: *(insert Internet address)*

   Bridge Page URL: *(insert Internet address)*

2. Revenue Sharing Formulas: *(insert details of formulas)*

3. Term of Agreement: *(insert term)*

4. Competitors of XYZ: *(insert list of competitors)*

5. Competitors of ABC: *(insert list of competitors)*

6. ABC's Bridge Page Development Terms:

(Insert terms similar to those found in the Web Site and Content Development contract, See Chapter 5 Form 5A)

GLOSSARY

Absolute Link. See *Hyper-Link.*

ActiveX means a type of object-oriented program. See also *Java Applet.*

ADSL. See *Asymmetric Digital Subscriber Line.*

Algorithm means a mathematical function, procedure or formula. Computer software is an elaborate algorithm.

Analog means the technology used to transmit *Data* as electronic signals of varying volume (amplitude) and pitch (frequency of wave change) that are added to carrier waves of a given frequency.

Anchor. See *Hyper-Link.*

Applet means a small software application. Applets are often embedded software in a *Web Site* and used to retrieve *Data* from a *Server.* See also *Java Applet.*

Application Service Provider (ASP) means *Host* of computer software. An ASP runs software on its *Servers,* usually for a fee, and provides the service of permitting access to the software or *Data* processing to others who do not have the software. A *Web Site Host* is also a type of ASP, that *Hosts* a *Web Site* for *Internet Users* to be able to access and view.

ASP. See *Application Service Provider.*

Asymmetric Digital Subscriber Line (ADSL) means a digital subscriber line that provides continuous asymmetric transmission, meaning more information flowing one way, i.e., down to the *Internet User* than up from the *Internet User,* which is common with multimedia.

B2B means business to business.

B2C means business to consumer.

Backbone means a large *Data* transmission line or set of lines that span long distances and carry *Data* gathered from smaller lines or local *Networks* that are connected to it.

Bandwidth is a term commonly used to describe how fast *Data* flows. In *Digital* systems, bandwidth is expressed in *bits per second*. In analog systems, bandwidth is expressed in terms of the width of a range of electromagnetic frequencies that an electronic signal occupies or hertz.

Binary means a numbering scheme in which there are only two possible values for each digit (the weight of which increases by powers of 2, rather than by powers of 10): 0 and 1.

Bit means a *Binary* digit and it is the smallest unit of *Data* in a computer. A Bit has a single *Binary* value, either 0 or 1.

Bits Per Second (BPS) means the number of *Bits* of *Data* transmitted or received each second. It is a common measure of *Data* speed for computer modems and transmission carriers.

Bps. See *Bits Per Second*.

Bridge means a connection between computers or *Networks* that use the same *Protocol*.

Browser means the software that enables an *Internet User* to view documents on the *World Wide Web*, to follow *Hyper-Links* among them, or to transfer files to and from *Web Sites*.

Bulletin Board System (BBS) means an interactive *Host* computer accessible by dial-up phone and used for sharing or exchanging messages or other files between users. See also *Chat Room*.

Cache means temporary storage of *Data*.

Canadian Internet Registration Authority (CIRA) means the not-for-profit corporation that is responsible for the administration of .ca *Domain Names*.

Certification Authority means the entity or *Trusted Third Party* (*TTP*) that maintains records of private and public *Keys* or *Algorithms*, for identifying, encrypting, decoding and authenticating electronic documents and their authors.

Chat Room means an interactive *Web Page* used for sharing or exchanging messages or other files with other *Internet Users*. See also *Bulletin Board*.

CIRA. See *Canadian Internet Registration Authority*.

Client means the requesting computer, program or user in a *Client/Server Relationship*. A Client is often a local computer, or *personal computer* that is connected to a *Network*.

Client/Server Relationship means the relationship between two computers or programs in which one computer or program, the *Client*, makes a service request from another computer or program, the *Server*, which fulfills the request. This relationship is common on a *Network*.

Closed System is another word used to describe a private *Network* or *Intranet*.

Content means the *Data*, files and embedded software (including *Hyper-Links*) on a *Web Site*, which result in the display and hearing by *Internet Users* of text, video, pictures, sound or other multimedia. The Content may be embedded directly into a *Web Site*, or it may be retrieved indirectly via a *Hyper-Link* from another *Web Site*, *Web Page*, database or file source. Content may be visible to *Internet Users* or it may be transparent, as in the case of *Java Applets* or other embedded software that retrieve *Data* from a *Server*.

Content Provider means a supplier of *Content*. A Content Provider may act as a service provider providing access to *Content* to customers who have subscribed to the Content Provider's service; license *Content* to customers for use on customers' *Web Sites*; or may develop *Content* specifically for a particular customer and transfer ownership of all intellectual property rights in the *Content* to such customer.

Context and Marketplace Providers mean providers of *Web Sites* or Portals (*including Web Site* owners, e-malls, on-line exchanges and auctions) which businesses and consumers can access via the *Internet* in order to enter into transactions among themselves.

Cookies are *Data* files that store various types of information and that are put into an *Internet User's* computer when the *Internet User* visits a *Web Site*. See also *Passport* and *Shopping Cart*.

CRM means Customer Relations Management. A CRM provider acts as a *Host* in running software on its *Servers* to process customer *Data* for businesses. They may also provide additional customer relations services as an *Outsourcer* for businesses, such as help desks for customer questions or service.

Data means information that has been converted into a form that is more convenient to transmit or process, such as *Analog*, *Binary* or *Digital* form.

Digital means the electronic technology that generates, stores, and processes *Data* in terms of two states: positive or "high" and non-positive or "low". Positive is represented by the number 1 and non-positive by the number 0.

Digital Signature means a cryptographic transformation of *Data* that, when associated with an electronic file or other *Data* unit, can confirm both the origin and the integrity of the *Data.*

Digital Subscriber Line (DSL) means a technology used on existing *Analog* (voice) phone lines to provide for transmission of large amounts of *Digital* information at a high *Bandwidth.* With a DSL, *Digital Data* does not require a modem to change it into *Analog* form and back.

DNS. See *Domain Name System.*

Domain Name means an alphanumeric *Internet* address that is assigned to a binary *IP* address through the process of registering for the service with a domain name registration authority, such as *CIRA.*

Domain Name Registration Authority means an entity that is responsible for the administration of *Domain* Names, such as *CIRA* in Canada.

Domain Name System (DNS) means a system that gives computers and *Web Sites* on the *Internet* alphanumeric addresses, much like postal addresses, known as *Domain Names* or *Uniform Resource Locators* (*URLs*).

DSL. See *Digital Subscriber Line.*

e-Commerce means commercial activity (such as the delivery of information, products, services, or payments) using computer systems, information technology and communications. More narrowly, e-Commerce is business to consumer (*B2C*) and business to business (*B2B*) transactions conducted over computer *Networks,* whether public (such as the *Internet*) or private *Networks.*

EDI. See *Electronic Data Interchange.*

Electronic Data Interchange (EDI) means a format for exchanging business *Data.*

Embedded Link or **In-Line Link** means a hidden *Hyper-Link* containing code that automatically performs a function as soon as a *Web Page* is loaded, such as the display of graphic images or information being stored in files on a *server* or another data base, without any action on behalf of the *Internet User.*

Enabler means a service provider that assists with the processing of *e-Commerce* transactions and helps to minimize the risks of e-contracting

Exchange. See *Portal.*

Extranet means an *Intranet* that is set up external to an organization, to allow access to only those *Internet Users* outside the organization who have been given access, usually by paying a fee, to subscribe to the information contained on the Extranet, and excluding non-subscribers from access.

File Transfer Protocol (FTP) means a *Protocol* that was created in the 1970s to increase file-sharing between multiple users and is still in use today.

FTP. See *File Transfer Protocol.*

Gateway means a point on a *Network* that acts as an entrance or control point to another *Network*, computer or program.

Header means, in general, something that goes in front of something and is usually repeated as a standard part of the units of the thing.

High-speed Backbone means a *Network* that interconnects a number of *Backbones.*

Homepage means the first *Web Page* of a *Web Site*, which *Web Page* usually acts as the introduction to the *Web Site* and should contain the legal terms and disclaimers.

Host means either: (1) a *Server* that serves software such as the *Web Pages* for a *Web Site;* or (2) the entity that provides *Web Site* or software hosting services (see also *ASP, CRM* and *Outsourcer*).

HTML means the computer language commonly known as *Hypertext Markup Language*. It is used in the programing of *Web Pages* and *Web Sites* to indicate how *Browsers* should display *Data* and files to *Internet Users*, and how to run embedded software and respond to *Internet User* actions.

HTTP means the *Client/Server* Protocol commonly known as Hypertext Transfer Protocol used to exchange information or files.

Hub means a central place where *Data* comes together from many directions and, through the use of a *Switch* or *Router*, is forwarded out to other directions.

Hyper-Link means an *HTML* code embedded into a *Web Site* that directs a *Browser* to retrieve information from another location either on the same *Web Server* (known as a *"Relative Link"*) or on an external *Web Server* (known as an *"Absolute Link"*). Hyper-Links must generally be activated by the *Internet User* by clicking on an icon, highlighted or underlined text (any of which is referred to as an *Anchor*) that is displayed on the *Client* screen by the *Browser*. However, sometimes, Hyper-Linking occurs seamlessly with the *Browser*, such as in the case of advertisements or *Content* displayed on a *Web Site* using *Embedded Links* or *In-Line Links*.

Hypertext Markup Language. See *HTML*.

Hypertext Transfer Protocol. See *HTTP*.

ICP. See *Internet Content Provider*.

In-Line Link. See *Embedded Link*.

Integrated Services Digital Network. See *ISDN*.

Internet means the publicly available world wide *Network* of computers that communicate with each other, also referred to as the net, *World Wide Web* or sometimes an *Extranet*.

Internet Content Provider means a *Content Provider* for *Web Sites*.

Internet Service Provider (ISP) means a service provider that sells connections to various telecommunications systems and high-speed backbones that link the worldwide *Network* of computers. An ISP provides more services than just access to the *Internet*. It usually offers services such as *Bulletin Boards, Chat Rooms,* or indexed databases.

Internet User means a person on the *Internet*.

Intranet means a private *Network* of computers in a closed system.

IP Address means a 32-Bit[1] number in the form of a series of numbers separated by periods (dots) that identifies the physical point on the *Internet* of each sender

---

1 The new *Internet Protocol* Version 6 (also called Next Generation Internet Protocol or IPng) will lengthen *IP Addresses* from 32 Bits to 128 Bits. IPv6 is a set of specifications made as a draft standard on August 10, 1998, by the Internet Engineering Task Force (IETF), the body that defines standard Internet operating protocol and is supervised by the Internet Society, an

or receiver of information that is sent in a *Packet* across the *Internet*. Each *Web Site* on the *Internet* has an IP Address.

ISDN means Integrated Services Digital Network and is a *Network* that permits the integrated transmission of both *Analog* or voice *Data* together with *Digital Data* over ordinary telephone lines (copper wire).

ISP. See *Internet Service Provider*.

Java means an object-oriented software programing language expressly designed for use in the *Internet*.

Java Applet means a small software application written using *Java*. It is often embedded software in a *Web Site* that performs functions, such as animations, immediate calculations, and other simple tasks.

JavaScript means a higher level programing code than *Java*.

Kbps means kilo bits per second.

Key means an *Algorithm* used for identifying, encrypting, decoding and authenticating electronic documents and their authors.

LAN means a local area network and is a *Network* of computers that are connected together by common communications over a close distance, such as in the same building or geographically limited area.

Link. See *Hyper-Link*.

Linking. See *Hyper-Link*.

Local Area Network. See *LAN*.

MacTCP. See *Socket*.

Mbps means million bits per second.

Meta means an underlying definition, set of rules or description.

Meta File means a file that is required to display certain *Content* on a *Web Site*.

---

international non-profit organization based in Reston, Virginia, that guides Internet architecture and technical issues.

Meta Tag means a *Tag* in the *HTML* of a *Web Page* that contains some information (e.g., keywords or description about the *Content* of the *Web Page*), which *Tag* is used by search engines to index the *Web Page* so that an *Internet User* searching for the information with a *Browser* will be able to find the *Web Page*.

Net. See *Internet*.

Network means a system of two or more computers or *Nodes* that are able to communicate with one another via telephone lines, satellite connections, cables, fibers, or other telecommunications media.

Network and Technology Infrastructure Providers mean those providers of network and technology products and services that make the *Internet* and *e-Commerce* function, including hardware and equipment manufacturers, *ISPs, ASPs, Hosts, Outsourcers, Web Site Hosts, Customer Relations Management* providers, telecommunications providers and software and *Web Site* developers.

Node means a connection point for *Data* transmissions that is programed or engineered with the capability to recognize and process or forward transmissions to other Nodes.

Object-Oriented Programing means a computer program development language organized around "objects" or units of code.

On-line Service Provider (OSP) means a service provider that leases space on *Internet* telecommunications systems, lines or *Backbones* and sells connections or access to the *Internet* to businesses and consumers.

Open System is another word used to describe interoperability between hardware and software.

OSP. See *On-Line Service Provider*.

Outsourcer means a third-party service provider.

Packet means a unit of *Data* that contains a specified destination address and is sent between computers and *Nodes* on the *Internet*.

Passport is a personal profile file created by the *Internet User* that is used for gathering and sharing information about the *Internet User* as it visits various *Web Sites*.

PC means personal computer and is often used to refer to a desktop computer or *Client*.

PKI. See *Public Key Infrastructure*.

Plug-In means software that is required to run or display certain *Content* on a *Web Site*.

Portal means a *Web Site* or gateway that brings together buyers and sellers of products or services. Portals can be connecting *B2C* or *B2B*. Examples of Portals include on-line market places, exchanges, shopping malls and auctions.

Protocol means a set of rules, and it is commonly used to describe communications standards. See also *TCP/IP*.

Public Key Infrastructure (PKI) means a central repository for administering certificates and private and public *Keys* or *Algorithms* for identifying, encrypting, decoding and authenticating electronic documents and their authors.

Public Network means a *Network* that is publicly accessible.

Regional Network. See *WAN*.

Registrant means a person who has registered a *Domain Name* with the applicable *Domain Name Registration Authority*, such as *CIRA* in Canada.

Registrar means a provider of *Domain Name* information, registration, transfer, renewal and modification services to *Internet Users*. In Canada, registrars must be certified by *CIRA*.

Relative Link. See *Hyper-Link*.

Repeater means a receiver and/or an amplifier on a *Network* that receives a signal, removes unwanted noise and amplifies and retransmits it along the *Network*.

Rotating with respect to an *Internet* advertisement means an advertisement that randomly rotates to different locations and may or may not be seen by an *Internet User*.

Router means a piece of hardware or, in some cases, software, at a *Gateway* that determines the route and next *Network* point, *Node* or Router to which a *Packet* should be sent to toward its ultimate destination. A Router is similar to, but more complicated than, a *Switch*, since the Router requires knowledge about the *Network* and how to determine the route.

Server means a computer or program that serves other computers, programs or users, known as *Clients*, in a *Client/Server Relationship* by providing services or functionality using Server software. Also referred to as a *Host*.

Shopping Cart is a file or *Cookie* used for keeping track of purchases selected or completed by an *Internet User* on a *Web Site.*

Sniffers are computers that sit on the *Internet* between *Internet Users* and *Web Sites* that use software to analyze *Internet* traffic to and from *Web Sites*. They collect information from *Cookies, Passports* or *IP Addresses* about *Internet Users,* such as their identities, when and what actions are taken, where requests for *Web Pages* are coming from and where *Web Pages* are sent.

Socket means a particular rule or program for interfacing with and exchanging data between two software applications, computers or networks, such as Winsock for the Windows operating systems or MacTCP for Macintosh.

Static with respect to an *Internet* advertisement means an advertisement that is displayed without rotation, such as a banner ad that appears constantly across the top of a *Web Page*.

Switch means a piece of hardware that determines where to forward a *Packet* towards its next destination. A Switch may also include the function of a *Router,* but differs from a *Router* in that it is a simpler and faster mechanism that requires no knowledge about the *Network* and how to determine the route.

T1 line is the most commonly used *Digital* line in Canada, the United States and Japan. In these countries, it carries 1.544 *Mbps* and is used to span distances within and between major metropolitan areas.

T3 line is a *Digital* line that carries 44.736 *Mbps*.

Tag means a language element descriptor or coding statement.

Targeted with respect to an *Internet* advertisement means an advertisement that is seen by an *Internet User* who either enters specific information or who browses to specific advertising areas on the *Internet*.

T-carrier System means a *Digital* transmission service offered by telecommunications carriers using pulse code modulation and time-division multiplexing technology. See also *T1 Line* and *T3 Line*.

TCP/IP means Transmission Control Protocol/Internet Protocol and is the *Internet's* basic *Protocol* for communicating *Packets*.

Top Level with respect to a *Domain Name* means that part of a *Domain Name* that specifies the type of entity or country of registration, e.g., .gov, .com, .ca.

Transmission Control Protocol/Internet Protocol. See *TCP/IP*.

Trusted Third Party. See *Certification Authority*.

TTP means Trusted Third Party. See *Certification Authority*.

Uniform Resource Locator. See *URL*.

URL means Uniform Resource Locator and it is the address of a file or software (including an individual *Web Page*) on the *Internet*. The URL generally contains the name of the *Protocol* required to access the file or software (e.g., *HTTP*), a *Domain Name* and, if applicable, specific *Web Page* or file locations. For example, http://www.blakes.ca is a URL that uses the *Hypertext Transfer Protocol* and retrieves the Blakes' *Homepage*.

WAN means a Wide Area Network and is a *Network* of computers or *LANs* connected together by common communications over a larger distance. A regional *Network* is a type of *WAN*.

Web Browser. See *Browser*.

Web Page is a simple computer program (software) written in a language, such as *Hypertext Markup Language*, which may contain *Data*, files and other embedded software, that is intended to be accessed by *Internet Users* with a *Browser*.

Web Server means the computer or computers that an *ISP* uses to make *Web Sites* accessible to *Internet Users*.

Web Site is a simple computer program (software) written in a language, such as *Hypertext Markup Language*, which may contain *Data*, files and other embedded software, that is intended to be accessed by *Internet Users* with a *Browser*. A *Web Site* is usually organized into multiple *Web Pages* or sections that are *Hyper-Linked* together in layers to permit *Internet Users* to efficiently find what they are looking for on the *Web Site*, using their *Browsers*.

Wide Area Network. See *WAN*.

Winsock. See *Socket*.

World Wide Web means, in a broad sense, the publicly available world wide *Network* of computers that communicate with one another, also referred to as the *Internet*. More narrowly, it means all the *HTTP* compliant *Web Servers* that contain *HTML* documents.

INDEX

L

M

O

P

Q

R

S

T

U

W